THE
PHILOS

THE SIGNIFICANCE OF PHILOSOPHICAL SCEPTICISM

BARRY STROUD

CLARENDON PRESS · OXFORD

Oxford University Press, Walton Street, Oxford OX2 6DP
Oxford New York Toronto
Delhi Bombay Calcutta Madras Karachi
Kuala Lumpur Singapore Hong Kong Tokyo
Nairobi Dar es Salaam Cape Town
Melbourne Auckland
and associated companies in
Beirut Berlin Ibadan Nicosia

Oxford is a trade mark of Oxford University Press

Published in the United States by
Oxford University Press, New York

First published 1984
Reprinted 1985

British Library Cataloguing in Publication Data

Stroud, Barry
The significance of philosophical scepticism.
1. Scepticism.
I. Title
121'.5 BD201

ISBN 0-19-824730-3
ISBN 0-19-824761-3 Pbk

Library of Congress Cataloging in Publication Data

Stroud, Barry
The significance of philosophical scepticism.
Includes index.
1. Scepticism. 2. Knowledge, Theory of. I. Title.
B837.S87 1984 121 83-25244

ISBN 0-19-824730-3
ISBN 0-19-824761-3 (pbk.)

Printed in Great Britain
at the University Press, Oxford
by David Stanford
Printer to the University

For Martha

Preface

Philosophical scepticism goes back to antiquity, and in writing of it as I do in this book I am not doing justice to that tradition. For the followers of Pyrrho of Elis, for example, a life of contentment or tranquillity was to be the reward for giving oneself up to 'appearances' and adopting no beliefs at all as to how things are. Suspending judgement was a way of freeing oneself from the anxieties and disturbances inevitably involved in seeking the truth and then encountering conflict among the things one feels forced to believe. Scepticism as a way of life is not my subject here. But some of the steps by which suspension of judgement was to have been achieved, and the difficulty of achieving it on *all* questions as to how things are, lie closer to my theme. The contrast implicit in sceptical practice between 'appearances' and 'the way things are' is also perhaps one version of an elusive distinction I examine from several different angles in what follows. My concerns are to that extent continuous with those of ancient scepticism, but I do not discuss such historical questions here. That is a subject I wish I knew more about.

In modern, and especially recent, times scepticism in philosophy has come to be understood as the view that we know nothing, or that nothing is certain, or that everything is open to doubt. That is a thesis or doctrine about the human condition, not itself a way of life. It is thought to rest on many of the same considerations ancient sceptics might have invoked in freeing themselves from their opinions or opposing the doctrines of others, but as a philosophical thesis it does not obviously lead to any one way of life rather than another, let alone to tranquillity or human happiness. One issue I raise in this book is just what relation philosophical scepticism does bear to the familiar concerns of everyday life.

As an account of human knowledge, scepticism in this modern form need not apply to everything we believe.

Knowledge or reliable belief might be possible about some things or in some areas and not others. Thus we could perhaps endorse scepticism about the claims of morality or religion without for the same reasons having to abandon mathematics or medicine or the science of nature.

In this book I examine the sceptical philosophical view that we can know nothing about the physical world around us. That thesis is found to be the only answer to a problem about how knowledge of the world is possible. Most philosophical theories of knowledge in modern times have taken a stand on that problem, very few of them an explicitly sceptical stand. The extent to which any of those theories could possibly be correct is therefore also at the centre of my interest. But it is not merely a question of finding the best theory of knowledge. By examining philosophical scepticism about the external world I hope to bring into question our very understanding of what a philosophical theory of knowledge is supposed to be. That is something that I believe is not as well understood as the apparently endless proliferation of more and more such 'theories' might lead one to suppose. It is time to stop and ask what *any* philosophical theory of knowledge is supposed to do.

I am concerned, then, with the *significance* of philosophical scepticism, and in several different ways. Something can be said to be significant as opposed to being insignificant or unimportant, and I want to illustrate the importance of scepticism for the philosophical study of knowledge. Not everyone would appear to agree; scepticism in philosophy has been found uninteresting, perhaps even a waste of time, in recent years. The attempt to meet, or even to understand, the sceptical challenge to our knowledge of the world is regarded in some circles as an idle academic exercise, a wilful refusal to abandon outmoded forms of thinking in this new post-Cartesian age. When this attitude is not based on ignorance or a philistine impatience with abstract thought it often rests on the belief that we already understand quite well just how and why traditional philosophical scepticism goes wrong. One aim of this book is to suggest that that comfortable belief is not true.

I think many philosophers who show little interest in

scepticism are in fact committed to it by their own theories of knowledge, and that others who would simply avoid the issue cannot give a satisfactory explanation of how it is to be overcome. I do not mean to legislate intellectual taste. I do not suggest that everyone should be interested in scepticism, or even that all philosophers should be interested in understanding how human knowledge is possible. But I do think that those who ponder this latter question at all are wrong to suppose they can now be indifferent to the workings of philosophical scepticism. There are those on the other hand who take no interest in scepticism because they think it is so obviously true as not to bear repeating. I find that reaction equally unsatisfactory, although more perceptive than its opposite, for reasons I hope will emerge.

Something can also be said to be significant as opposed to being meaningless or incoherent or unintelligible, and that is another dimension of my interest in the significance of philosophical scepticism. It could be that the sceptical thesis that we know nothing about the world around us turns out on investigation not to mean what it seems to mean, or perhaps not to mean anything at all. The question of what it does mean, if anything, runs throughout this book, and not only in Chapter Five where the issue of meaninglessness is discussed directly. If the sceptical thesis does turn out to be incoherent, all those who are bored either by its obvious falsity or by its obvious truth must be mistaken. They will not really understand why it is a non-issue even if it is.

We can also speak of the significance of something in the sense of what it signifies or what it indicates or what it shows. In that way too, perhaps above all, I am interested in the significance of philosophical scepticism. Even if the thesis means nothing, or not what it seems to mean, can the study of scepticism about the world around us nevertheless reveal something deep or important about human knowledge or human nature or the urge to understand them philosophically? I am pretty sure that the answer is 'Yes', but I do not get as far as I would like towards showing why that is so. Nor do I ever manage to state precisely what the lesson or moral of a study of philosophical scepticism might be. Aside from the usual contingencies of limited space and limited insight and understanding, there might be good, even philosophical, reasons for my failure to do that. Perhaps an unambiguous moral can never be stated. If so, that fact itself would be something worth explaining. I try to take some steps in that direction.

This book is written in the belief that the study of philosophical problems can itself be philosophically illuminating. Of course no one would deny the need for a clear understanding of the problem at hand if there is to be real intellectual progress. But I do not just mean that solving or answering philosophical questions can be illuminating. Of course it could be, if you happened to get the right answer and knew that you had, or even if you failed and knew that you had failed, and perhaps even had some idea why. I mean that the study of the very nature of a philosophical problem can be an illuminating activity quite independently of whether it ever leads to a better answer.

The attempt to understand what I am calling the nature of a philosophical problem can be expected to illuminate not only the problem itself, but also the very 'phenomenon'—morality, religion, knowledge, action, or whatever it might be—out of which the philosophical problem arises. It is surprising to me how few people writing philosophy in this day and age actually concentrate on the problems themselves and where they come from. There seems to be widespread confidence about what the problems are, what sort of thing a successful philosophical doctrine or theory would be, and what it would take to give us the kind of understanding philosophy can give us of the phenomena it has traditionally been concerned with. I do not share that confidence. I think that whatever we seek in philosophy, or whatever leads us to ask philosophical questions at all, must be something pretty deep in human nature, and that what leads us to ask just the questions we do in the particular ways we now ask them must be something pretty deep in our tradition. Studying the sources of philosophical problems as they now present themselves to us can therefore perhaps be expected to yield some degree of understanding, illumination, satisfaction, or whatever it is we seek in philosophy, even if we never arrive at something we can regard as a solution to a philosphical problem. In fact the two might even work against each other; adopting something we take to be an acceptable answer to a philosophical problem might be just what prevents us from learning the lesson that a deeper understanding of the source of the problem could reveal.

In any case the idea that the source of philosophical problems is not well understood and might promise something of philosophical interest is a hypothesis worth putting to the test. I hope I give some reasons for thinking it plausible in the case of one philosophical problem, but nothing I say is carried far enough to support a final verdict even in that single case. Perhaps a final verdict is too much to aspire to when it is a question of how much illumination can be gained from a certain kind of investigation. One of the attractions, and one of the perils, of the kind of task I recommend is that there is no telling in advance where it might lead or what it might yield. For that reason alone I hope the kind of investigation I try to encourage here will be pursued further. But the pages that follow should not be expected to culminate in a set of doctrines or conclusions about philosophical scepticism or about the problem to which it is an answer. At best they can take us some way towards understanding and appreciating its significance.

I expound and examine the writings of several particular philosophers in what follows, and I hope what I have to say about them can be seen to apply more widely than to their views alone. In fact I think each of the positions I discuss represents one or another of the several types of theory or approach now current in epistemology, even if I do not always discuss the latest instance of the type. I have been strongly tempted, and in some cases actually convinced, by each of them at one time or another. Dissatisfaction with each of them in turn no doubt contributed to my present preoccupation with the nature or point—or even the possibility—of a philosophical theory of knowledge as such. Again I offer nothing definitive about what a philosophical theory is. I exhibit some specimens and examine them in the light of the problem of our knowledge of the external world. Perhaps a certain pattern can eventually be discerned.

Over the years that I have been working, lecturing, and writing on these topics I have enjoyed the support of the Humanities Research Fellowships of the University of California, Berkeley, the American Council of Learned Societies, and the John Simon Guggenheim Memorial Foundation. I am extremely grateful to each. Without them this book would not exist.

I have presented versions of this or related material in a great many universities and colleges in eight countries. The variety of response and sympathetic criticism I received has had good effects on the pages that follow, even if I myself can no longer identify them and individually thank those responsible. I think the idea of a book-length study of scepticism along present lines first occurred to me for a series of talks I gave in a seminar in Berkeley in the spring of 1977. There was another in the winter of 1983 in which the penultimate draft of this book was given close scrutiny by a number of shrewd Berkeley graduate students. I would like to thank both groups, and several more-or-less captive lecture-course audiences in Berkeley as well, for their help. Without the opportunity to develop my material before such perceptive and outspoken students this project would never have got off the ground.

Everything here is newly written, but in places it overlaps, sometimes closely, with papers of mine published earlier. 'The Significance of Scepticism', written in 1977 for a conference in Bielefeld on Transcendental Arguments and the Conceptual Foundations of Science, gives a rough sketch of the general line I try to develop here in more detail. It appears in the proceedings of the conference, *Transcendental Arguments and Science*, edited by P. Bieri, R. P. Horstmann, and L. Krüger (Reidel, Dordrecht, 1981). The main ideas in my interpretation of Kant in Chapter Four can be found in 'Kant and Skepticism', my contribution to *The Skeptical Tradition*, edited by M. F. Burnyeat (University of California Press, Berkeley, 1983). Chapter Six is a revised and expanded version of 'The Significance of Naturalized Epistemology', which appeared in *Midwest Studies in Philosophy, Volume Six: The Foundations of Analytic Philosophy*, edited by P. A. French, T. E. Uehling, Jr., H. K. Wettstein (University of Minnesota Press, Minneapolis, 1981). Part of Chapter Seven is drawn from my contribution to an American Philosophical Association symposium, 'Reasonable Claims: Cavell and the Tradition', published in *The Journal of Philosophy*, 1980. I would like to thank the editors and publishers involved for permission to publish the present version.

It is by now quite impossible for me to list every friend, acquaintance, colleague, and critic who has influenced this work. I can therefore offer only rather sweeping thanks to all. In recent years I know I have profited from discussions with Rogers Albritton, Myles Burnyeat, Stanley Cavell, Donald Davidson, Burton Dreben, Linda Foy, Gil Harman, Lorenz Krüger, Thomas Nagel, Mark Platts, W. V. Quine, Tim Scanlon, Sam Scheffler, and Judith Thomson. Janet Broughton has been especially helpful in reading and commenting on parts of the manuscript at different stages of its composition and always giving me good advice. Michael Frede is a constant stimulus and support from whom I always learn more than I can make use of.

In a quite special relation to this book stands my friend and colleague Thompson Clarke. It is simply impossible for me fully to identify and acknowledge my debt to him over the years. Much of the substance of Chapter One has been taken for granted as common ground between us for a long time. I first presented some of the ideas of Chapter Two in a joint seminar with him in the late 1960s in response to writings of his which I saw at the time as conceding too much to Austin despite the effort to come to terms with linguistic philosophy in support of traditional epistemology. It is something we have continued to discuss in one form or another ever since. The basic conception of G. E. Moore in Chapter Three, aside from details of application, can be found in his 'The Legacy of Skepticism'. Our extended discussion of issues raised in that paper eventually gave me a grip on the distinction between what he calls 'the plain' and 'the philosophical' which in one form or another runs throughout the book. It then helped me to understand Kant's notion of the 'transcendental' as I try to explain it in Chapter Four. Verificationism gave me another, perhaps clearer, instance of the same kind of distinction, and I came to see that some of the dissatisfactions with it I express in Chapter Five were probably behind my 'Transcendental Arguments' of 1968. Chapter Six began in discussions of Quine in joint classes Clarke and I held in the late 1970s, and I developed in my own way ideas about the 'internal' and the 'external' that I think we had both been pursuing. Chapter Seven contains part of my response to 'The Legacy of Skepticism' at an American Philosophical Association meeting in 1972 and part of an interpretation of Stanley Cavell, both of which we discussed together many times.

But a list of particular chapters or topics in which his effect on this book can be identified would never be enough; I have been too close to his work over the last twenty years to measure what I have got from him in that way. By now there have undoubtedly been influences in both directions, but the effects of our association are much more pervasive and more unspecifiable in my case than in his. It is no exaggeration at all to say that my whole way of thinking about philosophy, and not just about traditional epistemology, has been affected by him in untold ways, and I am happy to have the chance to acknowledge it here. He would not deal with the questions I investigate in the way I do, but I would not proceed as I do had it not been for him. I would be pleased if what I have presented here of our shared conception of the subject helps make his own quite special contributions to these questions more available to the philosophical world.

Beyond these philosophical debts, I would like finally to say a word of gratitude to Venice, La Serenissima herself, where the book was first written. Probably no place on earth is more conducive to contemplating the problem of the reality of the external world, and without the undeniably real warmth and friendliness of the people I came to know there I might have returned to *terraferma* with a case rather than a treatment of scepticism.

BS

Contents

I

The Problem of the External World

Since at least the time of Descartes in the seventeenth century there has been a philosophical problem about our knowledge of the world around us.[1] Put most simply, the problem is to show how we can have any knowledge of the world at all. The conclusion that we cannot, that no one knows anything about the world around us, is what I call 'scepticism about the external world', so we could also say that the problem is to show how or why scepticism about the external world is not correct. My aim is not to solve the problem but to understand it. I believe the problem has no solution; or rather that the only answer to the question as it is meant to be understood is that we can know nothing about the world around us. But how is the question meant to be understood? It can be expressed in a few English words familiar to all of us, but I hope to show that an understanding of the special philosophical character of the question, and of the inevitability of an unsatisfactory answer to it, cannot be guaranteed by our understanding of those words alone. To see how the problem is meant to be understood we must therefore examine what is perhaps best described as its source—how the problem arises and how it acquires that special character that makes an unsatisfactory negative answer inevitable. We must try to understand the *philosophical* problem of our knowledge of the external world.

The problem arose for Descartes in the course of reflecting on everything he knows. He reached a point in his life at which he tried to sit back and reflect on everything he had ever been taught or told, everything he had learned or discovered or believed since he was old enough to know or

[1] It has been argued that the problem in the completely general form in which I discuss it here is new in Descartes, and that nothing exactly similar appears in philosophy before that time. See M. F. Burnyeat, 'Idealism and Greek Philosophy: What Descartes Saw and Berkeley Missed', *The Philosophical Review*, 1982.

believe anything.[2] We might say that he was reflecting on his knowledge, but putting it that way could suggest that what he was directing his attention to was indeed knowledge, and whether it was knowledge or not is precisely what he wanted to determine. 'Among all the things I believe or take to be true, what amounts to knowledge and what does not?'; that is the question Descartes asks himself. It is obviously a very general question, since it asks about everything he believes or takes to be true, but in other respects it sounds just like the sort of question we are perfectly familiar with in everyday life and often know how to answer.

For example, I have come to accept over the years a great many things about the common cold. I have always been told that one can catch cold by getting wet feet, or from sitting in a draught, or from not drying one's hair before going outdoors in cold weather. I have also learned that the common cold is the effect of a virus transmitted by an already infected person. And I also believe that one is more vulnerable to colds when over-tired, under stress, or otherwise in less than the best of health. Some of these beliefs seem to me on reflection to be inconsistent with some others; I see that it is very unlikely that all of them could be true. Perhaps they could be, but I acknowledge that there is much I do not understand. If I sit back and try to think about all my 'knowledge' of the common cold, then, I might easily come to wonder how much of it really amounts to knowledge and how much does not. What do I really know about the common cold? If I were sufficiently interested in pursuing the matter it would be natural to look into the source of my beliefs. Has there ever been any good reason for thinking that colds are even correlated with wet hair in cold weather, for example, or with sitting in a draught? Are the people from whom I learned such things likely to have believed them for good reasons? Are those beliefs just old wives' tales, or are they really true, and perhaps even known to be true by some people? These are questions I might ask myself, and I have at least a general idea of how to go about answering them.

[2] See the beginning of the first of his *Meditations on First Philosophy* in *The Philosophical Works of Descartes*, edited and translated by E. S. Haldane and G. R. T. Ross (2 vols., New York, 1955), vol. I, p. 145. (Hereafter cited as HR.)

Apart from my impression of the implausibility of all my beliefs about the common cold being true together, I have not mentioned any other reason for being interested in investigating the state of my knowledge on that subject. But for the moment that does not seem to affect the intelligibility or the feasibility of the reflective project. There is nothing mysterious about it. It is the sort of task we can be led to undertake for a number of reasons, and often very good reasons, in so far as we have very good reasons for preferring knowledge and firm belief to guesswork or wishful thinking or simply taking things for granted.

Reflection on or investigation of our putative knowledge need not always extend to a wide area of interest. It might be important to ask whether some quite specific and particular thing I believe or have been taking for granted is really something I know. As a member of a jury I might find that I have been ruling out one suspect in my mind because he was a thousand miles away, in Cleveland, at the time of the crime. But I might then begin to ask myself whether that is really something that I know. I would reflect on the source of my belief, but reflection in this case need not involve a general scrutiny of everything I take myself to know about the case. Re-examining the man's alibi and the credentials of its supporting witnesses might be enough to satisfy me. Indeed I might find that its reliability on those counts is precisely what I had been going on all along.

In pointing out that we are perfectly familiar with the idea of investigating or reviewing our knowledge on some particular matter or in some general area I do not mean to suggest that it is always easy to settle the question. Depending on the nature of the case, it might be very difficult, perhaps even impossible at the time, to reach a firm conclusion. For example, it would probably be very difficult if not impossible for me to trace and assess the origins of many of those things I believe about the common cold. But it is equally true that sometimes it is not impossible or even especially difficult to answer the question. We do sometimes discover that we do not really know what we previously thought we knew. I might find that what I had previously believed is not even true—that sitting in draughts is not even correlated with catching a cold, for example. Or I might find that there is not or perhaps never was any good reason to believe what I believed—that the man's alibi was concocted and then falsely testified to by his friends. I could reasonably conclude in each case that I, and everyone else for that matter, never did know what I had previously thought I knew. We are all familiar with the ordinary activity of reviewing our knowledge, and with the experience of reaching a positive verdict in some cases and a negative verdict in others.

Descartes's own interest in what he knows and how he knows it is part of his search for what he calls a general method for 'rightly conducting reason and seeking truth in the sciences'.[3] He wants a method of inquiry that he can be assured in advance will lead only to the truth if properly followed. I think we do not need to endorse the wisdom of that search or the feasibility of that programme in order to try to go along with Descartes in his general assessment of the position he is in with respect to the things he believes. He comes to find his putative knowledge wanting in certain general respects, and it is in the course of that original negative assessment that the problem I am interested in arises. I call the assessment 'negative' because by the end of his *First Meditation* Descartes finds that he has no good reason to believe anything about the world around him and therefore that he can know nothing of the external world.

How is that assessment conducted, and how closely does it parallel the familiar kind of review of our knowledge that we all know how to conduct in everyday life? The question in one form or another will be with us for the rest of this book. It is the question of what exactly the problem of our knowledge of the external world amounts to, and how it arises with its special philosophical character. The source of the problem is to be found somewhere within or behind the kind of thinking Descartes engages in.

One way Descartes's question about his knowledge differs from the everyday examples I considered is in being

[3] See his *Discourse on the Method of Rightly Conducting Reason and Seeking Truth in the Sciences* in HR, pp. 81 ff.

concerned with *everything* he believes or takes to be true. How does one go about assessing all of one's knowledge all at once? I was able to list a few of the things I believe about the common cold and then to ask about each of them whether I really know it, and if so how. But although I can certainly list a number of the things I believe, and I would assent to many more of them as soon as they were put to me, there obviously is no hope of assessing everything I believe in this piecemeal way. For one thing, it probably makes no sense, strictly speaking, to talk of the number of things one believes. If I am asked whether it is one of my beliefs that I went to see a film last night I can truly answer 'Yes'. If I were asked whether it is one of my beliefs that I went to the movies last night I would give the same answer. Have I thereby identified two, or only one, of my beliefs? How is that question ever to be settled? If we say that I identified only one of my beliefs, it would seem that I must also be said to hold the further belief that going to see a film and going to the movies are one and the same thing. So we would have more than one belief after all. The prospects of arriving even at a principle for counting beliefs, let alone at an actual number of them, seem dim.

Even if it did make sense to count the things we believe it is pretty clear that the number would be indefinitely large and so an assessment of our beliefs one by one could never be completed anyway. This is easily seen by considering only some of the simplest things one knows, for example in arithmetic. One thing I know is that one plus one equals two. Another thing I know is that one plus two is three, and another, that one plus three is four. Obviously there could be no end to the task of assessing my knowledge if I had to investigate separately the source of each one of my beliefs in that series. And even if I succeeded I would only have assessed the things I know about the addition of the number one to a given number; I would still have to do the same for the addition of two, and then the addition of three, and so on. And even that would exhaust only my beliefs about addition; all my other mathematical beliefs, not to mention all the rest of my knowledge, would remain so far unexamined. Obviously the job cannot be done piecemeal, one by one.

Some method must be found for assessing large classes of beliefs all at once.

One way to do this would be to look for common sources or channels or bases of our beliefs, and then to examine the reliability of those sources or bases, just as I examined the source or basis of my belief that the suspect was in Cleveland. Descartes describes such a search as a search for 'principles' of human knowledge, 'principles' whose general credentials he can then investigate (HR, 145). If some 'principles' are found to be involved in all or even most of our knowledge, an assessment of the reliability of those 'principles' could be an assessment of all or most of our knowledge. If I found good reason to doubt the reliability of the suspect's alibi, for example, and that was all I had to go on in my belief that he was in Cleveland, then what I earlier took to be my knowledge that he was in Cleveland would have been found wanting or called into question. Its source or basis would have been undermined. Similarly, if one of the 'principles' or bases on which all my knowledge of the world depends were found to be unreliable, my knowledge of the world would to that extent have been found wanting or called into question as well.

Are there any important 'principles' of human knowledge in Descartes's sense? It takes very little reflection on the human organism to convince us of the importance of the senses—sight, hearing, touch, taste, and smell. Descartes puts the point most strongly when he says that 'all that up to the present time I have accepted as most true and certain I have learned either from the senses or through the senses' (HR, 145). Exactly what he would include under 'the senses' here is perhaps somewhat indeterminate, but even if it is left vague many philosophers would deny what Descartes appears to be saying. They would hold that, for example, the mathematical knowledge I mentioned earlier is not and could not be acquired from the senses or through the senses, so not *everything* I know is known in that way. Whether Descartes is really denying the views of those who believe in the non-sensory character of mathematical knowledge, and whether, if he were, he would be right, are issues we can set aside for the moment. It is clear that the senses are at least very important for human knowledge. Even restricting ourselves to the traditional five senses we can begin to appreciate their importance by reflecting on how little someone would ever come to know without them. A person blind and deaf from birth who also lacked taste buds and a sense of smell would know very little about anything, no matter how long he lived. To imagine him also anaesthetized or without a sense of touch is perhaps to stretch altogether too far one's conception of a human organism, or at least a human organism from whom we can hope to learn something about human knowledge. The importance of the senses as a source or channel of knowledge seems undeniable. It seems possible, then, to acknowledge their importance and to assess the reliability of that source, quite independently of the difficult question of whether *all* our knowledge comes to us in that way. We would then be assessing the credentials of what is often called our 'sensory' or 'experiential' or 'empirical' knowledge, and that, as we shall see, is quite enough to be going on with.

Having found an extremely important 'principle' or source of our knowledge, how can we investigate or assess *all* the knowledge we get from that source? As before, we are faced with the problem of the inexhaustibility of the things we believe on that basis, so no piecemeal, one-by-one procedure will do. But perhaps we can make a sweeping negative assessment. It might seem that as soon as we have found that the senses are one of the sources of our beliefs we are immediately in a position to condemn all putative knowledge derived from them. Some philosophers appear to have reasoned in this way, and many have even supposed that Descartes is among them. The idea is that if I am assessing the reliability of my beliefs and asking whether I really know what I take myself to know, and I come across a large class of beliefs which have come to me through the senses, I can immediately dismiss all those beliefs as unreliable or as not amounting to knowledge because of the obvious fact that I can sometimes be wrong in my beliefs based on the senses. Things are not always as they appear, so if on the basis of the way they appear to me I believe that they really are a certain way, I might still be wrong. We have all found at one time or another that we have been misled by appearances; we know that the senses are not always reliable. Should we not conclude, then, that as a general source of knowledge the senses are not to be trusted? As Descartes puts it, is it not wiser never 'to trust entirely to any thing by which we have once been deceived' (HR, 145)? Don't we have here a quite general way of condemning as not fully reliable *all* of our beliefs acquired by means of the senses?

I think the answer to that question is 'No, we do not', and I think Descartes would agree with that answer. It is true that he does talk of the senses 'deceiving' us on particular occasions, and he does ask whether that is not enough to condemn the senses in general as a source of knowledge, but he immediately reminds us of the obvious fact that the circumstances in which the senses 'deceive' us might be special in certain ascertainable ways, and so their occasional failures would not support a blanket condemnation of their reliability.

Sometimes, to give an ancient example, a tower looks round from a distance when it is actually square. If we relied only on the appearances of the moment we might say that the distant tower is round, and we would be wrong. We also know that there are many small organisms invisible to the naked eye. If the table before me is covered with such organisms at the moment but I look at it and say there is nothing on the table at all, once again I will be wrong. But all that follows from these familiar facts, as Descartes points out, is that there are things about which we can be wrong, or there are situations in which we can get false beliefs, if we rely entirely on our senses at that moment. So sometimes we should be careful about what we believe on the basis of the senses, or sometimes perhaps we should withhold our assent from any statement about how things are—when things are too far away to be seen properly, for example, or too small to be seen at all. But that obviously is not enough to support the policy of never trusting one's senses, or never believing anything based on them. Nor does it show that I can never know anything by means of the senses. If my car starts promptly every morning for two years in temperate weather at sea level but then fails to start one morning in freezing weather at the top of a high mountain, that does not support the policy of never trusting my car to start again once I return to the temperate lower altitude from which I so foolishly took it. Nor does it show that I can never know whether my car will ever start again. It shows only that there are certain circumstances in which my otherwise fully reliable car might not start. So the fact that we are sometimes wrong or 'deceived' in our judgements based on the senses is not enough in itself to show that the senses are never to be trusted and are therefore never reliable as a source of knowledge.

Descartes's negative assessment of all of his sensory knowledge does not depend on any such reasoning. He starts his investigation, rather, in what would seem to be the most favourable conditions for the reliable operation of the senses as a source of knowledge. While engaging in the very philosophical reflections he is writing about in his *First Meditation* Descartes is sitting in a warm room, by the fire, in a dressing gown, with a piece of paper in his hand. He finds that although he might be able to doubt that a distant tower that looks round really is round, it seems impossible to doubt that he really is sitting there by the fire in his dressing gown with a piece of paper in his hand. The fire and the piece of paper are not too small or too far away to be seen properly, they are right there before his eyes; it seems to be the best kind of position someone could be in for getting reliable beliefs or knowledge by means of the senses about what is going on around him. That is just how Descartes regards it. Its being a best-possible case of that kind is precisely what he thinks enables him to investigate or assess at one fell swoop all our sensory knowledge of the world around us. The verdict he arrives at about his putative knowledge that he is sitting by the fire with a piece of paper in his hand in that particular situation serves as the basis for a completely general assessment of the senses as a source of knowledge about the world around us.

How can that be so? How can he so easily reach a general verdict about all his sensory knowledge on the basis of a single example? Obviously not simply by generalizing from one particular example to all cases of sensory knowledge, as one might wildly leap to a conclusion about all red-haired men on the basis of one or two individuals. Rather, he takes the particular example of his conviction that he is sitting by the fire with a piece of paper in his hand as representative of the best position any of us can ever be in for knowing things about the world around us on the basis of the senses. What is true of a representative case, if it is truly representative and does not depend on special peculiarities of its own, can legitimately support a general conclusion. A demonstration that a particular isosceles triangle has a certain property, for example, can be taken as a demonstration that all isosceles triangles have that property, as long as the original instance was typical or representative of the whole class. Whether Descartes's investigation of the general reliability of the senses really does follow that familiar pattern is a difficult question. Whether, or in precisely what sense, the example he considers can be treated as representative of our relation to the world around us is, I believe, the key to understanding the problem of our knowledge of the external world. But if it turns out that there is nothing illegitimate about the way his negative conclusion is reached, the problem will be properly posed.

For the moment I think at least this much can be said about Descartes's reasoning. He chooses the situation in which he finds himself as representative of the best position we can be in for knowing things about the world in the sense that, if it is impossible for him in that position to know that he is sitting by the fire with a piece of paper in his hand then it is also impossible for him in other situations to know anything about the world around him on the basis of his senses. A negative verdict in the chosen case would support a negative verdict everywhere else. The example Descartes considers is in that sense meant to be the *best* kind of case there could be of sensory knowledge about the world around us. I think we must admit that it is very difficult to see how Descartes or anyone else could be any better off with respect to knowing something about the world around him on the basis of the senses than he is in the case he considers. But if no one could be in any better position for knowing, it seems natural to conclude that any negative verdict arrived at about this example, any discovery that Descartes's beliefs in this case are not reliable or do not amount to knowledge, could safely be generalized into a negative conclusion about all of our sensory 'knowledge' of the world. If candidates with the best possible credentials are found wanting, all those with less impressive credentials must fall short as well.

It will seem at first sight that in conceding that the whole question turns on whether Descartes knows in this particular case we are conceding very little; it seems obvious that Descartes on that occasion does know what he thinks he knows about the world around him. But in fact Descartes finds that he cannot know in this case that he is sitting by the fire with a piece of paper in his hand. If the case is truly representative of our sensory knowledge in general, that will show that no one can know anything about the world around us. But how could he ever arrive at that negative verdict in the particular case he considers? How could anyone possibly doubt in such a case that the fire and the piece of paper are there? The paper is in Descartes's hand, the fire is right there before his open eyes, and he feels its warmth. Wouldn't anyone have to be mad to deny that he can know something about what is going on around him in those circumstances? Descartes first answers 'Yes'. He says that if he were to doubt or deny on that occasion that he is sitting by the fire with a piece of paper in his hand he would be no less mad than those paupers who say they are kings or those madmen who think they are pumpkins or are made of glass. But his reflections continue:

> At the same time I must remember that I am a man, and that consequently I am in the habit of sleeping, and in my dreams representing to myself the same things or sometimes even less probable things, than do those who are insane in their waking moments. How often has it happened to me that in the night I dreamt that I found myself in this particular place, that I was dressed and seated near the fire, whilst in reality I was lying undressed in bed! At this moment it does indeed seem to me that it is with eyes awake that I am looking at this paper; that this head which I move is not asleep, that it is deliberately and of set purpose that I extend my hand and perceive it; what happens in sleep does not appear so clear nor so distinct as does all this. But in thinking over this I remind myself that on many occasions I have in sleep been deceived by similar illusions, and in dwelling carefully on this reflection I see so manifestly that there are no certain indications by which we may clearly distinguish wakefulness from sleep that I am lost in astonishment. And my astonishment is such that it is almost capable of persuading me that I now dream. (HR, 145–6.)

With this thought, if he is right, Descartes has lost the whole world. He knows what he is experiencing, he knows how things appear to him, but he does not know whether he is in fact sitting by the fire with a piece of paper in his hand. It is, for him, exactly as if he were sitting by the fire with a piece of paper in his hand, but he does not know whether there really is a fire or a piece of paper there or not; he does not know what is really happening in the world around him. He realizes that if everything he can ever learn about what is happening in the world around him comes to him through the senses, but he cannot tell by means of the senses whether or not he is dreaming, then all the sensory experiences he is having are compatible with his merely dreaming of a world around him while in fact that world is very different from the way he takes it to be. That is why he thinks he must find some way to tell that he is not dreaming. Far from its being mad to deny that he knows in this case, he thinks his recognition of the possibility that he might be dreaming gives him 'very powerful and maturely considered' (HR, 148) reasons for withholding his judgement about how things are in the world around him. He thinks it is eminently reasonable to insist that if he is to know that he is sitting by the fire he must know that he is not dreaming that he is sitting by the fire. That is seen as a necessary condition of knowing something about the world around him. And he finds that that condition cannot be fulfilled. On careful reflection he discovers that 'there are no certain indications by which we may clearly distinguish wakefulness from sleep'. He concludes that he knows nothing about the world around him because he cannot tell that he is not dreaming; he cannot fulfil one of the conditions necessary for knowing something about the world.

The Cartesian problem of our knowledge of the external world therefore becomes: how can we know anything about the world around us on the basis of the senses if the senses give us only what Descartes says they give us? What we gain through the senses is on Descartes's view only information that is compatible with our dreaming things about the world around us and not knowing anything about that world. How then can we know anything about the world by means of the senses? The Cartesian argument presents a challenge to our knowledge, and the problem of our knowledge of the external world is to show how that challenge can be met.

When I speak here of the Cartesian argument or of Descartes's sceptical conclusion or of his negative verdict about his knowledge I refer of course only to the position he finds himself in by the end of his *First Meditation.* Having at that point discovered and stated the problem of the external world, Descartes goes on in the rest of his *Meditations* to try to solve it, and by the end of the *Sixth Meditation* he thinks he has explained how he knows almost all those familiar things he began by putting in question. So when I ascribe to Descartes the view that we can know nothing about the world around us I do not mean to suggest that that is his final and considered view; it is nothing more than a conclusion he feels almost inevitably driven to at the early stages of his reflections. But those are the only stages of his thinking I am interested in here. That is where the philosophical problem of our knowledge of the external world gets posed, and before we can consider possible solutions we must be sure we understand exactly what the problem is.

I have described it as that of showing or explaining how knowledge of the world around us is possible by means of the senses. It is important to keep in mind that that demand for an explanation arises in the face of a challenge or apparent obstacle to our knowledge of the world. The possibility that he is dreaming is seen as an obstacle to Descartes's knowing that he is sitting by the fire, and it must be explained how that obstacle can either be avoided or overcome. It must be shown or explained *how* it is possible for us to know things about the world, given that the sense-experiences we get are compatible with our merely dreaming. Explaining how something is nevertheless possible, despite what looks like an obstacle to it, requires more than showing merely that there is no impossibility involved in the thing—that it is consistent with the principles of logic and the laws of nature and so in that sense *could* exist. The mere possibility of the state of affairs is not enough to settle the question of how our knowledge of the world is possible; we must understand how the apparent obstacle is to be got round.

Descartes's reasoning can be examined and criticized at many different points, and has been closely scrutinized by many philosophers for centuries. It has also been accepted by many, perhaps by more than would admit or even realize that they accept it. There seems to me no doubt about the force and the fascination—I would say the almost overwhelming persuasiveness—of his reflections. That alone is something that needs accounting for. I cannot possibly do justice to all reasonable reactions to them here. In the rest of this first chapter I want to concentrate on deepening and strengthening the problem and trying to locate more precisely the source of its power.

There are at least three distinct questions that could be pressed. Is the possibility that Descartes might be dreaming really a threat to his knowledge of the world around him? Is he right in thinking that he must know that he is not dreaming if he is to know something about the world around him? And is he right in his 'discovery' that he can never know that he is not dreaming? If Descartes were wrong on any of these points it might be possible to avoid the problem and perhaps even to explain without difficulty how we know things about the world around us.

On the first question, it certainly seems right to say that if Descartes were dreaming that he is sitting by the fire with a piece of paper in his hand he would not then know that he is sitting by the fire with a piece of paper in his hand. When you dream that something is going on in the world around you you do not thereby know that it is. Most often, of course, what we dream is not even true; no one is actually chasing us when we are lying asleep in bed dreaming, nor are we actually climbing stairs. But although usually what we dream is not really so, that is not the real reason for our lack of knowledge. Even if Descartes were in fact sitting by the fire and actually had a piece of paper in his hand at the very time he was dreaming that he is sitting by the fire with a piece of paper in his hand, he would not thereby know he was sitting there with that paper. He would be like a certain Duke of Devonshire who, according to G. E. Moore, once dreamt he was speaking in the House of Lords and woke up to find that he *was* speaking in the House of

Lords.[4] What he was dreaming was in fact so. But even if what you are dreaming is in fact so you do not thereby know that it is. Even if we allow that when you are dreaming that something is so you can be said, at least for the time being, to think or to believe that it is so, there is still no real connection between your thinking or believing what you do and its being so. At best you have a thought or a belief which just happens to be true, but that is no more than coincidence and not knowledge. So Descartes's first step relies on what seems to be an undeniable fact about dreams: if you are dreaming that something is so you do not thereby know that it is so.

This bald claim needs to be qualified and more carefully explained, but I do not think that will diminish the force of the point for Descartes's purposes. Sometimes what is going on in the world around us has an effect on what we dream; for example, a banging shutter might actually cause me to dream, among other things, that a shutter is banging. If my environment affects me in that way, and if in dreams I can be said to think or believe that something is so, would I not in that case know that a shutter is banging? It seems to me that I would not, but I confess it is difficult to say exactly why I think so. That is probably because it is difficult to say exactly what is required for knowledge. We use the term 'know' confidently, we quite easily distinguish cases of knowledge from cases of its absence, but we are not always in a position to state what we are going on in applying or withholding the term in the ways we do. I think that in the case of the banging shutter it would not be knowledge because I would be *dreaming*, I would not even be awake. At least it can be said, I think, that even if Descartes's sitting by the fire with a piece of paper in his hand (like the banging shutter) is what in fact causes him to dream that he is sitting by the fire with a piece of paper in his hand, that is still no help to him in coming to know what is going on in the world around him. He realizes that he could be dreaming that he is sitting by the fire even if he is in fact sitting there, and that is the possibility he finds he has to rule out.

I have said that if you are dreaming that something is so

[4] G. E. Moore, *Philosophical Papers* (London, 1959), p. 245.

you do not thereby know that it is so, and it might seem as if that is not always true. Suppose a man and a child are both sleeping. I say of the child that it is so young it does not know what seven times nine is, whereas the grown man does know that. If the man happens at that very moment to be dreaming that seven times nine is sixty-three (perhaps he is dreaming that he is computing his income tax), then he is a man who is dreaming that something is so and also knows that it is so. The same kind of thing is possible for knowledge about the world around him. He might be a physicist who knows a great deal about the way things are which the child does not know. If the man also dreams that things are that way he can once again be said to be dreaming that something is so and also to know that it is so. There is therefore no incompatibility between dreaming and knowing. That is true, but I do not think it affects Descartes's argument. He is led to consider how he knows he is not dreaming at the moment by reflecting on how he knows at that moment that he is sitting by the fire with a piece of paper in his hand. If he knows that at all, he thinks, he knows it on the basis of the senses. But he realizes that his having the sensory experiences he is now having is compatible with his merely dreaming that he is sitting by the fire with a piece of paper in his hand. So he does not know on the basis of the sensory experiences he is having at the moment that he is sitting by the fire. Nor, of course, did the man in my examples know the things he was said to know on the basis of the sensory experiences he was having at that moment. He knew certain things to be so, and he was dreaming those things to be so, but in dreaming them he did not *thereby* know them to be so.

But as long as we allow that the sleeping man does know certain things about the world around him, even if he does not know them on the basis of the very dreams he is having at the moment, isn't that enough to show that Descartes must nevertheless be wrong in his conclusion that no one can know anything about the world around him? No. It shows at most that we were hasty or were ignoring Descartes's conclusion in conceding that someone could know something about the world around him. If Descartes's reasoning is correct the dreaming physicist, even when he is awake, does not really know any of the things we were uncritically crediting him with knowing about the way things are—or at least he does not know them on the basis of the senses. In order to know them on the basis of the senses there would have to have been at least some time at which he knew something about what was going on around him at that time. But if Descartes is right he could not have known any such thing unless he had established that he was not dreaming at that time; and according to Descartes he could never establish that. So the fact about dreams that Descartes relies on—that one who dreams that something is so does not thereby know that it is so—is enough to yield his conclusion if the other steps of his reasoning are correct.

When he first introduces the possibility that he might be dreaming Descartes seems to be relying on some knowledge about how things are or were in the world around him. He says 'I remind myself that on many occasions I have in sleep been deceived by similar illusions', so he seems to be relying on some knowledge to the effect that he has actually dreamt in the past and that he remembers having been 'deceived' by those dreams. That is more than he actually needs for his reflections about knowledge to have the force he thinks they have. He does not need to support his judgement that he has actually dreamt in the past. The only thought he needs is that it is now *possible* for him to be dreaming that he is sitting by the fire, and that if that possibility were realized he would not know that he is sitting by the fire. Of course it was no doubt true that Descartes had dreamt in the past and that his knowledge that he had done so was partly what he was going on in acknowledging the possibility of his dreaming on this particular occasion. But neither the fact of past dreams nor knowledge of their actual occurrence would seem to be strictly required in order to grant what Descartes relies on—the possibility of dreaming, and the absence of knowledge if that possibility were realized. The thought that he *might* be dreaming that he is sitting by the fire with a piece of paper in his hand, and the fact that if he were he wouldn't know he was sitting there, is what gives Descartes pause. That would worry him in the way it does even if he had never actually had any dreams exactly like it in the past—if he had never dreamt about fires and pieces of paper at all. In fact, I think he need never have actually dreamt of anything before, and certainly needn't know that he ever has, in order to be worried in the way he is by the thought that he might be dreaming now.

The fact that the possibility of dreaming is all Descartes needs to appeal to brings out another truth about dreams that his argument depends on—that anything that can be going on or that one can experience in one's waking life can also be dreamt about. This again is only a statement of possibility—no sensible person would suggest that we *do* at some time dream of everything that actually happens to us, or that everything we dream about does in fact happen sometime. But it is very plausible to say that there is nothing we *could* not dream about, nothing that could be the case that we *could* not dream to be the case. I say it is very plausible; of course I cannot prove it to be true. But even if it is not true with complete generality, we must surely grant that it is possible to dream that one is sitting by a fire with a piece of paper in one's hand, and possible to dream of countless other equally obvious and equally mundane states of affairs as well, and those possibilities are what Descartes sees as threatening to his knowledge of the world around him.

There seems little hope, then, of objecting that it is simply not possible for Descartes to dream that he is sitting by the fire with a piece of paper in his hand. Nor is it any more promising to say that even if he were dreaming it would not follow that he did not know that he was sitting there. I think both those steps or assumptions of Descartes's reasoning are perfectly correct, and further defence of them at this stage is unnecessary. If his argument and the problem to which it gives rise are to be avoided, it might seem that the best hope is therefore to accept his challenge and show that it can be met. That would be in effect to argue that Descartes's alleged 'discovery' is no discovery at all: we *can* sometimes know that we are not dreaming.

This can easily seem to be the most straightforward and most promising strategy. It allows that Descartes is right in thinking that knowing that one is not dreaming is a condition of knowing something about the world around us, but wrong in thinking that that condition can never be met. And that certainly seems plausible. Surely it is not impossible for me to know that I am not dreaming? Isn't that something I often know, and isn't it something I can sometimes find out if the question arises? If it is, then the fact that I must know that I am not dreaming if I am to know anything about the world around me will be no threat to my knowledge of the world.

However obvious and undeniable it might be that we often do know that we are not dreaming, I think this straightforward response to Descartes's challenge is a total failure. In calling it straightforward I mean that it accepts Descartes's conditions for knowledge of the world and tries to show that they can be fulfilled. That is what I think cannot be done. To put the same point in another way: I think Descartes would be perfectly correct in saying 'there are no certain indications by which we may clearly distinguish wakefulness from sleep', and so we could never tell we are not dreaming, *if* he were also right that knowing that one is not dreaming is a condition of knowing something about the world around us. That is why I think one cannot accept that condition and then go on to establish that one is not dreaming. I do not mean to be saying simply that Descartes is right—that we can never know that we are not dreaming. But I do want to argue that either we can never know that we are not dreaming or else what Descartes says is a condition of knowing things about the world is not really a condition in general of knowing things about the world. The straightforward strategy denies both alternatives. I will try to explain why I think we must accept one alternative or the other.

When Descartes asks himself how he knows that he is sitting by the fire with a piece of paper in his hand why does he immediately go on to ask himself how he knows he is not dreaming that he is sitting by the fire with a piece of paper in his hand? I have suggested that it is because he recognizes that if he were dreaming he would not know on the basis of his senses at the moment that he is sitting there, and so he thinks he must know that that possibility does not obtain if he is to know that he is in fact sitting there.

But this particular example was chosen, not for any peculiarities it might be thought to possess, but because it could be taken as typical of the best position we can ever be in for coming to know things about the world around us on the basis of the senses. What is true of this case that is relevant to Descartes's investigation of knowledge is supposed to be true of all cases of knowledge of the world by means of the senses; that is why the verdict arrived at here can be taken to be true of our sensory knowledge generally. But what Descartes thinks is true of this particular case of sensory knowledge of the world is that he must know he is not dreaming if he is to know that he is sitting by the fire with a piece of paper in his hand. That is required, not because of any peculiarities of this particular case, but presumably because, according to Descartes, it is a necessary condition of any case—even a best possible case—of knowledge of the world by means of the senses. That is why I ascribed to Descartes the quite general thesis that knowing that one is not dreaming is a condition of knowing something about the world around us on the basis of the senses. Since he thinks the possibility of his dreaming must be ruled out in the case he considers, and the case he considers is regarded as typical and without special characteristics of its own, he thinks that the possibility that he is dreaming must be ruled out in every case of knowing something about the world by means of the senses.

If that really is a condition of knowing something about the world, I think it can be shown that Descartes is right in holding that it can never be fulfilled. That is what the straightforward response denies, and that is why I think that response must be wrong. We cannot accept the terms of Descartes's challenge and then hope to meet it.

Suppose Descartes tries to determine that he is not dreaming in order to fulfil what he sees as a necessary condition of knowing that he is sitting by the fire with a piece of paper in his hand. How is he to proceed? He realizes that his seeing his hand and seeing and feeling a piece of paper before him and feeling the warmth of the fire—in fact his getting all the sensory experiences or all the sensory information he is then getting—is something that could be happening even if he were dreaming. To establish that he is not dreaming he would therefore need something more than just those experiences or that information alone. He would also need to know whether those experiences and that information are reliable, not merely dreamt. If he could find some operation or test, or if he could find some circumstance or state of affairs, that indicated to him that he was not dreaming, perhaps he could then fulfil the condition—he could know that he was not dreaming. But how could a test or a circumstance or a state of affairs indicate to him that he is not dreaming *if* a condition of knowing *anything* about the world is that he know he is not dreaming? It could not. He could never fulfil the condition.

Let us suppose that there is in fact some test which a person can perform successfully only if he is not dreaming, or some circumstance or state of affairs which obtains only if that person is not dreaming. Of course for that test or state of affairs to be of any use to him Descartes would have to know of it. He would have to know that there is such a test or that there is a state of affairs that shows that he is not dreaming; without such information he would be no better off for telling that he is not dreaming than he would be if there were no such test or state of affairs at all. To have acquired that information he would at some time have to have known more than just something about the course of his sensory experience, since the connection between the performance of a certain test, or between a certain state of affairs, and someone's not dreaming is not itself just a fact about the course of that person's sensory experience; it is a fact about the world beyond his sensory experiences. Now strictly speaking if it is a condition of knowing *anything* about the world beyond one's sensory experiences that one know that one is not dreaming, there is an obvious obstacle to Descartes's ever having got the information he needs about that test or state of affairs. He would have to have known at some time that he was not dreaming in order to get the information he needs to tell at *any* time that he is not dreaming—and that cannot be done.

But suppose we forget about this difficulty and concede that Descartes does indeed know (somehow) that there is a test or circumstance or state of affairs that unfailingly indicates that he is not dreaming. Still, there is an obstacle to his ever using that test or state of affairs to tell that he is not dreaming and thereby fulfilling the condition for knowledge of the world. The test would have to be something he could know he had performed successfully, the state of affairs would have to be something he could know obtains. If he completely unwittingly happened to perform the test, or if the state of affairs happened to obtain but he didn't know that it did, he would be in no better position for telling whether he was dreaming than he would be if he had done nothing or did not even know that there was such a test. But how is he to know that the test has been performed successfully or that the state of affairs in question does in fact obtain? Anything one can experience in one's waking life can also be dreamt about; it is possible to dream that one has performed a certain test or dream that one has established that a certain state of affairs obtains. And, as we have seen, to dream that something about the world around you is so is not thereby to know that it is so. In order to know that his test has been performed or that the state of affairs in question obtains Descartes would therefore have to establish that he is not merely dreaming that he performed the test successfully or that he established that the state of affairs obtains. How could that in turn be known? Obviously the particular test or state of affairs already in question cannot serve as a guarantee of its own authenticity, since it might have been merely dreamt, so some further test or state of affairs would be needed to indicate that the original test was actually performed and not merely dreamt, or that the state of affairs in question was actually ascertained to obtain and not just dreamt to obtain. But this further test or state of affairs is subject to the same general condition in turn. *Every* piece of knowledge that goes beyond one's sensory experiences requires that one know one is not dreaming. This second test or state of affairs will therefore be of use only if Descartes knows that he is not merely dreaming that he is performing or ascertaining it, since merely to dream that he had established the authenticity of the first test is not to have established it. And so on. At no point can he find a test for not dreaming which he can know has been successfully performed or a state of affairs correlated with not dreaming which he can know obtains. He can therefore never fulfil what Descartes says is a necessary condition of knowing something about the world around him. He can never know that he is not dreaming.

I must emphasize that this conclusion is reached *only* on the assumption that it is a condition of knowing anything about the world around us on the basis of the senses that we know we are not dreaming that the thing is so. I think it is his acceptance of that condition that leads Descartes to 'see so manifestly that there are no certain indications by which we may clearly distinguish wakefulness from sleep'. And I think Descartes is absolutely right to draw that conclusion, *given* what he thinks is a condition of knowledge of the world. But all I have argued on Descartes's behalf (he never spells out his reasoning) is that we cannot both accept that condition of knowledge and hope to fulfil it, as the straightforward response hopes to do. And of course if one of the necessary conditions of knowledge of the world can never be fulfilled, knowledge of the world around us will be impossible.

I think we have now located Descartes's reason for his negative verdict about sensory knowledge in general. If we agree that he must know that he is not dreaming if he is to know in his particular case that he is sitting by the fire with a piece of paper in his hand, we must also agree that we can know nothing about the world around us.

Once we recognize that the condition Descartes takes as necessary can never be fulfilled if he is right in thinking it is indeed necessary, we are naturally led to the question whether Descartes is right. Is it really a condition of knowing something about the world that one know one is not dreaming? That is the second of the three questions I distinguished. It is the one that has received the least attention. In asking it now I do not mean to be going back on something I said earlier was undeniably true, viz., that if one is dreaming that something about the world is so one does not thereby know that it is so. That still seems to me undeniable, but it is not the same as Descartes's assumption that one must know that one is not dreaming if one is to know something about the world. The undeniable truth says only that you lack knowledge if you are dreaming; Descartes says that you lack knowledge if you don't know that you are not dreaming. Only with the stronger assumption can his sceptical conclusion be reached.

Is that assumption true? In so far as we find Descartes's reasoning convincing, or even plausible, I think it is because we too on reflection find that it is true. I said that not much attention had been paid to that particular part of Descartes's reasoning, and I think that too is because, as he presents it, the step seems perfectly convincing and so only other parts of the argument appear vulnerable. Why is that so? Is it because Descartes's assumption is indeed true? Is there anything we can do that would help us determine whether it is true or not? The question is important because I have argued so far that *if* it is true we can never know anything about the world around us on the basis of the senses, and philosophical scepticism about the external world is correct. We would have to find that conclusion as convincing or as plausible as we find the assumption from which it is derived.

Given our original favourable response to Descartes's reasoning, then, it can scarcely be denied that what I have called his assumption or condition *seems* perfectly natural to insist on. Perhaps it seems like nothing more than an instance of a familiar commonplace about knowledge. We are all aware that, even in the most ordinary circumstances when nothing very important turns on the outcome, we cannot know a particular thing unless we have ruled out certain possibilities that we recognize are incompatible with our knowing that thing.

Suppose that on looking out the window I announce casually that there is a goldfinch in the garden. If I am asked how I know it is a goldfinch and I reply that it is yellow, we all recognize that in the normal case that is not enough for knowledge. 'For all you've said so far,' it might be replied, 'the thing could be a canary, so how do you know it's a goldfinch?'. A certain possibility compatible with everything I have said so far has been raised, and if what

I have said so far is all I have got to go on and I don't know that the thing in the garden is not a canary, then I do not know that there is a goldfinch in the garden. I must be able to rule out the possibility that it is a canary if I am to know that it is a goldfinch. Anyone who speaks about knowledge and understands what others say about it will recognize this fact or condition in particular cases.

In this example what is said to be possible is something incompatible with the truth of what I claim to know—if that bird were a canary it would not be a goldfinch in the garden, but a canary. What I believe in believing it is a goldfinch would be false. But that is not the only way a possibility can work against my knowledge. If I come to suspect that all the witnesses have conspired and made up a story about the man's being in Cleveland that night, for example, and their testimony is all I have got to go on in believing that he was in Cleveland, I might find that I no longer know whether he was there or not until I have some reason to rule out my suspicion. If their testimony were all invented I would not know that the man was in Cleveland. But strictly speaking his being in Cleveland is not incompatible with their making up a story saying he was. They might have invented a story to protect him, whereas in fact, unknown to them, he was there all the time. Such a complicated plot is not necessary to bring out the point; Moore's Duke of Devonshire is enough. From the fact that he was dreaming that he was speaking in the House of Lords it did not follow that he was not speaking in the House of Lords. In fact he was. The possibility of dreaming—which was actual in that case—did not imply the falsity of what was believed. A possible deficiency in the basis of my belief can interfere with my knowledge without itself rendering false the very thing I believe. A hallucinogenic drug might cause me to see my bed covered with a huge pile of leaves, for example.[5] Having taken that drug, I will know the actual state of my bed only if I know that what I see is not just the effect of the drug; I must be able to rule out the possibility that I am hallucinating the bed and the leaves. But however improbable

[5] A memorable example H. H. Price gave in a lecture in 1962. It is my impression that Price was reporting on an actual hallucination of his.

it might be that my bed is actually covered with leaves, its not being covered with leaves does not follow from the fact that I am hallucinating that it is. What I am hallucinating could nevertheless be (unknown to me) true. But a goldfinch simply could not be a canary. So although there are two different ways in which a certain possibility can threaten my knowledge, it remains true that there are always certain possibilities which must be known not to obtain if I am to know what I claim to know.

I think these are just familiar facts about human knowledge, something we all recognize and abide by in our thought and talk about knowing things. We know what would be a valid challenge to a claim to know something, and we can recognize the relevance and force of objections made to our claims to know. The question before us is to what extent Descartes's investigation of his knowledge that he is sitting by the fire with a piece of paper in his hand follows these recognized everyday procedures for assessing claims to know. If it does follow them faithfully, and yet leads to the conclusion that he cannot know where he is or what is happening around him, we seem forced to accept his negative conclusion about knowledge in general just as we are forced to accept the conclusion that I do not know it is a goldfinch or do not know the witness was in Cleveland because I cannot rule out the possibilities which must be ruled out if I am to know such things. Is Descartes's introduction of the possibility that he might be dreaming just like the introduction of the possibility that it might be a canary in the garden or that the alibi might be contrived or that it might be a hallucination of my bed covered with leaves?

Those possibilities were all such that if they obtained I did not know what I claimed to know, and they had to be known not to obtain in order for the original knowledge-claim to be true. Does Descartes's dream-possibility fulfil both of those conditions? I have already said that it seems undeniable that it fulfils the first. If he *were* dreaming Descartes would not know what he claims to know. Someone who is dreaming does not thereby know anything about the world around him even if the world around him happens to be just the way he dreams or believes it to be. So his dreaming *is* incompatible with his knowing. But does it fulfil the second condition? Is it a possibility which must be known not to obtain if Descartes is to know that he is sitting by the fire with a piece of paper in his hand? I think it is difficult simply to deny that it is. The evident force of Descartes's reasoning when we first encounter it is enough to show that it certainly strikes us as a relevant possibility, as something that he should know not to obtain if he is to know where he is and what is happening around him.

When that possibility strikes us as obviously relevant in Descartes's investigation we might come to think that it is because of a simple and obvious fact about knowledge. In the case of the goldfinch we immediately recognize that I must know that it is not a canary if I am to know it is a goldfinch. And it is very natural to think that that is simply because its being a canary is incompatible with its being a goldfinch. If it were a canary it would not be a goldfinch, and I would therefore be wrong in saying that it is; so if I am to know it is a goldfinch I must rule out the possibility that it is a canary. The idea is that the two conditions I distinguished in the previous paragraph are not really separate after all. As soon as we see that a certain possibility is incompatible with our knowing such-and-such, it is suggested, we immediately recognize that it is a possibility that must be known not to obtain if we are to know the such-and-such in question. We see that the dream-possibility satisfies that first condition in Descartes's case (if he were dreaming, he wouldn't know), and that is why, according to this suggestion, we immediately see that it is relevant and must be ruled out. Something we all recognize about knowledge is what is said to make that obvious to us.

But is the 'simple and obvious fact about knowledge' appealed to in this explanation really something that is true of human knowledge even in the most ordinary circumstances? What exactly is the 'fact' in question supposed to be? I have described it so far, as applied to the case of the goldfinch, as the fact that if I know something p (it's a goldfinch) I must know the falsity of all those things incompatible with p (e.g., it's a canary). If there were one of those things that I did not know to be false, and it were in fact true, I would not know that p, since in that case something incompatible with *p* would be true and so *p* would not be true. But to say that I must know that all those things incompatible with *p* are false is the same as saying that I must know the truth of all those things that must be true if *p* is true. And it is extremely implausible to say that that is a 'simple and obvious fact' we all recognize about human knowledge.

The difficulty is that there are no determinate limits to the number of things that follow from the things I already know. But it cannot be said that I now know all those indeterminately many things, although they all must be true if the things that I already know are true. Even granting that I now know a great deal about a lot of different things, my knowledge obviously does not extend to everything that follows from what I now know. If it did, mathematics, to take only one example, would be a great deal easier than it is—or else impossibly difficult. In knowing the truth of the simple axioms of number theory, for example, I would thereby know the truth of everything that follows from them; every theorem of number theory would already be known. Or, taking the pessimistic side, since obviously no one does know all the theorems of number theory, it would follow that no one even knows that those simple axioms are true.

It is absurd to say that we enjoy or require such virtual omniscience, so it is more plausible to hold that the 'simple and obvious fact' we all recognize about knowledge is the weaker requirement that we must know the falsity of all those things that we *know* to be incompatible with the things we know. I know that a bird's being a canary is incompatible with its being a goldfinch; that is not some far-flung, unknown consequence of its being a goldfinch, but something that anyone would know who knew anything about goldfinches at all. And the idea is that that is why I must know that it is not a canary if I am to know that it is a goldfinch. Perhaps, in order to know something, *p*, I do not need to know the falsity of all those things that are incompatible with *p*, but it can seem that at least I must know the falsity of all those things that I *know* to be incompatible with *p*. Since I claim to know that the bird is a goldfinch, and I know that its being a goldfinch implies that it is not a canary,

I must for that reason know that it is not a canary if my original claim is true. In claiming to know it is a goldfinch I was, so to speak, committing myself to knowing that it is not a canary, and I must honour my commitments.

This requirement as it stands, even if it does explain why I must know that the bird is not a canary, does not account for the relevance of the other sorts of possibilities I have mentioned. The reason in the goldfinch case was said to be that I know that its being a canary is incompatible with its being a goldfinch. But that will not explain why I must rule out the possibility that the witnesses have invented a story about the man's being in Cleveland, or the possibility that I am hallucinating my bed covered with a pile of leaves. Nor will it explain why Descartes must rule out the possibility that he is dreaming. What I claimed to know in the first case is that the man was in Cleveland that night. But, as we saw earlier, it is not a consequence of his being in Cleveland that no one will invent a story to the effect that he was in Cleveland; they might mistakenly believe he was not there and then tell what they think is a lie. Nor is it a consequence of my bed's being covered with leaves that I am not hallucinating that it is. But we recognize that in order to know in those cases I nevertheless had to rule out those possibilities. Similarly, as the Duke of Devonshire reminds us, it is not a consequence of Descartes's sitting by the fire with a piece of paper in his hand that he is not dreaming that he is. So if it is obvious to us that Descartes must know that he is not dreaming if he is to know that he is sitting by the fire, it cannot be simply because the possibility in question is known to be incompatible with what he claims to know. It is not.

If there is some 'simple and obvious fact about knowledge' that we recognize and rely on in responding to Descartes's reasoning it must therefore be more complicated than what has been suggested so far. Reflecting even on the uncontroversial everyday examples alone can easily lead us to suppose that it is something like this: if somebody knows something, *p*, he must know the falsity of all those things incompatible with his knowing that *p* (or perhaps all those things he knows to be incompatible with his knowing that *p*). I will not speculate further on the qualifications or emendations needed to make the principle less implausible. The question now is whether it is our adherence to any such principle or requirement that is responsible for our recognition that the possibility that the bird is a canary or the possibility that the witnesses made up a story must be known not to obtain if I am to know the things I said I knew in those cases. What exactly are the procedures or standards we follow in the most ordinary, humdrum cases of putative knowledge? Reflection on the source of Descartes's sceptical reasoning has led to difficulties in describing and therefore in understanding even the most familiar procedures we follow in everyday life. That is one of the rewards of a study of philosophical scepticism.

The main difficulty in understanding our ordinary procedures is that no principle like those I have mentioned could possibly describe the way we proceed in everyday life. Or, to put it less dogmatically, if our adherence to some such requirement were responsible for our reactions in those ordinary cases, Descartes would be perfectly correct, and philosophical scepticism about the external world would be true. Nobody would know anything about the world around us. If, in order to know something, we must rule out a possibility which is known to be incompatible with our knowing it, Descartes is perfectly right to insist that he must know that he is not dreaming if he is to know that he is sitting by the fire with a piece of paper in his hand. He knows his dreaming is incompatible with his knowing. I have already argued that if he is right in insisting that that condition must be fulfilled for knowledge of the world around us he is also right in concluding that it can never be fulfilled; fulfilling it would require knowledge which itself would be possible only if the condition were fulfilled. So both steps of Descartes's reasoning would be valid and his conclusion would be true.

That conclusion can be avoided, it seems to me, only if we can find some way to avoid the requirement that we must know we are not dreaming if we are to know anything about the world around us. But that requirement cannot be avoided if it is nothing more than an instance of a general procedure we recognize and insist on in making and assessing knowledge-claims in everyday and scientific life. We have no notion of knowledge other than what is embodied in those procedures and practices. So if that requirement is a 'fact' of our ordinary conception of knowledge we will have to accept the conclusion that no one knows anything about the world around us.

Before going more fully in subsequent chapters into the question of how closely Descartes's reasoning does follow the familiar procedures of everyday life I want to say a few more words about the position we would all be in if Descartes's conclusion as he understands it were correct. I described him earlier as having lost the whole world, as knowing at most what he is experiencing or how things appear to him, but knowing nothing about how things really are in the world around him. To show how anyone in that position could come to know anything about the world around him is what I am calling the problem of our knowledge of the external world, and it is worth dwelling for a moment on just how difficult a problem that turns out to be if it has been properly raised.

If we are in the predicament Descartes finds himself in at the end of his *First Meditation* we cannot tell by means of the senses whether we are dreaming or not; all the sensory experiences we are having are compatible with our merely dreaming of a world around us while that world is in fact very different from the way we take it to be. Our knowledge is in that way confined to our sensory experiences. There seems to be no way of going beyond them to know that the world around us really is this way rather than that. Of course we might have very strongly-held beliefs about the way things are. We might even be unable to get rid of the conviction that we are sitting by the fire holding a piece of paper, for example. But if we acknowledge that our sensory experiences are all we ever have to go on in gaining knowledge about the world, and we acknowledge, as we must, that given our experiences as they are we could nevertheless be simply dreaming of sitting by the fire, we must concede that we do not know that we are sitting by the fire. Of course, we are in no position to claim the opposite either. We cannot conclude that we are not sitting by the fire; we simply cannot tell which is the case. Our sensory experience gives us no basis for believing one thing about the world around us rather than its opposite, but our sensory experience is all we have got to go on. So whatever unshakeable conviction we might nevertheless retain, that conviction cannot be knowledge. Even if we are in fact holding a piece of paper by the fire, so that what we are convinced of is in fact true, that true conviction is still not knowledge. The world around us, whatever it might be like, is in that way beyond our grasp. We can know nothing of how it is, no matter what convictions, beliefs, or opinions we continue, perhaps inevitably, to hold about it.

What *can* we know in such a predicament? We can perhaps know what sensory experiences we are having, or how things seem to us to be. At least that much of our knowledge will not be threatened by the kind of attack Descartes makes on our knowledge of the world beyond our experiences. What we can know turns out to be a great deal less than we thought we knew before engaging in that assessment of our knowledge. Our position is much more restricted, much poorer, than we had originally supposed. We are confined at best to what Descartes calls 'ideas' of things around us, representations of things or states of affairs which, for all we can know, might or might not have something corresponding to them in reality. We are in a sense imprisoned within those representations, at least with respect to our knowledge. Any attempt to go beyond them to try and tell whether the world really is as they represent it to be can yield only more representations, more deliverances of sense experience which themselves are compatible with reality's being very different from the way we take it to be on the basis of our sensory experiences. There is a gap, then, between the most that we can ever find out on the basis of our sensory experience and the way things really are. In knowing the one we do not thereby know the other.

This can seem to leave us in the position of finding a barrier between ourselves and the world around us. There would then be a veil of sensory experiences or sensory objects which we could not penetrate but which would be no reliable guide to the world beyond the veil. If we were in such a position, I think it is quite clear that we could not know what is going on beyond the veil. There would be no possibility of our getting reliable sensory information about the world beyond the veil; all such reports would simply be more representations, further ingredients of the ever-more-complicated veil. We could know nothing but the veil itself. We would be in the position of someone waking up to find himself locked in a room full of television sets and trying to find out what is going on in the world outside. For all he can know whatever is producing the patterns he can see on the screens in front of him might be something other than well-functioning cameras directed on to the passing show outside the room. The victim might switch on more of the sets in the room to try to get more information, and he might find that some of the sets show events exactly similar or coherently related to those already visible on the screens he can see. But all those pictures will be no help to him without some independent information, some knowledge which does not come to him from the pictures themselves, about how the pictures he does see before him are connected with what is going on outside the room. The problem of the external world is the problem of finding out, or knowing how we could find out, about the world around us if we were in that sort of predicament. It is perhaps enough simply to put the problem this way to convince us that it can never be given a satisfactory solution.

But putting the problem this way, or only this way, has its drawbacks. For one thing, it encourages a facile dismissive response; not a solution to the problem as posed, but a rejection of it. I do not mean that we should not find a way to reject the problem—I think that is our only hope—but this particular response, I believe, is wrong, or at the very least premature. It is derived almost entirely from the perhaps overly dramatic description of the predicament I have just given.

I have described Descartes's sceptical conclusion as implying that we are permanently sealed off from a world we can never reach. We are restricted to the passing show on the veil of perception, with no possibility of extending our knowledge to the world beyond. We are confined to appearances we can never know to match or to deviate from the imperceptible reality that is forever denied us. This way of putting it naturally encourages us to minimize the seriousness of the predicament, to try to settle for what is undeniably available to us, or perhaps even to argue that nothing that concerns us or makes human life worthwhile has been left out.

If an imperceptible 'reality', as it is called on this picture, is forever inaccessible to us, what concern can it be of ours? How can something we can have no contact with, something from which we are permanently sealed off, even make sense to us at all? Why should we be distressed by an alleged limitation of our knowledge if it is not even possible for the 'limitation' to be overcome? If it makes no sense to aspire to anything beyond what is possible for us, it will seem that we should give no further thought to this allegedly imperceptible 'reality'. Our sensory experiences, past, present, and future, will then be thought to be all we are or should be concerned with, and the idea of a 'reality' lying beyond them necessarily out of our reach will seem like nothing more than a philosopher's invention. What a sceptical philosopher would be denying us would then be nothing we could have ordinary commerce with or interest in anyway. Nothing distressing about our ordinary position in the familiar world would have been revealed by a philosopher who simply invents or constructs something he calls 'reality' or 'the external world' and then demonstrates that we can have no access to it. That would show nothing wrong with the everyday sensory knowledge we seek and think we find in ordinary life and in scientific laboratories, nor would it show that our relation to the ordinary reality that concerns us is different from what we originally thought it to be.

I think this reaction to the picture of our being somehow imprisoned behind the veil of our own sensory experiences is very natural and immediately appealing. It is natural and perhaps always advisable for a prisoner to try to make the best of the restricted life behind bars. But however much more bearable it makes the prospect of life-imprisonment, it should not lead him to deny the greater desirability, let alone the existence, of life outside. In so far as the comfort of this response to philosophical scepticism depends on such a denial it is at the very least premature and is probably based on misunderstanding. It depends on a particular diagnosis or account of how and why the philosophical argument succeeds in reaching its conclusion. The idea is that the 'conclusion' is reached only by contrivance. The inaccessible 'reality' denied to us is said to be simply an artefact of the philosopher's investigation and not something that otherwise should concern us. That is partly a claim about how the philosophical investigation of knowledge works; as such, it needs to be explained and argued for. We can draw no consolation from it until we have some reason to think it might be an accurate account of what the philosopher does. So far we have no such reason. On the contrary; so far we have every reason to think that Descartes has revealed the impossibility of the very knowledge of the world that we are most interested in and which we began by thinking we possess or can easily acquire. In any case, that would be the only conclusion to draw if Descartes's investigation does indeed parallel the ordinary kinds of assessments we make of our knowledge in everyday life.

We saw that I can ask what I really know about the common cold, or whether I really know that the witness was in Cleveland on the night in question, and that I can go on to discover that I do not really know what I thought I knew. In such ordinary cases there is no suggestion that what I have discovered is that I lack some special, esoteric thing called 'real knowledge', or that I lack knowledge of some exotic, hitherto-unheard-of domain called 'reality'. If I ask what I know about the common cold, and I come to realize that I do not really know whether it can be caused by sitting in a draught or not, the kind of knowledge I discover I lack is precisely what I was asking about or taking it for granted I had at the outset. I do not conclude with a shrug that it no longer matters because what I now find I lack is only knowledge about a special domain called 'reality' that was somehow invented only to serve as the inaccessible realm of something called 'real knowledge'. I simply conclude that I don't really know whether colds are caused by sitting in draughts or not. If I say in a jury-room on Monday that we can eliminate the suspect because we know he was in Cleveland that night, and I then discover by reflection on Tuesday that I don't really know he was in Cleveland that night, what I am denying I have on Tuesday is the very thing I said on Monday that I had.

There is no suggestion in these and countless similar everyday cases that somehow in the course of our reflections on whether and how we know something we are inevitably led to change or elevate our conception of knowledge into something else called 'real knowledge' which we showed no signs of being interested in at the beginning. Nor is it plausible to suggest that our ordinary assessments of knowledge somehow lead us to postulate a 'reality' that is simply an artefact of our inquiries about our knowledge. When we ask whether we really know something we are simply asking whether we know that thing. The 'really' signifies that we have had second thoughts on the matter, or that we arc subjecting it to more careful scrutiny, or that knowledge is being contrasted with something else, but not that we believe in something called 'real knowledge' which is different from or more elevated than the ordinary knowledge we are interested in. Knowing something differs from merely believing it or assuming it or taking it for granted or simply being under the impression that it is true, and so forth, so asking whether we really know something is asking whether we know it as opposed to, for example, merely believing it or assuming it or taking it for granted or simply being under the impression that it is true.

If that is true of our ordinary assessments of knowledge, and if Descartes's investigation of his knowledge that he is sitting by the fire with a piece of paper in his hand is just like those ordinary cases, his discovery that he doesn't know in the case he considers will have the same significance as it has in those ordinary cases. And if that example is indeed representative of our knowledge of the world around us, the kind of knowledge we are shown to lack will be the very kind of knowledge we originally thought we had of things like our sitting by the fire holding a piece of paper. Without a demonstration that Descartes's philosophical investigation differs from our ordinary assessments in some way that prevents its negative conclusion from having the kind of significance similar conclusions are rightly taken to have in everyday life, we can derive no consolation from the ungrounded idea that the reality from which he shows our knowledge is excluded does not or should not concern us anyway. It is the investigation of his everyday knowledge, and not merely the fanciful picture of a veil of perception, that generates Descartes's negative verdict.

But even if we did try to console ourselves with the thought that we can settle for what we *can* know on Descartes's account, how much consolation could it give us? The position Descartes's argument says we are in is much worse than what is contemplated in the optimistic response of merely shrugging off any concern with an imperceptible 'reality'.

For one thing, we would not in fact be left with what we have always taken to be the familiar objects of our everyday experience—tables and chairs, trees and flowers, bread and wine. If Descartes is right we know nothing of such things. What we perceive and are in direct sensory contact with is never a physical object or state of affairs, but only a representation—something that could be just the way it is even if there were no objects at all of the sort it represents. So if we were to settle for the realm of things we could have knowledge about even if Descartes's conclusion were correct, we would not be settling for the comfortable world with which we began. We would have lost all of that, at least as something we can know anything about, and we would be restricted to facts about how things seem to us at the moment rather than how they are.

It might still be felt that after all nothing is certain in this changing world, so we should not aspire to firm truths about how things are. As long as we know that all or most of us agree about how things seem to us, or have seemed to us up till now, we might feel we have enough to give our social, cultural, and intellectual life as much stability as we can reasonably expect or need. But again this reaction does not really acknowledge the poverty or restrictedness of the position Descartes's sceptical conclusion would leave each of us in. Strictly speaking, there is no community of acting, experiencing and thinking persons I can know anything about if Descartes is correct. Other people, as I understand them, are not simply sensory experiences of mine; they too, if they exist, will therefore inhabit the unreachable world beyond my sensory experiences, along with the tables and chairs and other things about which I can know nothing. So at least with respect to what I can know I could not console myself with thoughts of a like-minded community of perceivers all working together and cheerfully making do with what a communal veil of perception provides. I would have no more reason to believe that there are any other people than I have to believe that I am now sitting in a chair writing. The representations or sensory experiences to which Descartes's conclusion would restrict my knowledge could be no other than my own sensory experiences; there could be no communal knowledge even of the veil of perception itself. If my own sensory experiences do not make it possible for me to know things about the world around me they do not make it possible for me to know even whether there are any other sensory experiences or any other perceiving beings at all.

The consequences of accepting Descartes's conclusion as it is meant to be understood are truly disastrous. There is no easy way of accommodating oneself to its profound negative implications. But perhaps by now we have come far enough to feel that the whole idea is simply absurd, that ultimately it is not even intelligible, and that there can be no question of 'accepting' Descartes's conclusion at all. I have no wish to discourage such a reaction. I would only insist that the alleged absurdity or unintelligibility must be identified and made out. I think that is the only way we can hope to learn whatever there is to be learned from Descartes's investigation. In the next chapter I consider a powerful form of criticism along these lines and try to sketch a certain conception of the relation between the philosophical investigation of knowledge and our everyday standards and procedures for assessing knowledge. If that conception can be explained and defended, the sceptical conclusion will remain intact and its scope and negative significance will be undiminished.

II

Philosophical Scepticism and Everyday Life

I think that when we first encounter the sceptical reasoning outlined in the previous chapter we find it immediately gripping. It appeals to something deep in our nature and seems to raise a real problem about the human condition. It is natural to feel that either we must accept the literal truth of the conclusion that we can know nothing about the world around us, or else we must somehow show that it is not true. Accepting it and holding to it consistently seem disastrous, and yet rejecting it seems impossible. But what *is* the 'literal truth' of that conclusion? Both responses depend on a firm understanding of what it says and means; without that there would be nothing determinate to accept as true or to reject as false. That proper understanding of the sceptical conclusion is what I want to concentrate on. That is why I suggest we look to the source of that conclusion—how it is arrived at and how it becomes so unavoidable—and in particular at just how closely Descartes's requirement that the dream-possibility must always be eliminated corresponds to our ordinary standards or requirements for knowledge in everyday life.

In suggesting that we try to determine exactly what the sceptical reasoning manages to establish I do not mean to deny that it does raise deep problems about the human condition and can reveal something of great significance about human knowledge. It might seem as if that is not so, since it might seem that as soon as we even glance in the direction of the standards and procedures we follow in everyday life we will find that there is nothing at all in Descartes's argument. It is obvious that we do not always insist that people know they are not dreaming before we allow that they know something in everyday life, or even in science or a court of law, where the standards are presumably stricter. So it can easily look as if Descartes reaches his sceptical conclusion only by violating our ordinary standards and requirements for knowledge, perhaps substituting a new and different set of his own. If that were so his conclusion would not have the consequences it seems to have for our everyday and scientific knowledge and beliefs. So understood, it would not have the significance we originally take it to have.

One example of a diagnosis of scepticism along these lines goes as follows. Suppose someone makes the quite startling announcement that there are no physicians in the city of New York. That certainly seems to go against something we all thought we knew to be true. It would really be astonishing if there were no physicians at all in a city that size. When we ask how the remarkable discovery was made, and how long this deplorable state of affairs has obtained, suppose we find that the bearer of the startling news says it is true because, as he explains, what he means by 'physician' is a person who has a medical degree and can cure any conceivable illness in less than two minutes.[1] We are no longer surprised by his announcement, nor do we find that it contradicts anything we all thought we knew to be true. We find it quite believable that there is no one in the whole city who fulfils all the conditions of that peculiar 're-definition' of 'physician'. Once we understand it as it was meant to be understood, there is nothing startling about the announcement except perhaps the form in which it was expressed. It does not deny what on first sight it might seem to deny, and it poses no threat to our original belief that there are thousands and thousands of physicians in New York.

The suggestion is that the sceptical conclusion is in the same boat. It too is said to rest on a misunderstanding or distortion of the meanings of the words in which it is expressed. It is at first astonishing to be told that no one can ever know anything about the world around us, but once we learn that the 'knowledge' in question is 'knowledge' that requires the fulfilment of a condition which is not in fact required for the everyday or scientific knowledge we are

[1] See P. Edwards, 'Bertrand Russell's Doubts About Induction' in A. Flew (ed.), *Logic and Language*, First Series (Oxford, 1955).

interested in, we will no longer be surprised or disturbed by that announcement. We do not insist that the dream-possibility must always be known not to obtain in order to know things in everyday or scientific life. When we find that Descartes's sceptical reasoning does insist on that requirement, we will find that his sceptical conclusion does not contradict anything we thought we knew at the outset. We might find it quite believable that there is no knowledge of the world fulfilling all the conditions of Descartes's special 're-definition' of knowledge. But properly understood, his conclusion would not deny what its peculiar linguistic form originally led us to suppose it denies, and it would pose no threat to our everyday knowledge and beliefs. Any exhilaration or disquiet we might have felt on first encountering it must therefore have been due to nothing but illusion.

If there were nothing more behind Descartes's sceptical conclusion than there is behind the peculiar announcement about physicians in New York it would indeed be profoundly uninteresting. If Descartes simply imposes on knowledge an unreasonable or outrageous requirement, and then points out (even quite correctly) that it can never be fulfilled, there will be no reason to go along with him, even temporarily. What he says would reveal nothing more about the everyday or scientific knowledge that we want a philosophical theory to illuminate than that crazy announcement manages to reveal about physicians in New York. Someone is no less a physician even though there are many patients he never happens to cure, and if Descartes is simply distorting the requirements for knowledge, what we possess in everyday life and in science will be no less knowledge even though we do not usually fulfil the outrageous condition that we must know we are not dreaming. I think many philosophers find philosophical scepticism uninteresting and the study of it unprofitable on grounds such as these. Descartes's assessment of his own position is thought to deviate so radically and so obviously from our familiar assessments that it cannot be expected to reveal anything of deep or lasting significance about the human knowledge we are interested in.

It is perhaps not so immediately obvious that a change or distortion of meaning has occurred in the philosophical case as it is in the announcement about physicians in New York. If we are at all taken in by the sceptical reasoning, the misunderstanding must be to that extent hidden from us, just as it is presumably hidden from the sceptical philosopher himself. Giving that special meaning to the word 'physician' is nothing more than a crazy whim. But the philosopher's alleged change in the meaning of the word 'know' might not be unmotivated; certainly it is not just a personal whim. What lies behind the sceptical conclusion might therefore turn out to be more interesting and more worthy of investigation than what lies behind that 're-definition' of 'physician'.

But still, it will be felt, the philosophical case will be interesting only to the extent to which it is interesting to find out how and why philosophers so persistently go wrong—why they continue to insist, as they apparently do, on misunderstanding or distorting the meanings of the familiar words they examine and use. The investigation of philosophical scepticism would then be of pathological interest only. Aside from revealing how easy it is for philosophers to fall into confusion or make mistakes, it could not be expected to reveal anything deep or of lasting significance about human knowledge itself.

J. L. Austin, for example, thought an inquiry into the sources of the sceptical conclusion was 'a matter of unpicking, one by one, a mass of seductive (mainly verbal) fallacies, or exposing a wide variety of concealed motives—an operation which leaves us, in a sense, just where we began'.[2] In a positive vein, he thought we might at most learn something about the meanings of certain English words that are interesting in their own right.[3] Many recent philosophers who care less than Austin did about the meanings of those English words would hold that if we simply keep our wits about us and guard against the errors that have led older philosophers astray we will find no reason to follow them down the garden path to philosophical scepticism. The misguided sceptical conclusion is held to reveal nothing about our everyday or scientific knowledge and beliefs because it is not really about that knowledge or those beliefs at all, any more than

[2] J. L. Austin, *Sense and Sensibilia* (Oxford, 1962), pp. 4–5.

[3] *Sense and Sensibilia*, p. 5.

that crazy announcement is really about the physicians in New York.

I have tried so far to suggest that the best strategy in the face of the sceptical argument is to examine more carefully the requirement that we must know we are not dreaming if we are to know anything about the world around us. I think that is much more promising than accepting Descartes's condition as a genuine condition of knowledge and trying to show that it can be fulfilled. I argued that that strategy cannot succeed. If it is in general a necessary condition of our knowing something about the world around us that we know we are not dreaming, it follows that we can never know that we are not dreaming. That is why I think the only hope lies in avoiding that condition. But I do not share the impression that what Descartes says is a condition of knowledge of the world is obviously no such condition at all. There seems to me to be no question that the meaning of 'physician' has been changed in that trivial example, but in Descartes's reasoning I think much deeper and more complex issues are raised. And what is at stake is more than simply a mass of avoidable mistakes or confusions by traditional philosophers. I think the right kind of investigation into the sources of Descartes's requirement promises to illuminate something about our actual conception of knowledge, or about what we seek when we try to understand it, or perhaps even about human knowledge itself.

Let us suppose for the moment that the critics are right, and that what Descartes says is a requirement for knowledge of the world is really no such requirement at all. How could that be known, if it were true? What shows or would show that Descartes is or must be distorting or misunderstanding what knowledge is when he insists that we must know we are not dreaming if we are to know anything about the world around us? When critics of Descartes's conclusion argue that the meaning of 'know' does not in fact require what Descartes apparently requires of it, that knowledge is not 'closed under logical consequence', or that the word 'know' does not 'penetrate' to all the logical consequences of what is known, or to what are known to be its logical consequences, or even to what are known to be the consequences of knowing it,[4] how are such claims about knowledge or about the meaning of the word 'know' themselves to be supported? I will try to bring out some of the difficulties this question raises by looking at one of the most persuasive and most influential versions of that line of criticism.

The sceptical conclusion is reached in the course of an assessment of our knowledge of the world—an investigation of how we know the things we think we know about the world around us. J. L. Austin thinks philosophers in the course of such assessments have not paid sufficient attention to 'what sort of thing does actually happen when ordinary people are asked "How do you know?" ',[5] and in his 'Other Minds' he tries to show how the typical philosophical investigation deviates from our normal practices.

If asked how I know there is a goldfinch in the garden, for example, I might reply by explaining how I have come to know about goldfinches, or about small British birds in general, or I might explain how I came to be in a position to recognize and hence to know about the goldfinch in the garden in this particular case. This second kind of reply to the question 'How do you know?' might be inadequate because my system of classification is wrong—what I think are goldfinches are really something else—or my response might be challenged on the grounds that what I have said about how I know is not enough. If I said I knew it was a goldfinch by its red head, it might be objected 'But that's not enough: plenty of other birds have red heads. What you say doesn't prove it. For all you know, it may be a woodpecker' (OM, 51). This amounts to raising a possibility compatible with everything I have said but which, if actual, would imply that I do not know that there is a goldfinch in the garden. It therefore brings us close to the kind of objection Descartes raises against our ordinary knowledge of the world around us.

[4] Many recent philosophers have argued against scepticism on some such grounds. One version of the idea is worked out in some detail in F. Dretske, 'Reasons and Consequences', *Analysis*, 1968; 'Epistemic Operators', *The Journal of Philosophy*, 1971. For a more recent version along the same lines see R. Nozick, *Philosophical Explanations* (Cambridge, Mass., 1981), ch. 3. I believe the basic idea is to be found in Austin.

[5] J. L. Austin, 'Other Minds', in his *Philosophical Papers* (Oxford, 1961), p. 45. (Hereafter cited as OM.)

Austin thinks philosophers in their assessments tend to concentrate on questions about 'reality' and to some extent about 'sureness and certainty', and that although questions of those kinds are of course raised about knowledge in everyday life, the philosopher's special investigation of knowledge distorts or abandons our everyday procedures for answering them. In objecting to a piece of putative knowledge on the grounds that what has been said is not enough or does not prove what is claimed to be known, he says, we all ordinarily accept that:

(a) If you say 'That's not enough', then you must have in mind some more or less definite lack . . . . If there is no definite lack, which you are at least prepared to specify on being pressed, then it's silly (outrageous) just to go on saying 'That's not enough'.
(b) Enough is enough: it doesn't mean everything. Enough means enough to show that (within reason, and for present intents and purposes) it 'can't' be anything else, there is no room for an alternative, competing description of it. It does *not* mean, for example, enough to show it isn't a *stuffed* goldfinch. (OM, 52.)

When philosophers go on to raise questions about 'reality' ('But do you know it's a *real* goldfinch?') they intend to question the reliability of the 'facts' put forward in support of the original claim to know. That too, of course, is something we do in everyday life. Austin thinks philosophers do not always satisfy the above conditions when they press our ordinary knowledge-claims in this way.

The doubt or question 'But is it a *real* one?' has always (must have) a special basis, there must be some 'reason for suggesting' that it isn't real, in the sense of some specific way, or limited number of specific ways, in which it is suggested that this experience or item may be phoney. Sometimes (usually) the context makes it clear what the suggestion is: . . . If the context doesn't make it clear, then I am entitled to ask 'How do you mean? Do you mean it may be stuffed or what? *What are you suggesting*?' (OM, 55.)

Austin suggests that a philosopher interested in knowledge —or at any rate someone he calls 'the metaphysician'— does not fulfil this condition in his typical challenges. His 'wile' consists in asking 'Is it a real table?' without specifying or limiting the ways he has in mind in which it might not be real. This leaves us at a loss in trying to answer him, just as we are left baffled and uneasy by the conjurer's invitation 'Will some gentleman kindly satisfy himself that this is a perfectly ordinary hat?' (OM, 55n). It is no wonder we feel the philosophical objection to our ordinary knowledge cannot be met if this is what it trades on.

It should be clear that this unflattering description of the philosopher's or 'metaphysician's' procedure does not apply to Descartes's argument as I have outlined it. In his assessment of his claim to know that he is sitting by the fire with a piece of paper in his hand he does not simply complain in general terms that his grounds are not sufficient to prove that he is really sitting there. He is fully prepared to specify, in fact the whole force of his argument turns on his explicitly specifying, a particular way in which his grounds are inadequate, a particular possibility compatible with the facts he is relying on but incompatible with his knowing that he is really sitting there. His grounds are found inadequate in a perfectly determinate way; he might be dreaming. The 'wile of the metaphysician' as Austin describes it cannot explain why it is difficult or impossible to meet Descartes's objection to our knowledge of the world.

Austin might still be right that Descartes does violate our ordinary standards or procedures in another closely-related way. Once it has been made determinate precisely what question must be answered before one can be said to know in a particular case, Austin says, the question can then be answered 'by means of recognized procedures (more or less roughly recognized, of course) appropriate to the particular type of case' (OM, 55). In fact Austin strongly suggests, without saying so explicitly, that the existence of such 'recognized procedures' is a simple consequence of the determinateness of the original criticism of the knowledge-claim; as soon as it is made clear what doubt or deficiency the critic of knowledge has in mind (e.g., 'How do you know you are not dreaming?'), it will follow that there are recognized procedures for making up the deficiency or allaying the doubt.[6] 'There are recognized ways of distinguishing between

[6] Austin's reason for believing that this connection holds is probably to be found in his conception of what he calls 'the normal procedure of language', which he 'schematizes' as follows: if that complex of features originally taken

dreaming and waking', Austin says, '(how otherwise should we know how to use and to contrast the words?), and of deciding whether a thing is stuffed or live, and so forth' (OM, 55).

Austin does not say much about what he thinks the 'procedures' or 'recognized ways' of telling that one is not dreaming actually are. He seems content with the idea that there must be such procedures or else we would not be able to use and to contrast the words 'dreaming' and 'waking' as we do. I find that particular claim dubious, or at the very least difficult to establish, partly for reasons I will return to later.[7] The reason he gives in his lectures is even less persuasive. In *Sense and Sensibilia* he denies the philosopher's contention that there is no 'qualitative difference' between normal waking experience and dream experience. He argues that actually being presented to the Pope is not 'qualitatively indistinguishable' from dreaming that I am being presented to the Pope on the grounds that:

> After all, we have the phrase 'a dream-like quality'; some waking experiences are said to have this dream-like quality, and some artists and writers occasionally try to impart it, usually with scant success, to their works. But of course, if the fact here alleged *were* a fact, the phrase would be perfectly meaningless, because applicable to everything. If dreams were not 'qualitatively' different from waking experiences, then *every* waking experience would be like a dream; the dream-like quality would be, not difficult to capture, but impossible to avoid.[8]

Someone who believed that our ability to tell that we are not dreaming on particular occasions is guaranteed by the very meaningfulness of certain English expressions would

to be sufficient for saying 'This is a C' comes to be 'accompanied or followed in definite circumstances by another special and distinctive feature or complex of features, which makes it seem desirable to revise our ideas' we will 'draw a distinction between "This looks like a C, but in fact is only a dummy, &c." and "This is a real C (live, genuine, &c.)" . . . If the special distinctive feature is one which does not have to manifest itself in *any* definite circumstances (on application of some specific test, after some limited lapse of time, &c.) then it is not a suitable feature on which to base a distinction between "real" and "dummy, imaginary, &c." ' (OM, 57).

[7] See pp. 72 ff.

[8] *Sense and Sensibilia*, pp. 48–9.

perhaps feel little need to describe those 'procedures' carefully or to explain exactly how they work. He would already be convinced that they must work, so even without a detailed description of those 'procedures' he would seem to be directly in conflict with Descartes's reasoning. For Descartes at the end of his first *Meditation* it is impossible to know that we are not dreaming, so it might look as if the whole issue between him and Austin turns on the cogency of this appeal to the meaningfulness of the expression 'a dream-like quality' or to our ability to use and to contrast the words 'dreaming' and 'waking' as we do. But in fact I think Austin's real opposition to the sceptical philosophical conclusion is to be found elsewhere.

Descartes's conclusion rests on the general requirement that we must know that we are not dreaming if we are to know anything at all about the world about us. That requirement is what renders inadequate any tests or procedures for determining that one is not dreaming; one would have to know that one was not simply dreaming that one was performing the test, and not dreaming that one was performing any of the other tests used to determine *that*, and so on. For Austin it is precisely in insisting on that strong general condition for knowledge that the real distortion or unreasonableness comes in. If it is not in general a condition of knowing things about the world around us that we must know that we are not dreaming, not only will Descartes have failed to show that we can never know that we are not dreaming (and that there can be no 'procedures' of the kind Austin has in mind), he will not have begun to show that we cannot know anything about the world around us either. Without Descartes's condition for knowledge, philosophical scepticism about the external world would be completely disarmed. Austin attacks what is really the heart of Descartes's position. Can it be shown that in insisting on his strong general condition for knowledge of the world Descartes is violating or abandoning the ordinary conditions or standards of knowledge?

I have already said that a moment's reflection seems enough to convince us that Descartes's condition is not in fact a condition of knowledge in everyday or scientific life.

After thinking about philosophical scepticism for some time we often tend to forget or distort what we actually do in everyday life, but if we insist on returning to a realistic account of how we actually behave there seems little doubt that we do not in fact impose that general condition on our knowledge-claims.

For example, suppose I remark to the bird-lovers at my cocktail party that a goldfinch has just appeared in the garden. 'Really? How do you know?', one of them asks, and I reply that I just saw it hop from one limb to another in that large pine tree. 'How do you know you're not dreaming?', asks another, in what would obviously be no better than a feeble attempt at a joke. There is no reason to take what he says seriously, and none of us would. We do not regard it as a threat to my knowledge. Suppose I am in a bird-recognition contest. I examine my specimen carefully, noting its differences from birds of similar but distinct species, and I announce that I now know that this one is a goldfinch. Could one of the judges at that point ask me how I know I didn't simply dream it, and then reject my answer because I cannot give a satisfactory defence? That would be perfectly outrageous, and I would feel no necessity to answer the question in order for my original claim to stand.

These are trivial examples, but the inappropriateness of insisting on Descartes's condition does not stem from the relative unimportance of the knowledge in question. Even when it matters a great deal, when it is literally a matter of life or death, as in a court of law, it is simply not true that the dream-possibility is always allowed as a relevant consideration for the claim to know some particular thing. If I testify on the witness stand that I spent the day with the defendant, that I went to the museum and then had dinner with him, and left him about midnight, my testimony under normal circumstances would not be affected in any way by my inability to answer if the prosecutor were then to ask 'How do you know you didn't dream the whole thing?'. The question is outrageous; it has no tendency to undermine my knowledge. It is nothing more than the desperate reaction of a hard-pressed lawyer with no case. Nor do we ever expect to find a careful report of the procedures and results of an elaborate experiment in chemistry followed by an account of how the experimenter determined that he was not simply dreaming that he was conducting the experiment. No such thing was in question; the issue is never raised, let alone settled. The point is obvious, and the multiplication of further examples is unnecessary. It seems clear that we simply do not insist on fulfilling Descartes's condition in order to know things in real life. Nor do we insist that someone cure every conceivable illness in less than two minutes in order to be regarded as a physician.

Of course it is sometimes relevant to ask how or whether we know we are not dreaming. When that is a relevant criticism of a claim to know something, failure to answer the question satisfactorily would imply that we do not know what we claim to know. If I am lying half-awake in bed early in the morning after a late night and seem to hear someone calling my name from outside the window, I might not be sure whether there really is someone out there or I am only dreaming that I hear the call. I do not know whether there is someone out there or not. But from the fact that that possibility is sometimes relevant it does not follow that on every occasion we must know that it does not obtain if we are to know anything about the world around us. When the alarm-clock has sounded and I have reached out and turned it off and got out of bed and gone over to the window and opened the curtains and found my friend calling and gesticulating in the garden, there is no question at that point that I might be dreaming or that I should check to see whether I am dreaming before I can know that he is really there—even though I can truly say to him that I didn't know he was there a few minutes ago because I didn't know whether or not I was dreaming.

As Austin puts it in the case of the goldfinch:

> Knowing it's a 'real' goldfinch isn't in question in the ordinary case when I say I know it's a goldfinch: reasonable precautions only are taken. But when it *is* called in question, in *special* cases, then I make sure it's a real goldfinch in ways essentially similar to those in which I made sure it was a goldfinch, . . . (OM, 56.)

That there are such ways of making sure that it is a real goldfinch does not of course guarantee that we can always tell that it is, nor is it a proof against 'miracles or outrages of nature' (OM, 56). Something might still go wrong, something completely unexpected might happen to the bird, but that by itself is no bar to saying, or having been right to say, that we know it is a real goldfinch.

It is only in *special* circumstances that certain kinds of possibilities are relevant to claims to know something. Austin makes the point in connection with claims to know something about the mind or feelings of another person. Worries about deception, or about whether the person is sufficiently like us to be feeling what we would feel, or about whether he is quite inadvertently behaving as he does, all arise only in 'special cases'. Again, there are (more or less roughly) established procedures for dealing with such cases when they arise, but:

> These special cases where doubts arise and require resolving, are contrasted with the normal cases which hold the field[1] *unless* there is some special suggestion that deceit &c., is involved, and deceit, moreover, of an intelligible kind in the circumstances, that is, of a kind that can be looked into because motive, &c., is specially suggested. There is no suggestion that I *never* know what other people's emotions are, nor yet that in particular cases I might be wrong for no special reason or in no special way.
>
> [[1]Austin's footnote: 'You cannot fool all of the people all of the time' is 'analytic'.] (OM, 81.)

Austin's stress here on the need for special reasons to doubt when questions of 'reality' are at issue is not the same as the earlier point that there must always be some 'special basis' for the doubt or question 'But is it a *real* one?'. That requirement was expressed as the demand that the critic have 'some "reason for suggesting" that it isn't real, in the sense of some specific way, or limited number of specific ways, in which it is suggested that this experience or item may be phoney' (OM, 55). Descartes in his reasoning meets that requirement as stated: he specifies dreaming as the way the experience might be 'phoney'. But here Austin is arguing that even if the way the experience or item might be 'phoney' has been specified, the doubt or question 'But is it a *real* one?' is relevant to the original knowledge-claim and must be answered only if there is some special reason for suggesting that that specified possibility might obtain. It is not simply that the critic of the knowledge-claim must specify some way in which knowledge would not be present on the occasion in question; he must also have some reason for thinking or suggesting that the possible deficiency he has in mind might be present on that occasion. In the absence of such a reason —that is, in the normal or non-special case—knowing it is a real goldfinch, for example, is not in question. The 'reasonable precautions' said to be taken in the ordinary case are precautions against only those possibilities that there is some special reason to think might obtain in that case. Whether or not such possibilities obtain is all that is in question.

The need for a special reason for doubt is also present when we cite authorities or rely on the testimony of others —a rich source of knowledge not much studied by philosophers.

> Naturally, we are judicious: we don't say we know (at second hand) if there is any special reason to doubt the testimony: but there has to be *some* reason. It is fundamental in talking (as in other matters) that we are entitled to trust others, except in so far as there is some concrete reason to distrust them. (OM, 50.)

The same holds for any other possibility of error or mistake. There can be no doubt that human beings are inherently liable to be mistaken in particular claims to know things— and not just things we know 'at second hand' or from testimony. But the question 'How do you know?' is not a successful challenge if it is based only on such general human fallibility. That is not to deny that knowledge precludes error or mistake.

> 'When you know you can't be wrong' is perfectly good sense. You are prohibited from saying 'I know it is so, but I may be wrong', just as you are prohibited from saying 'I promise I will, but I may fail'. If you are aware you may be mistaken, you ought not to say you know, . . . But of course, being aware that you may be mistaken doesn't mean merely being aware that you are a fallible human being: it means that you have some concrete reason to suppose that you may be mistaken in this case . . . It is naturally *always* possible ('humanly' possible) that I may be mistaken or may break my word, but that by itself is no bar against

using the expressions 'I know' and 'I promise' as we do in fact use them. (OM, 66.)

It would be no easy matter to give a precise formulation of the requirement that there must be some special reason to think a certain possibility might obtain before the raising of that possibility is allowed as a relevant criticism of a claim to know something. Is it enough for there simply to be such a reason, or must someone actually have that reason, and raise the possibility for that reason? How concrete or specific must the reason be, and how good a reason must there be for thinking something is amiss in the particular case? I want to leave aside all such questions of detail and ask about the conflict between *any* requirement along those general lines and the condition that Descartes insists on for knowledge about the world around us. I therefore want to grant everything Austin says about what sort of thing does actually happen when ordinary people are asked 'How do you know?', and everything else that could be discovered about how we respond to the questions or would-be challenges of others with respect to our knowledge. I want to concentrate on the question: do such facts about our everyday and scientific practices show that Descartes's reasoning deviates from our everyday procedures and standards for acquiring and assessing knowledge?

It certainly looks as if Descartes could not be right in insisting that we must rule out the dream-possibility in order to know something about the world around us if Austin is right about how the raising of such possibilities can work against our knowledge in everyday life. If there must be some special reason for suggesting or suspecting that one is dreaming before that reason for doubt is even allowed as relevant in everyday life, the most that is true of the dream-possibility with respect to our knowledge of the world is that it must be known not to obtain whenever there is some special reason to think it might obtain. That is to say, if there is some special or concrete reason to believe that one might be dreaming, one cannot know some particular thing about the world around us unless one knows that one is not dreaming. That is obviously weaker than Descartes's general requirement which says that one cannot know any particular thing about the world around us unless one knows that one is not dreaming. Descartes's reasoning imposes a condition on knowledge of the world which must be fulfilled in every case, whether there is any special reason to believe one might be dreaming or not. The weaker requirement says that that condition must be fulfilled only in some cases, when the 'special reason' condition is also fulfilled, but that otherwise the dream-possibility is not even relevant to our claims to know things about the world around us.

Another way to put the difference is that the weaker requirement allows for the possibility of knowledge of the world in a way that Descartes's requirement does not. I have tried to show how Descartes's requirement is strong enough to make knowledge of the world around us impossible; it precludes fulfilment of the very condition it holds to be necessary for knowledge of the world. For all the weaker requirement says, one *could* know things about the world around us without knowing that one is not dreaming. With no special reason to think one might be dreaming, that alleged possibility is simply not in question at all, so the possibility Descartes invokes would present no obstacle to knowing things about the world in those cases. It therefore looks as if the sceptical reasoning cannot succeed if only the weaker requirement, and not Descartes's condition for knowledge, is what is true of our ordinary conception of knowledge.

Descartes's reasoning itself cannot be said to fulfil only the weaker requirement. He considers his knowledge of the world around him in general by considering the particular case of his sitting by the fire with a piece of paper in his hand. That single case is chosen to serve as a representative of all of our knowledge of the world. It could sustain a quite general conclusion about all of our knowledge of the world only if it were a perfectly normal case, without special features. If Descartes had had some special reason to doubt the deliverances of his senses at that particular time and place—if it were early morning, for example, and he was not quite sure whether he was fully awake or not—his verdict could not support the kind of general conclusion he draws from it about our sensory knowledge in general. It would just be one special, non-representative case in which, as it turns out, he fails to know. But if there is nothing special about the case, if he had no special reason to think he might be dreaming at that particular time and place, his challenge 'How do I know I am not dreaming?' will have no special basis. The possibility will be raised without any special or concrete reason for supposing in this case that he might be dreaming, so it would seem that it must violate what Austin says is a condition of its being a serious or even a relevant challenge to a knowledge-claim in everyday life.

Despite this apparently obvious conflict between our everyday practices and Descartes's requirement I still want to press the question whether all the facts about how we speak and respond to the questions or would-be challenges of others in everyday life are enough to show that Descartes in his reasoning deviates from our everyday standards and procedures and changes or distorts the meaning of the word 'know' or any of the other words he uses. I think those facts would not have that anti-sceptical consequence if a certain conception of everyday life, and hence a certain conception of the relation between the philosophical problem of the external world and what goes on in everyday life, were correct. In looking at the significance of those facts I will therefore be looking from a different angle at the significance of the philosophical problem itself and at what, if anything, it can reveal about our position and procedures in everyday life. If the philosophical sceptic's conception of everyday life is intelligible, everything that goes on in everyday life and in science would be compatible with the literal truth of the conclusion that no one knows anything about the world around us.

If only Austin's weaker, and not Descartes's stronger, requirement is true of our ordinary conception of knowledge, it nevertheless should state a truth about *knowledge*. What I mean by such an obvious remark is this. If we have a conception of knowledge that we employ in everyday life prior to and independently of all philosophizing, and if Descartes or some other philosopher is to be shown to have changed or distorted that conception in the course of his philosophizing, it must be shown that it is that very conception that he has distorted, and that that conception is a conception of knowledge. Austin's weaker requirement, for example, will state a condition of knowledge only if it implies that in those cases in which there is no special reason to think one might be dreaming, and one fulfils all the other conditions for knowing, one does indeed *know* something about the world around us without knowing that one is not dreaming. I stress the point because I think that speaking very strictly, or on a certain conception of our linguistic and other behaviour in everyday life, facts of the kind cited by Austin do not actually have that implication.

What Austin reminds us of are facts of speech, of linguistic usage. When he describes what sort of thing does actually happen when ordinary people are asked 'How do you know?' he tells us what people say, and what conditions must be fulfilled in order for them to say it, or to be speaking correctly in saying it. In the passages already quoted, for example, he says:

> If there is no definite lack, which you are at least prepared to specify on being pressed, then it's silly (outrageous) just to go on *saying* 'That's not enough'.
> Knowing it's a 'real' goldfinch isn't in question in the ordinary case when I *say* I know it's a goldfinch: we don't *say* we know . . . if there is any special reason to doubt . . .
> If you are aware you may be mistaken, you ought not to *say* you know . . .
> [Its being always possible that I may be mistaken] is no bar against *using the expressions* 'I know' and 'I promise' as we do in fact use them.

I have italicized the crucial words to show that in each case what is in question is how certain expressions are or should be used. Similar facts are appealed to when Austin says:

> we are often right to say we *know* even in cases where we turn out subsequently to have been mistaken. (OM, 66.)
> we may be perfectly justified in saying we know or we promise, in spite of the fact that things 'may' turn out badly, and it's a more or less serious matter for us if they do. (OM, 69.)

I have said that I want to grant all facts of the kind Austin here describes. But in order to move from such facts about the use of the expressions 'I know' or 'He knows' or 'How do you know?' to conclusions about knowledge we must at least know *why* those expressions are used as they are on those occasions.

There are also facts about our reactions to the raising of various possibilities in ordinary circumstances that seem to support Austin's conclusion. I pointed out in earlier examples that we simply ignore, perhaps with some embarrassment, the party guest's question how I know I didn't dream the goldfinch in the garden. We find the bird-contest judge's challenge incomprehensible, and do not regard it as affecting in any way the truth or reasonableness of my identification. We immediately throw out of court the desperate prosecutor's ridiculous challenge and proceed as if it never had been made. We do not expect, and would be astonished to find, dream-elimination tests appended to laboratory reports; they would not affect one way or the other our acceptance of the results reported. When something serious is in question we usually find it silly (outrageous) for someone to persist in asking how we know we are not dreaming and to insist that we don't know what we thought we knew until we can answer the question satisfactorily. These all seem to me undeniable facts of everyday life.

The question is whether all this linguistic and other behaviour is generated by or warranted by or even required by our everyday conception of knowledge. Whether that is so or not depends on why we behave in those ways in everyday life. It is admittedly bizarre, silly, outrageous, perhaps even incomprehensible, to raise the dream-possibility as a criticism of ordinary claims to know things in everyday and scientific life, but exactly what kind of outrageousness or inappropriateness is it? What is its source? Is it derived from our very conception of knowledge itself? Is anyone who raises the possibility in normal circumstances necessarily violating or rejecting the everyday meaning of the word 'know'?

These questions arise because there are two apparently distinct questions that can be asked about what someone says. We can ask whether it is true, or we can ask whether it was appropriately or reasonably said. The two questions do not always get the same answer; certainly it is possible for them to differ. All the conditions sufficient for appropriate or reasonable utterance can be fulfilled when what is said is not literally true. The distinction even more obviously can be made in the other direction; there are countless things that are now true which no one is now in a position reasonably to assert or believe—many people are busily engaged in trying to find out what some of them are. I do not mean to suggest that there is or must be some sort of conflict or opposition, let alone an unbridgeable gap, between reasonable utterance and truth. There is nothing in the distinction itself which suggests that the truth is forever —or ever—beyond us. Normally, we believe, the conditions of reasonable utterance coincide with the conditions of truth. We usually take it for granted that what we are in a good position to assert is in fact true and what we are in a good position to deny is in fact false. In trying to find out whether or not some particular thing is true we try to get into the best possible position for accepting and asserting it, or for rejecting and denying it. The point is only that the two sets of conditions can be distinguished. From the fact that someone carefully, reasonably and appropriately asserts something on a particular occasion it does not directly follow that what he says is true, and from the fact that someone quite inappropriately and with no good reason says something it does not immediately follow that what he says is false. This holds just as much for assertions or denials of knowledge as for other assertions and denials.

For example, suppose I am at a party and my host asks me if I know whether my friend John, who was ill last week, will be coming to the party. I reply that I know he will be there, and when asked how I know I explain that he has now recovered, I have just talked to him on the telephone and he said he was coming right over; there is someone at the party he is interested in talking to and he wouldn't miss it for anything. Suppose further that John is well-known to be generally trustworthy, reliable, and also a careful, sober driver—and he doesn't live very far away. All this puts my assertion that I know John will be at the party beyond criticism. There could hardly be more favourable grounds for claiming knowledge about something not currently under my direct observation. Suppose now that John for some reason unknown to me nevertheless fails to show up at the party. My saying that he would be there, in fact that I knew he would be there, was justified, reasonable, and appropriate in the circumstances, but it has turned out that what I said is not true. John is not at the party, so I did not know what I said I knew. The best possible conditions for asserting something, or that I knew something, did not coincide with the conditions under which what I said is true.

Suppose that as I am leaving the party at the end of the evening and John has still not appeared my host turns on me and says 'You should be more careful about what you claim to know. You said you knew John would be here and he isn't. You didn't know any such thing!' I think we find that response simply outrageous. It is absurd and improper and completely unjustified. It is difficult to find the right words to describe its degree of insensitivity and social obtuseness. It perhaps even shows incomprehension of how and why we claim to know things in the face of the normal vicissitudes of life. But aside from the unreasonable abuse and insensitivity conveyed by it, the remark cannot be said to be totally false or without foundation. Part of what the host said was 'You said you knew John would be here and he isn't. You didn't know any such thing', and that is, at least, the literal truth, however harsh or inappropriate it might have been for him to say it. I did say I knew, and I didn't know. What the cruel host says is an accurate description of my position.

It is clear that the host's remarks are outrageous or unreasonable as criticisms of *me*, or of my having *said* that I know John will be there. My response when asked whether I knew John would be at the party was justified, reasonable, appropriate, and perfectly proper. It is not open to the kind of attack the host tries to subject it to. But what is invulnerable to those absurd attacks is my act of *saying* something, and also perhaps my coming to believe or to accept something. My asserting it is beyond criticism even if what I assert is (of course unknown to me) not true. And the host's remark about the state of my knowledge is true even if his making it is outrageous, unreasonable, and unjustified. So even if we know that a certain attempt to criticize a knowledge-claim is outrageous or unreasonable or would not be listened to in everyday life, we cannot immediately infer that the knowledge-claim does not suffer from the deficiency stated in the criticism, or that the person does nevertheless know what he claims to know. Whether that is so or not will depend on the nature and source of the outrageousness or inappropriateness in question. The inappropriately-asserted objection to the knowledge-claim might not be an outrageous violation of the conditions of knowledge, but rather an outrageous violation of the conditions for the appropriate assessment and acceptance of *assertions* of knowledge. John's being at the party is an admitted condition of my knowing that he will be at the party—since he is not there I do not know what I said I knew—but his not being there does not warrant any and all criticisms of my saying or believing what I did. My saying and believing in those circumstances is beyond criticism. But still I did not know.

Suppose that in fact the reason John never arrived at the party was that just as he stepped out his front door he was struck down by a meteorite, the only one of lethal size known to have hit the earth in a century and a half. Of course there was no special reason—no reason at all—for me or for anyone else to expect such a thing. Certainly I never thought of it (nor of its not happening) when I said I knew John would be at the party, and it is safe to say that no one else at the party did either. If the news of John's fate had been conveyed to all of us just as I was about to leave the party, the host's parting shot as I described it a moment ago would be if anything even more outrageous and inappropriate. When we all discover why John never got to the party and hence why I failed to know, and we see how bizarre and how completely unforeseeable his not getting there was, it is even more difficult to understand what the host could think he was doing in saying to me 'You said you knew John would be here and he isn't. You didn't know any such thing!' But I think it cannot be denied that one thing the host was doing was speaking the truth.

My failure to know in this case as originally described

was due to the falsity of what I claimed to know. That necessary condition of knowledge was unfulfilled even though no one at the time was in a position to know that it was unfulfilled, and no one at the time was in a position appropriately or reasonably to criticize my claim on that basis. Perhaps the same is true of other necessary conditions of knowledge.

Imagine a slightly different sequence of events at the party from the one described so far. Suppose that, as soon as I had hung up the telephone from talking with John and had said that I knew he would be at the party, the boorish host had said 'But do you really know he'll be here? After all, how do you know he won't be struck down by a meteorite on the way over? You don't know he won't be.' We find this at least as outrageous as his response in the other story after the truth about John and the meteorite was known. Not only is this 'challenge' as unfair and as inappropriate as that other response, it is difficult to understand why he even brings up such a consideration at this point and thinks it is a relevant criticism. His doing so would normally suggest that he thinks there have been a lot of meteorites hitting the earth lately in this general area, some of them rather big and capable of causing harm. If that were so, perhaps I should have thought of it and considered it—or at least if I didn't know about it my ignorance might threaten my claim to know John would be there. But in the absence of any such special reason the 'challenge' seems just as outrageous as it did in the other story.

My act of asserting that I knew John would be at the party was made on just about the most favourable grounds one can have for claiming to know things. It is no reflection on me or on my saying what I did that I had not ruled out or even thought of the meteorite possibility. But once the question is asked, however inappropriately, can it be said that I do know that that possiblity will not obtain? It seems to me that it cannot. When I hung up the telephone I do not think I could be described as knowing that John will not be hit by a meteorite. As it turned out, of course, I did not know it because it wasn't true—he *was* hit by a meteorite. But even if things had turned out differently—even if John had actually arrived at the party—I do not think it was true when I hung up the telephone that I knew John would not be hit by a meteorite. So again, part of what the host says is true. I did not know any such thing. But still I said I knew John would be at the party.

I want to be careful here. I want to emphasize that I am not saying that in this second case I do not know that John will be at the party because I do not know when hanging up the telephone that he will not be struck down by a meteorite on the way over. I am concerned at the moment not so much with the truth about my state of knowledge in the example as with the question of how we arrive at conclusions about the state of my knowledge on the basis of admitted facts about how we speak and assess our assertions of knowledge and respond to the assertions and attempted criticisms of others. We agree that the imagined response of the host is outrageous and unjustified; it is something he has no specific reason to bring up as a possible objection to what I have said. All I am saying at the moment is that it does not follow directly from the admitted outrageousness of his introducing that possibility that my ruling out the meteorite possibility is simply *not* a condition of my knowing that John will be at the party. Its being a necessary condition of my knowledge is so far at least compatible with the host's remarks' being inappropriate or outrageous, just as John's being at the party is a necessary condition of my knowing he will be there even if it is inappropriate or outrageous for the host to say that I didn't know he would be there because in fact that condition was not fulfilled. A necessary condition of knowledge might remain unfulfilled even though it would be outrageous for anyone to assert that it is or inappropriate for anyone to criticize my knowledge-claim on that basis. The inappropriateness or outrageousness might have some source other than the falsity of what is said or implied about knowledge.

I emphasize a mere possibility here—that a certain conclusion about knowledge *might* not be true even granted the facts about how we speak and how we react to the speech of others—because I think philosophers who have investigated knowledge in Descartes's way have a conception of everyday life and everyday speech that would get between those facts of usage and that conclusion about knowledge. That is not to say that their conception must be correct, or even fully intelligible, but it should at least make us more cautious in inferring directly from a reasonable, justified, even exemplary assertion of knowledge on a particular occasion to the conclusion that on that occasion all the conditions of knowledge are in fact fulfilled. If it is possible for the conditions sufficient for appropriate or reasonable utterance to be fulfilled even though what is said is not literally true—and it does seem that that is possible—someone might be fully justified in saying he knows some particular thing about the world around him without its being true that he does know that thing. In particular, when someone claims to know something about the world without asking himself about or even thinking of a certain possibility, and that possibility, if realized, would mean that he does not know what he claims to know, he might fail to know in that situation precisely because he has not eliminated that possibility. If there were no special reason for him to consider that possibility, he might nevertheless be fully justified in saying he knows. I was fully justified in saying I knew John would be at the party even though I did not think of the possibility that a meteorite might strike him; there was no reason to think such a bizarre event might occur.

On the conception I have in mind, the requirement that there must be some 'special reason' for thinking a certain possibility might obtain in order for that possibility to be relevant to a particular knowledge-claim would be seen as a requirement on the appropriate or reasonable assertion of knowledge, but not necessarily as a requirement on knowledge itself. In the absence of such a 'special reason', one might perhaps be fully justified in saying 'I know that *p*' even though it is not true that one knows that *p*. Descartes reaches his sceptical conclusion about our knowledge of the world around us on the basis of a condition he holds is necessary for the truth of 'I know that *p*'. To show that our everyday notion of knowledge contains no such condition, but only the weaker requirement that would enable us to know things about the world without knowing we are not dreaming as long as there were no special reason to think we might be dreaming, it would have to be shown that when no such 'special reason' is present, 'I know that *p*' will sometimes be true and not just justifiably asserted.

How is it to be shown that that weaker requirement, or any other description of the way we actually speak and respond to the assertions of others, does in fact state a condition of knowledge, as opposed to a condition of appropriately or justifiably saying that one knows? As long as it is even intelligible to suppose that there is a logical gap between the fulfilment of the conditions for appropriately making and assessing assertions of knowledge on the one hand, and the fulfilment of the conditions for the truth of those assertions on the other, evidence from usage or from our practice will not establish a conclusion about the conditions of knowledge. The charge of violating or altering the meaning of the word 'know' (or any other word) can therefore be laid at the sceptical philosopher's doorstep on the basis of such evidence only if a certain conception of meaning, a certain conception of everyday speech, and a certain conception of the relation between them, can all be shown to be mistaken, perhaps even unintelligible. Rejecting such a conception would involve much more than the simple rejection of an isolated and idiosyncratic 're-definition' of knowledge, and even much more than a simple denial of the initially startling conclusion that no one can know anything about the world around us. That is why I think discovering the source of Descartes's requirement might reveal something deep and important.

Descartes and other philosophers who have examined knowledge in the same way and have been led to sceptical conclusions are fully aware that the kinds of doubts or criticisms they raise in their philosophical investigations would not always be appropriately raised in everyday or scientific activity. That in itself does not show that they must be changing or misunderstanding the meaning of the word 'know' or any other words. By invoking the conception I have just mentioned, they would attribute the inappropriateness to something other than the notion of knowledge itself.

Descartes, for example, insists that his procedure of asking what is beyond all possible doubt is to be followed only in the philosophical investigation of human knowledge and not in everyday life.

> . . . we are to make use of this doubt only when we are engaged in contemplating the truth. For, as regards the conduct of our life, we are frequently obliged to follow opinions which are merely probable, because the opportunities for action would in most cases pass away before we could deliver ourselves from our doubts. (HR, 219–20.)

C. I. Lewis, another philosopher whose Cartesian examination of knowledge proceeds by the raising of possible doubts to ordinary claims to know things about the world, writes:

> To quibble about such doubts will not, in most cases, be common sense. But we are not trying to weigh the degree of theoretical dubiety which common-sense practicality should take account of, but to arrive at an accurate analysis of knowledge.[9]

Both accounts stress the contrast between the practical and the theoretical, or between what is appropriate or required in action and what is appropriate or required in knowing the truth. The standards or procedures we follow in everyday life find their source in the exigencies of action and in the general conditions under which actions must be performed. In the case of action, unlike that of belief and knowledge, truth is not the only important consideration. Actions take place at different times and in changing conditions, so what is a perfectly reasonable thing to do in one situation is not equally reasonable—in fact, might be quite outrageous—to do in another. What is or is not an appropriate or reasonable thing to do is determined by the situation at hand, by one's aims or interests at the moment, by one's appraisal of the situation, and, as Descartes emphasizes, by the time at one's disposal. It would be silly to stand for a long time in a quickly filling bus trying to decide on the absolutely best place to sit. Since sitting somewhere in the bus is better than standing, although admittedly not as good as sitting in the best of all possible seats, the best thing to do is to sit down quickly. In general, our actions

[9] C. I. Lewis, *An Analysis of Knowledge and Valuation* (La Salle, Illinois, 1946), p. 180.

are more likely to succeed and to produce satisfaction to the extent to which we can deliberate longer and more rigorously and with more and more information, but it is part of the very nature of practical life that we often cannot carry that process far enough to give us the kind of certainty we would otherwise like to have. We do the best we can in the circumstances.

These platitudes show that there is no general answer to the question of how certain we should be before we act, or what possibilities of failure we should be sure to eliminate before doing something. It will vary from case to case, and in each case it will depend on how serious it would be if the act failed, how important it is for it to succeed by a certain time, how it fares in competition on these and other grounds with alternative actions which might be performed instead, and so on. This holds just as much for the action of saying something, or saying that you know something, or ruling out certain possibilities before saying that you know something, as for other kinds of action. There is no general answer to the question of which possibilities we should rule out before we assert something or say we know it to be true. Checking our beliefs or justifying our claims to know something is itself something we do, and the desirability or reasonableness of doing it beyond a certain point must always be weighed against the desirability or reasonableness of doing all those other things incompatible with it. It is a practical question how much time, effort and ingenuity we should spend on supporting and checking our beliefs, so we might easily find that it would be silly or outrageous on a particular occasion to go on trying to eliminate a certain possibility. That is to say, it would be silly or outrageous in the circumstances to act in that way.

The doubts or possibilities considered by the philosopher investigating human knowledge are not put forward as relevant to such practical questions as whether to assert something or to say that you know it or to raise an objection to what someone else has said. They are thought relevant only to the question of whether one knows something—whether it is true that one knows—and not whether it is appropriate or reasonable to say that one knows. And if the dream-possibility, for example, is a possibility that one must know not to obtain if one is to know some particular thing about the world around us, then one will simply not know that thing about the world if one has not been able to eliminate that possibility—even though it might be completely inappropriate or unreasonable on particular occasions in everyday life to insist on ruling out that possibility before saying that one knows.

One way to bring out what I think is the sceptical philosopher's conception of everyday life in relation to his epistemological project is to consider in some detail the following story adapted from an example of Thompson Clarke's.[10] Suppose that in wartime people must be trained to identify aircraft and they are given a quick, uncomplicated course on the distinguishing features of different planes and how to recognize them. They learn from their manuals, for example, that if a plane has features *x*, *y*, and *w* it is an E, and if it has *x*, *y*, and *z* it is an F. A fully-trained and careful spotter on the job will not say that a particular plane is an F until he has found all three features, *x*, *y*, *z*. If at a certain point he has found only *x* and *y* and cannot yet tell what other features the plane has got, he does not know whether it is an F or an E. Once he finds that it also has feature *z* he can report that the plane in the sky is an F. He might even be asked how he knows it is an F and reply 'Because it has *x*, *y*, *z*'. He has observed the plane in the sky very carefully, he has followed his training to the letter, and he is right that it has *x*, *y*, *z*. There seems no doubt that he knows the plane is an F.

Suppose that there are in fact some other airplanes, Gs say, which also have features *x*, *y*, *z*. The trainees were never told about them because it would have made the recognition of Fs too difficult; it is almost impossible to distinguish an F from a G from the ground. The policy of simplifying the whole operation by not mentioning Gs in the training manual might be justified by the fact that there are not many of them, or that they are only reconnaissance planes, or that in some other ways they are not as directly dangerous as Fs;

[10] Thompson Clarke, 'The Legacy of Skepticism', *The Journal of Philosophy*, 1972, pp. 759 ff.

it does not matter as much whether they fly over our territory.

When we are given this additional information I think we immediately see that even the most careful airplane-spotter does not know that a plane he sees is an F even though he knows that it has *x*, *y*, *z*. For all he knows, it might be a G. Just as he did not know the plane was an F when he had found only features *x* and *y*—for all he knew then, it might have been an E—so he does not know now that it is an F because all the features he has now found are also present on another kind of airplane. Of course there would be no point in telling him that he does not know; the same good reasons for not even mentioning Gs in the training manual would still apply. In saying that he does not know it is an F we would be making no criticism of his performance; he has followed his training perfectly and conscientiously. We ourselves might not even care whether the plane in the sky is an F or a G; it is precisely because Gs are not worth worrying about in the same way that the manual was written as it was. But I think it must nevertheless be admitted that the spotter does not know that the plane is an F.

In saying that he does not know the plane is an F I do not mean to deny that he can be said to know 'for all practical purposes'. Whether it is an F or a G does not matter much; that is why the training could afford to ignore the differences between them. All things considered, it is best to have a policy of not distinguishing between the two kinds of planes when deciding what to do, how to respond to their presence. So as a contribution to the war effort his recognition is beyond criticism. We might even be tempted to say something like 'As far as his training goes, he knows it is an F', or 'He knows that according to his manual it is an F'. But if we know the facts about Gs I think we cannot say simply 'He knows it is an F'. When I say that we cannot say that he knows it is an F I mean that we recognize that that would not be true. We recognize that he does not know it is an F even though there is absolutely nothing to be gained by pointing his ignorance out to him or to anyone else. For all practical purposes we can accept his saying that he knows it's an F. He can perhaps be said to know-for-all-practical-purposes. After all, there are more important things in wartime—and even in peacetime everyday life—than knowledge.

I think the sceptical philosopher sees our position in everyday life as analogous to that of the airplane-spotters. There might be very good reasons why we do not normally eliminate or even consider countless possibilities which nevertheless strictly speaking must be known not to obtain if we are to know the sorts of things we claim to know. We therefore cannot conclude simply from our having carefully and conscientiously followed the standards and procedures of everyday life that we thereby know the things we ordinarily claim to know. The philosophical investigation of our knowledge is concerned with whether and how it is true that we know, whether and how the conditions necessary and sufficient for our knowing things about the world are fulfilled. Descartes's argument turned on its being a condition of our knowing any particular thing about the world around us that we know we are not dreaming, and on this conception the admitted fact that we do not insist on eliminating that possibility in everyday life does not show that we do not need to eliminate it in order to know things about the world. The well-trained airplane-spotter is not required to rule out the possibility that the plane he sees with features *x, y, z* is a G; nor do his teachers or his fellow spotters insist on that possibility's being eliminated. But we recognize that it is nevertheless a condition of knowing that the plane is an F on the basis of *x, y, z* that one know that it is not a G. Facts about the way we speak and the procedures we follow in everyday life do not show that the sceptical philosopher has misunderstood or distorted the nature of knowledge if this conception of our everyday practices and procedures is correct.

The point is worth stressing. Many people are apparently disposed to think that if the philosopher holds that a certain condition must be met in order to know something, and we do not insist on that condition's being met in everyday life, then the philosopher simply *must* be imposing new or higher standards on knowledge or changing the meaning of the word 'know' or some other word. But if our position in everyday life is like that of the airplane-spotters that is not so. When we who know the facts about Gs say that the careful spotter does not really know that the plane he sees is an F I do not think we are imposing on him or inventing for ourselves some new and unreasonably strict conception of knowledge. If we explained the situation to the spotter himself (which admittedly would not help the war effort) he too would agree that he did not know whether the plane was an F or a G. Just as he recognized earlier that the presence of *x* and *y* alone was not enough to settle the question whether the plane was an F, so he would see, with the new information, that even *x*, *y*, and *z* are not enough. He would see that he has to do more in order to know that it is an F. The fact that there is nothing more that a mere airplane-spotter can do—that it is almost impossible to distinguish an F from a G from the ground—would not alter that judgement. He would see that with the resources currently available to him he simply cannot know whether a plane in the sky is an F or not. But in coming to that conclusion he would not have altered the conception of knowledge with which he began. He originally understood the word 'know' and applied that conception of knowledge fully reasonably and justifiably in particular cases, but (as we knew all along and he now would come to realize) he never knew on any of those occasions that the plane in the sky was an F.

That is how I think the philosopher who investigates human knowledge sees the relation between what he concludes about knowledge and the way we speak about knowledge in everyday life. We do not ordinarily insist on the dream-possibility's being ruled out unless there is some special reason to think it might obtain; the philosopher insists that it must always be known not to obtain in order to know anything about the world around us. But on his understanding of everyday life that difference is not to be explained by the philosopher's insisting on or inventing a conception of knowledge stricter or more demanding than that of the scientist or the lawyer or the plain man. Rather he claims to share with all of us one and the same conception of knowledge—that very conception that operates in everyday and scientific life.

One thing the sceptical philosopher can appeal to to show that he does not introduce a new or extraordinary conception of knowledge into his investigation, I think, is the ease with which we all acknowledge, when presented with the case, that Descartes ought to know that he is not dreaming if he is to know that he is sitting by the fire with a piece of paper in his hand. The force we feel in the sceptical argument when we first encounter it is itself evidence that the conception of knowledge employed in the argument is the very conception we have been operating with all along. If we become even half persuaded that Descartes really should eliminate the dream-possibility, I think we do not have the sense that the knowledge for which that is now felt to be required is something different from the knowledge expressed in Descartes's original conviction that he knew he was sitting by the fire with a piece of paper in his hand. Nor do we think it is something different from the kind of knowledge we take ourselves to seek and to possess in everyday life. That is why the sceptical argument can seem to threaten our everyday knowledge. We are originally inclined to respond to it in the way the careful airplane-spotter would respond to the news about Gs. We realize that, strictly speaking, we must be able to eliminate the dream-possibility if we are to know anything about the world around us.

But of course we are also strongly inclined to reject the sceptical reasoning because what it would require of us deviates so radically from what we require of ourselves and others in everyday life. The sceptical philosopher has an explanation of that difference. There is a single conception of knowledge at work both in everyday life and in the philosophical investigation of human knowledge, but that conception operates in everyday life under the constraints of social practice and the exigencies of action, co-operation and communication. The practical social purposes served by our assertions and claims to know things in everyday life explain why we are normally satisfied with less than what, with detachment, we can be brought to acknowledge are the full conditions of knowledge. From the detached point of view—when only the question of whether we know is at issue—our interests and assertions in everyday life are seen as restricted in certain ways. Certain possibilities are not even considered, let alone eliminated, certain assumptions are shared and taken for granted and so not examined, and our claims are made and understood as if they were restricted to the particular issues that have explicitly arisen. In the context of the war effort no one has any reason to challenge the careful airplane-spotter's claim to know that the plane he sees is an F. Within the restricted range of possibilities he was trained to consider he has chosen the right one. But we from our detached position can see that his 'knowledge' is confined or restricted to that range. He has been fully competent in doing what he must do, but he does not really know that the plane in the sky is an F.

I have said that we who know the facts about Gs and are in that way detached from the airplane-spotter's context would say that he does not know the plane is an F. Our verdict about his lack of knowledge is not arrived at on the same sorts of grounds as those within the situation might have for saying the very same thing. For those within the spotters' context, there is a contrast between the cases they describe as knowing and those they describe as not knowing. When a plane first appears in the sky, for example, the spotter might say 'I don't know yet what sort of plane it is. It has got *x* and *y*, but that is all I can see, so I don't know whether it is an F or not. It might be an E'. Those who are waiting at headquarters to act on his report will have to say that he does not know yet whether it is an F. After he gets a better look and notices that the plane also has *z* he is no longer in doubt. 'It's an F,' he says, 'I know it is. It has also got *z*, and that rules out the possibility that it is an E'. It can now be reported to headquarters that he knows it is an F, so appropriate action can be taken. There is obviously a real difference between the earlier and the later state of affairs.

A similar contrast exists between the report made by a careful spotter and that of a less conscientious trainee who finds features *x* and *y* and simply guesses that *z* is probably present too, or who concludes without further thought from the presence of *x* and *y* that the plane is an F. The careful spotter would be said by his colleagues and superiors to know, the careless spotter not to know, that the plane is an F. There is a real difference between them. We from our more detached position will agree that the careless spotter does not know, and that the careful spotter did not know when he had found only x and y, but we will also agree that the careful spotter does not know the plane is an F even when he has also found it has z. 'He knows it is an F' is always false, given the facts about Gs and the only way spotters can find out things about the planes in the sky.[11]

On this conception it is possible for a perfectly meaningful expression to be appropriately and justifiably applied in certain situations and for its negation to be equally appropriately and justifiably applied in others, even though what is said in each of the positive applications is never true. When those within the situation say 'He does not know it is an F' on some particular occasion they could be said to be relying on a distinction between that occasion and those occasions on which the conditions normally appropriate for asserting 'He knows it is an F' are fulfilled. What is important for the action of saying something is whether it is one sort of occasion or the other. When we, outside the restricted practical context, say that even the careful spotter does not know the plane is an F we are not simply drawing the same contrast. When we deny that knowledge is present we are not distinguishing the spotter's claim to know it is an F from those cases in which the conditions normally appropriate for the assertion of 'He knows it is an F' are fulfilled. We know that it is a case of just that kind; we know he is justified in saying what he does. Our grounds for denying he knows are different. We are distinguishing his position from one in which the conditions of knowledge are fulfilled—conditions of the truth of 'He knows it is an F'. But the fact that we say what we do on different grounds from those available to speakers within the restricted practice does not show that the notion of knowledge we use is different from theirs. When

[11] Of course the example will seem unrealistically restricted. Someone could presumably tell a plane was an F if he flew up next to it and read the label on the side, or shot it down and took it apart and checked its serial-number on a list at the factory. It is not impossible to know in that way that a particular plane is an F. But spotters confined to distant sightings in the sky can never know of any plane that it is an F. The point is that that limitation need have no effect on the meaning of what they say or their reasons for saying it.

they in their (justified) ignorance think that all the conditions of knowledge are in fact satisfied in the careful spotter's case, they mean by 'He knows it is an F' what we mean by it, but they are simply mistaken (through no fault of theirs). The careful spotter's case does indeed differ in easily discernible ways from the cases in which they say of someone 'He does not know it is an F'. Everyone within that practice can be aware of that difference. What we, in our detached position, realize is that that difference is not the difference between knowing and not knowing.

It is in this way, I think, that the sceptical philosopher would reply to any argument that starts from the premiss that each of a pair of expressions *S* and *not-S* is meaningfully applied on different occasions and reaches the conclusion that both *S* and *not-S* must sometimes apply truly to such occasions. That 'paradigm-case argument' had a brief vogue at the height of linguistic philosophy in the 1950s. Something like it seems to be appealed to in Austin's rhetorical question 'How could we use and contrast the words 'waking' and 'dreaming' as we do if there were not recognized ways of telling on particular occasions that we are not dreaming?'. But the argument fails because it takes no account of how and why the expressions we use come to be applied to the different sorts of occasions to which we apply them. There can be real and easily discernible differences between two sorts of occasions, and we might apply an expression, or its negation, to an occasion on the basis of just such discernible features. But if certain widely-shared but unexamined assumptions are what make it possible or desirable for us to proceed in that way, or if certain restrictions are in force which limit our interest simply to drawing a particular distinction between the two kinds of occasion, then although we will be marking a real difference between the occasion to which we apply *S* and that to which we apply *not-S*, it will not follow that the distinction we draw is in fact the distinction between *S*'s applying truly to a particular occasion and its not so applying. 'He knows it is an F' was appropriately applied to the airplane-spotters in situations differing in clearly recognizable ways from those in which 'He does not know it is an F' was correctly applied. But the difference drawn between those two sorts of situations within that practice was not the difference between knowing and not knowing. Even in the former cases what the careful spotter said was false; 'He knows it is an F' is never true under the conditions described.

If our own more general practices of gaining and assessing knowledge in everyday life also operated under a similar set of practical constraints or restrictions it looks as if it would also be possible for no one to know anything about the world around us even though our ordinary procedures are followed to the letter and our claims to know things are often beyond criticism. At least this much can be said: no anti-sceptical conclusion to the contrary could be drawn simply from the fact that we use the expressions 'I know . . .', 'He knows . . .', etc., as we do in fact use them. One would then be in a strong position to defend the sceptical conclusion against any objection to the effect that it distorts the meanings of the very words in which it is expressed since it conflicts with obvious facts about how those words are ordinarily used. The evidence from usage would not support that conclusion about meaning on the conception of the relation between meaning and use that I have tried to identify.[12]

[12] Peter Unger rightly insists on the importance of this distinction in his defence of scepticism. He identifies a class of terms he calls 'absolute terms' (like 'flat' and 'empty') which are appropriately applied on many occasions even though they are never literally true of any of the things to which they are applied. That is shown to be no bar to our using and understanding the expressions as we do. For Unger the same holds for 'certain' and, since knowledge implies certainty, for 'know' as well. Our use of such terms is therefore compatible with the literal truth of scepticism. I agree that Unger's conception of the relation between meaning and use can be used to defend scepticism against the charge that it conflicts with the facts of usage. I do not agree that Unger can *establish* scepticism on the basis of his theory of 'absolute terms' alone. I think his argument to show that no one is ever undogmatically certain of (and hence doesn't know) anything about the world makes essential use of a step that is equivalent in force to Descartes's requirement that we must know we are not dreaming if we are to know anything about the world around us. Without that requirement, the 'absoluteness' of 'certain' and 'know' will not yield the sceptical conclusion. And I have tried to show here that with that requirement we have all we need to generate the sceptical conclusion, so the doctrine of 'absolute terms' is not needed. For a slightly fuller version of this appreciation and criticism of Unger see my review of P. Unger, *Ignorance: a Case for Scepticism* (Oxford, 1975) in *The Journal of Philosophy*, 1977.

Pressing for the precise source of linguistic oddity or inappropriateness and

I have defended the sceptical conclusion against a certain line of attack in order to begin to reveal what I think is the sceptical philosopher's conception of everyday life and everyday assertions lying behind it. He sees those assertions as restricted in certain ways relative to what, with detachment, we can all recognize to be the full conditions of their truth. So now we are led to the question whether that conception is correct, or even fully intelligible. When we begin to understand how it would vindicate scepticism I think we feel it cannot be correct. We see that that conception must somehow be rejected if we are to show how and why the elimination of the dream-possibility is not always required for knowledge of the world around us. That would begin to account for what I feel to be the depth and importance of the sceptical reasoning. Coming to terms with it would eventually involve a great deal more than simply deciding whether somebody knows something in a particular case, or even whether anybody knows anything about the world around us. A whole way of thinking of ourselves and of our practices in everyday life, and perhaps even the possibility of our getting a certain kind of detached understanding of ourselves, would be at issue. On this conception of epistemology there is much more at stake than the question of what knowledge is, or whether and how we know things.

The idea of ourselves and of our relation to the world that lies behind the sceptical reasoning seems to me deeply powerful and not easily abandoned. As long as it is even an intelligible way of thinking the sceptical conclusion will seem to be defensible against attack. In trying to give expression to the idea it is natural to resort to what seems like nothing more than the merest platitudes. If that is so, trying to avoid scepticism by throwing over the old conception will not be easy—it will involve denying what seem to be obvious truths.

distinguishing between meaning and use in the way both Unger and I here rely on form the basis of a fundamental criticism of linguistic philosophy and a quite general theory of language and communication in the important work of H. P. Grice, to which I have been much indebted in my thinking on these and other matters. See his 'The Causal Theory of Perception', *The Aristotelian Society: Supplementary Volume* XXXV, 1961; 'Logic and Conversation' in D. Davidson and G. Harman (eds), *The Logic of Grammar* (Belmont, California, 1975); and the not-yet-published William James Lectures delivered at Harvard University in 1967.

The simplest way to put the idea that lies behind our concern with knowledge is that the world around us that we claim to know about exists and is the way it is quite independently of its being known or believed by us to be that way. It is an objective world. In fact, of course, much of the world we claim to know about was here long before we were and some of it will remain after we have gone. In many cases what we believe or think we know about the world does not require anyone's knowing or believing anything in order for it to be true. If I believe that there is a mountain more than five thousand metres high on the continent of Africa, for example, what I believe will be true, or false, depending solely on the heights of the mountains in Africa. Whether anyone knows or believes or has any special reason to suspect anything about those mountains is not part of what I believe when I believe there is a mountain more than five thousand metres high. If I do not know what to believe and I ask or wonder whether there are any mountains in Africa more than five thousand metres high, my question has an answer which is completely independent of anyone's knowing or believing or being in a position to assert anything. It is quite independent of whether any human or other animate beings have ever existed. What I ask or come to believe concerns only the distance above sea-level of certain mountains.

Of course, I would not have come to believe or even to understand what I now believe unless people had existed and had come to assert things and to know things. But what I believe or understand, viz., that there is a mountain more than five thousand metres high in Africa, does not itself require any such things in order to be true. No statement of precisely *what* I understand, therefore no account of what 'There is a mountain more than five thousand metres high in Africa' means, will include anything about human beings or human knowledge or human thought. In particular it will not include anything about whether that sentence itself is or can be known to be true or could be reasonably asserted in certain circumstances. That would introduce an extraneous reference to human beings or human knowledge into a statement solely about the non-human world.

I am trying to express a conception of the independence of the world, of the idea that the world is there quite independently of human knowledge and belief, that I think we all understand. It embodies a conception of objectivity, of things being a certain way whether anyone is affected by them or interested in them or knows or believes anything about them or not. There seems to be nothing in the conception itself to imply that knowledge or reasonable belief about the objective world is impossible, or that what we can discover or know things about is, or must always be, something different from the objective world so conceived. Quite the contrary. In seeking knowledge we are trying to find out what is true, to ascertain how the world is in this or that respect. Was the suspect in Cleveland that night? Does sitting in draughts contribute to catching cold? Is there a mountain more than five thousand metres high in Africa? What we want to find out in each case is what is true, what the objective facts of the matter are. And what we aspire to and eventually claim to know is the objective truth or falsity of, for example, 'There is a mountain more than five thousand metres high in Africa'. What we aspire to and eventually claim to know is something that holds quite independently of our knowing it or of our being in a position reasonably to assert it. That is the very idea of objectivity.

Many of the things we ask or believe or want to know about do involve human knowledge, human belief and human reasoning. We ask whether anyone knows or has any good reason to believe that sitting in a draught contributes to catching cold, and if so how they know it or what the reasons are. We believe that much more is now known about the properties of matter than was known two hundred years ago. We believe that the causes of cancer are still unknown. What we ask or believe or claim knowledge about in these cases do involve human beings and human knowledge and human thought. They are questions or assertions about what we might call the human world, as opposed to that non-human part of the world that would have been the way it is whether any human beings had existed or behaved in certain ways or not.

Even here, I think, with respect to knowledge and other

human institutions, we have the same conception of objectivity. We want to know whether it is objectively true that somebody knows or has good reason to believe that sitting in a draught contributes to catching cold. In saying that the causes of cancer are still unknown we take ourselves to be making a statement about the present state of human knowledge, and we think human knowledge is in whatever state it is in with respect to the causes of cancer quite independently of our now knowing or being in a position reasonably to assert that it is. Of course we do assert what we do about the present state of human knowledge because we believe we know or have good reason to assert that no one knows the causes of cancer, but we do not regard our being in the position to make that assertion as itself part of what we know or assert when we say that no one knows the causes of cancer. Most facts of human knowledge and belief are in that respect as objective and as independent of anyone's knowing what they are as are the facts about mountains in Africa. If it is an objective fact that the causes of cancer are not known at present then in stating that fact or claiming to know it I am stating or claiming to know an objective fact about human knowledge. And if I try to find out whether anyone knows of any connection between draughts and the common cold I am trying to ascertain what the objective facts about that aspect of human knowledge really are.

Looked at in this way, if I say that I myself know a certain thing, or if I ask or wonder whether I do, what I am saying or asking about will be true or not depending on the present state of my own knowledge with respect to that thing. So when I ask whether I really know that the witness was in Cleveland that night, or when Descartes asks whether he knows that he is sitting by the fire with a piece of paper in his hand, we are enquiring into the present state of our own knowledge with respect to the matter in question. We seek a certain kind of understanding of our state or our relation to the facts—what might be called an objective understanding of our position. Whether someone (even ourselves) knows a certain thing is in that respect as objective a matter of fact as whether there is a mountain of a certain height in Africa, and what we seek is knowledge of whether or not that objective matter obtains, and perhaps in addition some understanding of how the conditions necessary and sufficient for its obtaining have been fulfilled.

That is just how we understand the position of the airplane-spotters. When the careful spotter says 'That plane is an F' he is saying something only about the identity of that plane in the sky—something that would be true or false whether any spotters were watching or not. And when he says 'I know it is an F' he is stating something about his relation to that objective fact. He used the manual and his observation of the plane to bring him into the position he is now in, but in saying he knows it is an F he is not saying anything about the manual or about his observations. If asked how he knows it is an F, he will say that he saw that it had *x, y, z*, and he knows that the manual says that any plane with *x, y, z* is an F. But when he says 'I know it is an F', he is not saying simply 'I know it has *x, y, z*' and 'I know that according to the manual it is an F'.

We know that the careful spotter does not know that the plane he sees in the sky is an F. But we can agree that he does know that according to the manual it is an F. So the question of whether he knows what kind of plane it is is not the same as the question whether he knows what the manual says it is. A reflective airplane-spotter in his spare time might be expected to be aware of that distinction, just as we are. Of course, believing what he has been told in his training, he thinks the two questions get the same answer. But in asking himself how he knows what kinds of planes there are in the sky he would see that the manual and his observations are all he has got to go on, and he would admit that if the manual were incorrect in certain ways he would not know everything he now thinks he knows. This thought need not be relevant to the war effort; knowledge or truth are not the only values in time of war. But if he does think he knows that some planes in the sky are Fs, he will appeal to the correctness of the manual to explain that knowledge to himself or others. In the story as told, that assumption is not true—it is because we know that the manual is not correct that we know that he does not know that the plane is an F. But even if the assumption of the correctness of the manual were true, the reflective spotter would see that its being true is required for his knowing what kinds of planes there are in the sky in the way he does.

Whether the manual is correct or not is itself an objective fact. In this case we outsiders know it is not correct. The spotter who relies on the manual regards it as correct; and he can see that its objective correctness is essential to his knowing. It is because he believes in its correctness that he thinks he knows the plane is an F. We who have a more objective understanding of the spotter's position know that he does not know. We are in a position that he is not in with respect to one of the facts essential to his knowing. We are therefore in a better position for determining whether 'He knows it is an F' is objectively true or not. The reflective spotter thinks it is true, and he thinks he can explain how his knowledge is possible. If we told him what we know about Gs he would realize that he had not been in the best position for determining whether he knows or for explaining how his knowledge is possible. Even without our help, if it occurred to him that the manual might not be correct, he could see that he was not in the best position he could be in for explaining his putative knowledge. He would see that checking the reliability of the manual would put him in a better position for determining whether what he says when he says 'I know it is an F' is objectively true. It would give him a more objective understanding of his position.

The sceptical philosopher's conception of our own position and of his quest for an understanding of it is parallel to this reflective airplane-spotter's conception. It is a quest for an objective or detached understanding and explanation of the position we are objectively in. What is seen to be true from a detached 'external' standpoint might not correspond to what we take to be the truth about our position when we consider it 'internally', from within the practical contexts which give our words their social point. Philosophical scepticism says the two do not correspond; we never know anything about the world around us, although we say or imply that we do hundreds of times a day.

I think we do have a conception of things being a certain way quite independently of their being known or believed or said to be that way by anyone. I think the source of the philosophical problem of the external world lies somewhere within just such a conception of an objective world or in our desire, expressed in terms of that conception, to gain a certain kind of understanding of our relation to the world. But in trying to describe that conception I think I have relied on nothing but platitudes we would all accept—not about specific ways we all now believe the world to be, but just the general idea of what an objective world or an objective state of affairs would be. If those platitudes about objectivity do indeed express the conception of the world and our relation to it that the sceptical philosopher relies on, and if I am right in thinking that scepticism can be avoided only if that conception is rejected, it will seem that in order to avoid scepticism we must deny platitudes we all accept. I believe this sometimes has happened in philosophy.

But perhaps the commonplaces I have appealed to, if they really are uncontroversial, do not manage to express the full conception of objectivity and of everyday life that the philosopher relies on in his sceptical reasoning. Perhaps there is a way of taking them so that they express no philosophical conception at all, and so do not generate or exacerbate the philosophical problem of the external world. I want now to explore several different ways in which that might be thought to be true. They are in effect different ways of trying to explain what the philosophical problem of the external world amounts to.

III

G. E. Moore and Scepticism: 'Internal' and 'External'

Someone who doubts or denies that he knows a certain thing—the name of Lear's second daughter or the date of the battle of Waterloo, for example—can sometimes be reminded that he does know it after all. And the best response to someone who insists that he doesn't know a certain thing or that it is not known by anyone or perhaps is not even true would be to prove that very thing to him. G. E. Moore's approach to the problem of the external world embodies both of these forthright reactions. He seeks to remind philosophers that they do indeed know many things they say they doubt, and he thinks he can prove to those who doubt or deny it that there are indeed external things. We are perhaps familiar enough with the problem of the external world to be doubtful about the prospects of such a straightforward approach. I nevertheless want to look at what Moore does in his celebrated 'proof of an external world' and what he achieves by it. I think he can be seen to achieve a great deal even if it turns out not to be what he thinks he achieves.

He starts, characteristically, with some words he finds in Kant's *Critique of Pure Reason.*[1] He takes them to express the complaint that a proof of the existence of things outside us has never been given. Whether that is what Kant complains of in that passage is open to question, but Moore thinks there is no doubt he can meet the challenge he finds expressed there. He begins by explaining in considerable detail precisely what he is going to prove and what it would take to prove it—clearing off the table and rolling up his sleeves, as it were, while describing exactly what he is going to do before getting down to performing the remarkable feat itself.

[1] G. E. Moore, 'Proof of an External World', in his *Philosophical Papers* (London, 1959), p. 127. (This volume is hereafter cited as PP.)

He explains that by 'things outside us' he means things to be met with in space, and he carefully distinguishes that class of things from pains, after-images, double-images and the like, which are not to be met with in space. From the statement that such 'inner' things exist it follows that someone is having or has had some experience or other, but from the existence of things outside us no such inference can be drawn. Things outside us can in that sense be said to be independent of us—not dependent for their existence on being perceived or experienced. Examples of things outside us, so defined, are sheets of paper, shoes and socks, human hands, and soap bubbles. From the fact that things of that kind exist it does not follow that anyone is perceiving or experiencing anything. If at least two things of that kind could be proved to exist, the existence of things outside us would have been proved. That is precisely what Moore then tries to do.

The proof is short. It starts with his holding up his two hands and making a certain gesture with the right hand while saying 'Here is one hand' and a certain gesture with the left while saying 'And here is another'. He thereby proves that two human hands exist. But it was just explained that that would be sufficient for proving the existence of things outside us; anyone who proved what Moore claims to have proved has 'proved *ipso facto* the existence of external things' (PP, 146). So here is a 'perfectly rigorous' proof of the existence of external things; Moore thinks it is probably impossible to give a better or more rigorous proof of anything (PP, 146).

It certainly seems true, as he points out, that:

> we all of us do constantly take proofs of this sort as absolutely conclusive proofs of certain conclusions—as finally settling certain questions, as to which we were previously in doubt. (PP, 147.)

He gives an everyday example of proving that there are at least three misprints on a certain page. If there has been some dispute on the question—or even if there hasn't, for that matter—the issue can be conclusively settled in the affirmative by finding that here is one misprint and here is another and here is another. That does prove it. Our daily experience

—not to mention what goes on in scientific laboratories or in courts of law—is full of similar examples every day. The best proof we could possibly have of something's existence would be to find it right before our eyes.

That we do often prove things and come to know them in this way in everyday and scientific life seems to me undeniable; it must be kept clearly in mind in any discussion of Moore's proof. It is what I think makes his curious performance so important for an understanding of the philosophical problem of our knowledge of the external world. If Moore's proof is just like the proofs we give and accept of similar matters in everyday life, then by studying his proof and asking how it bears on the philosophical problem we can hope to clarify the relation between the philosophical problem and our ordinary procedures and claims to know things in everyday life. If Moore really does prove that there are external things, doesn't that settle the question of whether we know that such things exist? And if he does answer the question, isn't it also answered in the affirmative a thousand times a day by proofs we give in everyday life that are just as rigorous and conclusive as Moore's? Anyone trying to explain the philosophical problem of the external world would have to have convincing answers to these questions. If, on the other hand, we think Moore does not really establish what he sets out to prove, doesn't it follow that our ordinary attempts to know and prove things in everyday life are deficient in the same way? It would follow that nobody ever does establish that there are as many as three misprints on a certain page. But where exactly does Moore go wrong? And what mistake are all the rest of us making in everyday life when we give and accept proofs we regard as conclusive?

I considered one sort of answer to those questions in Chapter Two. On that account we would have to accept the sceptical conclusion that we never know anything about the world around us in everyday and scientific life. A consideration of Moore's proof gives us one way of testing the plausibility, or perhaps even the intelligibility, of that answer.

Moore points out that his proof satisfies three necessary conditions of a successful proof. (1) Its premiss is different from the conclusion it is used to prove. The proposition 'Two human hands exist' is different from 'Here is a human hand' and 'Here is another human hand'; that conclusion could be true even if both of those premisses were false. (2) The premisses are something known to be true. It would be quite absurd, Moore says, to suggest that he does not know that here is one hand and here is another, or that he only believes it to be true but is not or cannot be certain of it. 'You might as well suggest that I do not know that I am now standing up and talking—that perhaps after all I'm not, and that it's not quite certain that I am!', he replies (PP, 146–7). (3) The conclusion follows from the premisses. If it is true that here is one hand and here is another it could not possibly be false that two human hands exist at this moment. So Moore's proof is like other proofs in which a conclusion is validly drawn from premisses that differ from it and are known to be true.

Once we are familiar with the philosophical problem of our knowledge of the external world, I think we immediately feel that Moore's proof is inadequate. We are then most strongly inclined to object that he does not really satisfy the second of his three conditions for a successful proof—he does not really know that here is one hand and here is another. It seems hopeless to protest that the conclusion does not follow from the premisses—that even if it were true that here is a hand and here is another it still might not be true that two human hands exist—so his 'knowledge' of the premisses strikes us as the most questionable claim Moore makes for his proof.

It is worth looking into the source of this very natural reaction. I think it is more complicated than it might seem. We can distinguish two different questions that are not usually asked separately—probably because a certain answer to one of them is taken for granted. We can ask whether Moore's proof is a good one—whether he knows what he claims to know and legitimately establishes his conclusion on that basis. If so, he has proved that there are external things. We can also ask whether Moore refutes philosophical scepticism and answers affirmatively the philosophical problem of the external world. I think we do immediately feel that the answer to this second question is 'No'. But must we then conclude that the answer to the first question must be 'No' also; that there must be something wrong with Moore's proof? From the fact that Moore's performance does not answer a certain philosophical problem (assuming for the moment it does not) does it follow that there must be something wrong with that performance, that it does not succeed in doing what Moore intended it to do? I think it does not immediately follow. Explaining why that is so might help to illuminate the special character of the philosophical problem.

For one thing, if that conclusion did follow, it would be because what Moore says is inconsistent with what philosophical scepticism says, and because his proof was intended to refute that very philosophical thesis. It is of course extremely natural to assume that that is so. Moore says 'I know that there are at least two external things', and philosophical scepticism says 'No one knows whether there are any external things'; it is difficult to imagine how they could fail to be inconsistent with each other. And Moore does take himself to be refuting the very thing he thinks sceptical philosophers are saying. But—and here I only introduce the possibility—*if* there were in fact no incompatibility between them, and *if* what Moore claims to refute turned out not to be the thesis of philosophical scepticism at all, we would not be forced on the usual grounds to say that there is something wrong with his proof as a proof. Perhaps we could even say that he really does know that there are external things, and that it really can be proved that there are as many as three misprints on a certain page, as long as we do not imply in either case that it is thereby demonstrated that philosophical scepticism is not true. What philosophical scepticism could possibly amount to might then become much more difficult to understand, but at least we would have a less distorted picture of how we prove and know things in everyday life against which to try to illuminate it.

To begin to explore the question of the compatibility or incompatibility between everyday knowledge and the thesis of philosophical scepticism I want to look at some of the ways Moore's proof can get misinterpreted when it is judged too much in the light of a certain understanding of the philosophical problem. I take as illustrations two sympathetically-motivated but, it seems to me, ultimately unacceptable accounts of Moore's proof. Something can be learned from each of them.

Norman Malcolm has tried to identify the great force and philosophical importance of Moore's work despite the fact that, taken at face value, his proof seems simply to 'beg the question' against philosophical scepticism, and his reply to philosophical paradox 'does not seem to be a fruitful one' or 'one which ought to convince the philosopher that what he said was false'.[2] Moore says that he does know that there are hands before him, and so any arguments to the contrary must be wrong, but according to Malcolm, 'he does not say *how* they are wrong; so is he not begging the question?'[3] If Moore in his 'proof' were simply asserting that there are two human hands, Malcolm thinks he would not disprove what a sceptical philosopher says—'at least it seems a poor sort of refutation' (S, 348-9). In response to a philosopher who says we can never know whether there is a tree before us, for example, Malcolm thinks it would be 'pointless' for Moore to say 'I know there is a tree there because I have a clear, unobstructed view of it'.[4] But that seems to be just the sort of thing Moore does say.

Alice Ambrose also finds Moore's proof unsatisfactory when taken at face value. She thinks it would never convince a philosophical sceptic because he would require in addition that Moore prove his premisses that here is one hand and here is another. It is not simply that the philosopher has higher standards than Moore or that Moore is more easily convinced of things than he ought to be. Rather, it is the very possibility of knowing such things as Moore's premisses that Ambrose thinks the philosopher questions; that is what is involved in questioning the possibility of knowing whether any external things exist. Since the sceptical philosopher would agree with Moore that being a hand entails being an

[2] N. Malcolm, 'Moore and Ordinary Language', in P. A. Schilpp (ed.), *The Philosophy of G. E. Moore* (New York, 1952), p. 348. (This volume is hereafter cited as S.)

[3] N. Malcolm, 'George Edward Moore', in his *Knowledge and Certainty* (Englewood Cliffs, N.J., 1963), p. 177.

[4] N. Malcolm, 'Defending Common Sense', *The Philosophical Review*, 1949, p. 209.

external object, Ambrose thinks Moore's proof 'will not be to the point' if it demonstrates only that the existence of external things follows from the existence of human hands.[5] She concludes that if 'There are external things' is taken as a straightforward empirical proposition deduced from another proposition established by the evidence of the senses, it could never serve as a refutation of scepticism (S, 399).

Both responses start from the reaction that Moore's proof, taken as it stands, is unsuccessful as a refutation of philosophical scepticism about the external world. But both nevertheless regard the proof as extremely valuable and indeed correct when properly understood. For Malcolm it is a philosophical advance of great importance which does refute scepticism (S, 349); for Ambrose it is successful in making one see that scepticism is unacceptable (S, 418). They therefore conclude that it cannot be taken at face value; Moore must be doing something different from what he seems to be doing. His proof cannot be the ordinary empirical demonstration it appears to be.

For both Malcolm and Ambrose the real force of Moore's proof cannot be appreciated without understanding the peculiar nature of philosophical scepticism. They both think it is clear on reflection that for the philosophical sceptic nothing could possibly count as knowing by means of the senses that there are external things. It is not just that the evidence Moore gives for the existence of his hands is incomplete or inadequate in specifiable ways, but that all the empirical evidence there could possibly be would still not be enough. Ambrose thinks the philosophical sceptic cannot even describe what sort of thing could make one's evidence for 'There are external things' complete; there are for her no describable circumstances in which anyone could be said to know that there are external things. She concludes that the sceptic's claim 'No one knows external things exist' cannot be falsified and so cannot be an 'empirical assertion' about our inability to know (S, 402). She thinks this in turn shows that 'the sceptic is arguing for the *logical impossibility* of knowledge and not for any empirical fact' (S, 402). For him, every statement such as 'I do not know there is a dollar in

[5] A. Ambrose, 'Moore's "Proof of an External World"' (S, 399).

my purse' is 'necessarily true' (S, 402). Malcolm also holds that philosophical scepticism is the view that it is 'logically impossible' for anyone to know that that is a tree or that here is a human hand; for the sceptic there is a 'contradiction' involved in supposing that such things are known (S, 353). Malcolm and Ambrose agree about the philosophical sceptic's invulnerability to straightforward empirical refutation, and therefore about the source of the weakness or irrelevance of Moore's proof taken simply as a claim to know that there are hands before him and that therefore at least two external things exist. They also think the proof must therefore be understood to be something different from what on first sight it appears to be. Only then would it refute philosophical scepticism correctly understood. Both Malcolm and Ambrose assume that that is the only way it could have the profound philosophical significance it so obviously has for them.

What, then, is Moore really doing in his proof, and how does he succeed in refuting philosophical scepticism? According to Malcolm he is really pointing out that there is no contradiction involved in asserting that someone knows that there is a hand, and therefore an external object, before him. He does so in the only way Malcolm seems to allow it is possible to show that something is non-contradictory—by showing that it is 'perfectly correct language' to say on certain occasions things like 'I see a tree', or that 'it is a proper way of speaking to say that we know for certain that there are several chairs in this room' (S, 354). Moore appeals to 'our language-sense' (S, 354). By insisting that he knows the things he does Moore 'reminds us that there *is* an ordinary use of the phrase "know for certain" in which it is applied to empirical statements' (S, 355). That in itself 'constitutes a refutation of the philosophical statement that we can never have certain knowledge of material-thing statements' (S, 355). Moore's proof really makes a point about what is correct language, and from that in turn a conclusion about the possibility of a certain state of affairs is said to follow.

Ambrose's account agrees with most of what Malcolm says but goes one step further. She thinks the philosophical sceptic could not fail to be aware of the facts about how we speak. He knows that language is in fact so used that the sentence 'I know there is a dollar in my purse' describes something that could be the case. He would admit that it is not a necessary falsehood as language is now used to say that such a thing is known. That is why 'it will not settle the dispute for Moore to show the sceptic he is using language incorrectly' (S, 410). But philosophical scepticism according to Ambrose is really an insistence that such a sentence *should* be used to express a necessary falsehood. The sceptic argues *as if* the sentence 'No one knows that hands exist' expressed a necessary proposition, so for Ambrose he is really recommending or proposing that certain expressions of our language should be deprived of what he acknowledges is their current use. Moore's insistence that he knows that there are hands is therefore to be seen as working against scepticism because it 'constitutes an insistence on retaining present usage' (S, 411); it is a recommendation opposed to the recommendation of the philosophical sceptic. 'It is the sceptic's recommendation which makes Moore's insistence relevant' (S, 411).

These interpretations of Moore's proof are offered to explain how something which on the surface seems so inadequate as a reply to philosophical scepticism can nevertheless be of great philosophical force and importance. Moore certainly does not *seem* to be doing what they claim he is doing, so in order to increase the plausibility of their interpretations both Malcolm and Ambrose go on to argue directly against what Moore appears to be doing. Not only would his proof be ineffectual against scepticism if he were doing only what he seems to be doing, they argue, but (for different reasons in each case) Moore simply *could not* be doing what he appears to be doing. What he superficially seems to be doing simply cannot be done. To see why I think both these criticisms fail will take us a long way towards understanding Moore's proof as he understands it. That will leave us with the problem of its relation to philosophical scepticism.

Ambrose admits that Moore does seem to be trying to 'establish the proposition that there exist things external to our minds' (S, 397) by 'an ordinary empirical argument'

(S, 405) of a very common form. Just as one can establish an existential proposition such as 'There is a coin in the collection plate' by pointing out a specific instance—say, a particular dime in the collection plate—so Moore appears to be pointing out his hands as a way of establishing that there are external things. But for Ambrose what Moore does could not be of that form because pointing in the ordinary case 'calls attention to a thing with features differentiating this thing from things of other kinds' (S, 405), but one cannot point out an 'external thing' to someone in that way. It is impossible to point to something that is *not* an 'external thing'. There is therefore nothing from which 'external things' could be distinguished, no contrasting class of 'non-external things', and no features differentiating 'external things' from things of other kinds. Ambrose concludes that the term 'external thing' is not 'a general name for some kind of thing, designating features distinguishing that kind of thing from some other kind' (S, 406). It therefore is not simply a term that is more general than 'dime' or 'coin' or 'piece of money', all of which do serve to pick out things of certain sorts. But then one cannot establish the existence of external things by pointing to a human hand in the way one can establish the existence of a coin by pointing to a dime. So Moore's proof, whatever it is, cannot be a straightforward empirical demonstration of an empirical proposition. It cannot be an empirical refutation of a philosophical sceptic who denies that external things can be known. This objection to what Moore appears to be doing is meant to support Ambrose's claim that he is really doing something else in his proof—in particular that he is recommending a certain familiar linguistic usage, or resisting the sceptic's radical recommendation that certain words be used in new ways.

Fortunately we have Moore's reply to this interpretation, and it is not surprising to find that he repudiates it entirely. He insists that his assertion that there are external things is 'empirical' and was meant to be 'empirical', and that in proving it he meant to be proving that the proposition 'There are no external things' is actually false (S, 672). Consistent with that conception of his proof, he also says that he took the term 'external object' to be an 'empirical' term: producing or pointing to a dime can prove that at least one external object exists just as it can prove that at least one coin exists (S, 671). Moore admits that there are differences between the term 'external object' and the term 'coin', but he thinks the terms do not differ with respect to the possibility of pointing to instances that fall under them. It might be true that one cannot literally point with one's finger at something that is not an external object, but one can certainly draw someone's attention to, and in that sense point out to him, a sense-datum, an after-image, or some other object which is not 'external' in the sense Moore specified before giving his proof. So for Moore the term 'external object' has a significant empirical contrast within our experience; it denotes things which can be pointed out and distinguished from other things that do not fall into that class. That is why the proposition 'There are external things' follows directly and obviously from 'There are coins' or 'There are human hands' just as 'There are coins' follows directly and obviously from 'There are dimes'. The term 'external thing' as Moore understands it is just a more general empirical term than 'dime', 'coin', and 'piece of money', but not everything that exists falls under it.

Given this conception of his proof it is no wonder Moore thinks the only objection one could possibly make to it is that he has not proved his premisses that here is one hand and here is another. To object that the argument is not valid would be as silly as refusing to agree that there are coins while conceding that there are dimes. If the terms in which the conclusion is expressed are just more general than those in the premisses, the only possible objection would seem to be that the premisses are not really known. That is perhaps what Wittgenstein is conceding at the beginning of *On Certainty* when he says 'If you do know that *here is one hand*, we'll grant you all the rest'.[6]

Because Moore understands his proof and the proposition established by it to be 'empirical', he does not hesitate to dismiss Ambrose's interpretation of him as making a certain recommendation about the use of words. He sees himself

[6] L. Wittgenstein, *On Certainty* (Oxford, 1969), §1.

in his proof as appealing to one fact—that here is a hand and here is another—in order to prove another—that there are external objects. He thinks the fact he appeals to proves just what he wanted to prove, but 'I could not have supposed', Moore says, 'that the fact that I had a hand proved anything as to how the expression "external objects" ought to be used' (S, 674). When he finds that here is one hand and here is another, he proves that there are external things, just as one might find that here is one misprint and here is another and here is another and thereby prove that there are three misprints. In neither case is anything proved or even said about the *expression* 'hand', 'external thing', 'misprint', or even the expression 'I know that here is a hand' or 'I know that there are three misprints'. Moore takes himself to be appealing to a certain fact in order to prove something which itself is nothing linguistic. His proof as he understands it would be completely ineffectual against someone who was making a linguistic recommendation. Nothing about how words should be used follows one way or the other from his premisses.

This insistence of Moore's is important because it shows that if he is doing what he here claims to have been doing in his proof, not just Ambrose's interpretation, but Malcolm's interpretation as well, must be wrong. Just as the fact that here is a hand does not prove anything about how certain expressions *ought* to be used, so it does not prove anything about how certain expressions *are* used, or are correctly used, either. The point of Moore's proof could not be to show that such-and-such is 'perfectly correct language' or 'a proper way of speaking', if Moore is right about what he himself is doing in his proof. Malcolm believes that Moore never repudiated Malcolm's interpretation of the proof—he even suggests that Moore actually accepted it[7]—but it seems to me that that cannot be so if Moore was doing what he says he was doing. Of course Malcolm does have an additional argument to show that Moore *could not* have been doing what he says

[7] N. Malcolm, 'Moore and Wittgenstein on the Sense of "I Know"', in his *Thought and Knowledge* (Ithaca, N.Y., 1977), p. 171. (Hereafter cited as MW.)

he was doing. I will consider that additional argument in a moment. But on Moore's own understanding of his proof there is nothing to be said in favour of the idea that its premisses or conclusion 'may be interpreted as meaning "It is correct language to say . . ." ' (S, 350).

It might still be true, as Malcolm says, that the proof or Moore's other typical assertions against philosophers serve to 'remind' us that 'situations constantly occur which ordinary language allows us to describe by uttering sentences of the sort "I see my pen" ' (S, 351), or that he 'reminds us that there *is* an ordinary use of the phrase "know for certain" in which it is applied to empirical statements' (S, 355). Moore's remarks might serve to remind us of many things, but that does not show that those reminders are the very point or conclusion of his proof of an external world, or that they are what it is meant to achieve. If I ask whether there is anything to eat in the kitchen and am told that there is spaghetti and broccoli, I might be reminded that some English words for food are taken over from Italian. But that is not the point of the reply, nor would I have found out what I wanted to know if I had been told only the facts of language that the reply served to remind me of. Even if I *am* reminded of those facts of language, it would not be correct to say that the reply 'There is spaghetti and broccoli' may be interpreted as meaning 'Some English words for food are taken over from Italian'.

Behind both Malcolm's and Ambrose's interpretation of Moore's proof is the idea that the philosophical sceptic is not putting forward an empirical statement when he says that no one knows whether any external things exist. That is why they think Moore cannot be understood to be giving a straightforward empirical argument. Not only are their interpretations repudiated by Moore, as we have seen, but the inference on which they are based seems to be mistaken. Moore himself makes, or half makes, the point in his reply to Ambrose.

The philosophical sceptic might think he had *a priori* reasons for denying that there are external things or that anyone knows that there are. But even if he argues for his conclusion in that way, it does not follow that his conclusion cannot be refuted empirically. If someone claims to have established on *a priori* grounds that there are no Xs, or even that there could not possibly be, it would be sufficient refutation of his view to point to the presence of Xs right before our eyes. The statement that we know *a priori* that there are no Xs, or the statement that there could not possibly be any Xs, both do imply, after all, that there are no Xs. And if it is obviously or even discoverably true that there are Xs, the original claim will have been refuted, whatever the arguments for it might have been. Moore believes that there is no difficulty in refuting scepticism empirically even if the sceptic's reasons are thought to be, and actually are, *a priori* or non-empirical (S, 672–3). But with that *non sequitur* out of the way, Malcolm's and Ambrose's reasons for saying that Moore must be doing something different from what he seems to be doing in his proof reduce to nothing more than the reaction that the proof as it stands seems ineffective against philosophical scepticism. I suggest that that reaction, which I think we all share, is compatible with Moore's doing just what he appears to be doing in the proof.

Malcolm's direct argument to show that what Moore superficially appears to be doing simply cannot be done tries to explain Moore's repeated insistence to the contrary as due to confusion. He thinks Moore fails to see that if he had been simply asserting that he knows that here is a human hand and here is another in the circumstances in which he found himself, he would have been misusing the word 'know'; it is simply not possible in those circumstances to use the word 'know' as Moore says he was using it. To understand and evaluate this line of criticism will take us a long way towards understanding both Moore's proof and the philosophical problem of the external world. But it must be kept in mind throughout that this diagnosis of how and why Moore could not succeed in doing what he says he is doing is to be assessed quite independently of any feelings we might have about the ineffectiveness of his proof against philosophical scepticism. That will lead us closer to an examination of what Moore actually does that is uncoloured for the moment by expectations about what he should be doing if he wants to refute philosophical scepticism.

Malcolm's criticism of Moore's proof and other assertions against philosophers is that remarks like 'I know that here is a human hand' or 'I know that that is a tree' cannot be intelligibly made in just any situation, at any time, but require for their sense certain special conditions. In his paper 'Defending Common Sense' he says that for the proper use of the word 'know' there must be some question at issue or some doubt to be removed, the person saying he knows something must be able to give some reason for his assertion, and there must be some investigation which, if carried out, would settle the question.[8] Malcolm holds that Moore violates all three conditions in his proof and in his typical responses to sceptical philosophers. The philosopher who denies that anyone knows that there are external things is not in fact in doubt about the existence of external things, there is no question at issue, Moore cannot give anything that counts as a reason for what he claims to know, and there is no investigation that could ever settle the question. Malcolm concludes that Moore misuses the word 'know'. We cannot even ask whether it is true that Moore knows that here is a human hand, since he does not succeed in using the word 'know' correctly when he says that. His 'proof', understood straightforwardly, cannot get off the ground.

As a way of proving that Moore misuses the word 'know' this argument is obviously only as good as Malcolm's contention that the conditions he lists are necessary for the proper use of that word in an assertion of knowledge. It seems clear that they are not. The use of the word 'know' is more complicated than Malcolm's three examples and three conditions would indicate. In a more recent paper, he gives not three but twelve examples of ordinary uses of 'I know'. He admits that the twelve do not yield a complete account of the proper use of 'I know'; he now thinks 'there is no such thing as a "complete account"' (MW, 179). That makes it difficult to give a proof, in the old way, that Moore

[8] N. Malcolm, 'Defending Common Sense', *The Philosophical Review*, 1949, pp. 203 ff. It is not completely clear whether Malcolm regards each of the three conditions as necessary, or only their disjunction.

must be misusing 'know'. Nevertheless Malcolm goes on from his twelve examples to conclude that 'It is clear that Moore was not giving *any* everyday employment to the words "I know" ' (MW, 185).

Unfortunately Malcolm does not try to show precisely how and why Moore fails to say anything or misuses 'I know' in typical utterances against sceptical philosophers. He is more interested in a 'picture' of knowledge he thinks Moore must have been operating with and which must have led him astray. But that 'picture' can be shown to have led Moore astray only if it can be shown that Moore *was* led astray—that he was in fact misusing the expression 'I know' or not giving it any everyday employment. And that could be shown only by a more careful examination of what Moore was actually doing or trying to do.

In a letter quoted in Malcolm's paper, Moore points out that the only reason Malcolm gives for saying he misused 'I know' is that he did not use it in circumstances in which it would normally be used; for example, no doubt or uncertainty had been expressed which was then cleared up by some new-found knowledge. Moore concedes that it might serve no useful purpose to say a certain thing or to utter certain words on a certain occasion, but he insists that 'this is an entirely different thing from saying that the words in question don't, on that occasion "make sense" ' (MW, 174). He thinks 'it is perfectly possible that a person who uses [certain words] senselessly, in the sense that he uses them where no sensible person would use them because, under those circumstances, they serve no useful purpose, should be using them *in their normal sense*, and that what he asserts by so using them should be *true*' (MW, 174). Moore here seems to be invoking something like the distinction between the conditions for the appropriate or useful application of expressions and the conditions of their truth that I introduced in the sceptic's defence in Chapter Two. It might seem odd to find the anti-sceptical Moore insisting on a distinction that I argued makes scepticism invulnerable to the charge that it misuses or distorts the meanings of its terms. But that charge is never part of Moore's attack on philosophical scepticism. In his typical assertions against philosophers he is not making a point about the actual or proper use of expressions.

In this published letter to Malcolm he is of course making a point about the use of expressions; he is denying that he misused 'I know' in his proof or in his assertion that he knew that that was a tree before him. But he was not making a point about the use of expressions in making those assertions themselves. He does not even admit that the words he used against philosophers were 'senseless' in the sense of serving no useful purpose.

> Of course, in my case, I was using them with a purpose—the purpose of disproving a general proposition which many philosophers have made; so that I was not only using them in their usual sense, but also under circumstances where they might possibly serve a useful purpose, though not a purpose for which they would be commonly used. (MW, 174.)

This repeats Moore's insistence that in his proof he meant to be doing exactly what he appears to be doing—proving the truth of a certain proposition. We now need to ask whether he succeeds and if so, whether what he succeeds in disproving is 'a general proposition which many philosophers have made'.

I think there is a way of understanding Moore's assertions in which they are perfectly intelligible and legitimate and involve no misuse of 'I know' or any other expressions. Whether he thereby settles affirmatively the philosophical problem of the external world depends in part on what that problem amounts to and what the negative sceptical answer to it means. But if Moore does prove or know that there are external things, there must be some general proposition to the effect that there are no external things which he proves or knows to be false. We know that some philosophers have said or implied that no one knows whether there are external things. But if there is a way of understanding Moore's assertions as fully legitimate we are now faced with the possibility that what those philosophers meant to assert is not the same thing Moore proves to be false. This is precisely why I think G. E. Moore's proof of an external world is so important; he better than anyone else opens up this possibility for us. He of course would never explain the significance of his work in this way. He thinks he is refuting the very thing sceptical philosophers said or implied. But if there is nothing wrong with his saying what he says, he could be unwittingly presenting us with the possibility that what he and all the rest of us say and do in everyday life could be perfectly true and legitimate without thereby answering one way or the other the philosophical problem of our knowledge of the external world. If that were so, the philosophical problem and its sceptical answer would perhaps be seen to stand in a much more complicated and puzzling relation to what we say and do in everyday life than the traditional conception outlined in Chapter Two would imply. That in itself could be a philosophical advance of great importance.

Malcolm thinks 'it is evident that Moore was not giving *any* everyday employment to the words "I know . . ." ' in his typical assertions against philosophers, even though 'he was saying something of deep philosophical interest' (MW, 185). He was giving what Malcolm calls 'a *philosophical* employment to the words "I know . . ." ' (MW, 185). I agree that Moore does something of deep philosophical interest, but I would like to suggest that it might be possible to do something of deep philosophical interest without giving a 'philosophical' employment to one's words. Perhaps a steadfast refusal or inability to speak or think in a 'philosophical' or non-everyday way could reveal something of the greatest philosophical significance. Exploring that possibility will involve looking closely, and if possible without philosophical preconceptions, at the sort of thing Moore actually does and says in his typical assertions against philosophers.

Is it possible to use 'I know' as Moore does without misusing it? Could one then really fail to answer the philosophical problem of the external world? I think the answer to both questions is 'Yes'. Malcolm apparently thinks the answer to the second question is 'No', and perhaps that, along with his understanding of philosophical scepticism, is part of what leads him to conclude that it is not possible to use 'I know' in the way Moore tries to use it. To see that it is possible to use Moore's very words in contexts that appear nowhere in Malcolm's list of correct uses of 'know', we can recall Thompson Clarke's example of the physiologist lecturing on mental abnormalities. Near the beginning of his lecture he might say:

> Each of us who is normal knows that he is now awake, not dreaming or hallucinating, that there is a real public world outside his mind which he is now perceiving, that in this world there are three-dimensional animate and inanimate bodies of many shapes and sizes . . . . In contrast, individuals suffering from certain mental abnormalities each believes that what we know to be the real world is his imaginative creation.[9]

Here the lecturer uses the same words often used by philosophers who make or question general statements about the world and our knowledge of it. When he says that each of us knows that there is a public world of three-dimensional bodies, he is stating what can only be regarded as a straightforward empirical fact. Most of us do know the things he mentions, and those with the abnormalities he has in mind presumably do not. That is a real difference between people that can be observed or ascertained.

I think we do not regard the lecturer in this context as having settled affirmatively the philosophical problem of our knowledge of the external world. If we had once raised the philosophical question of whether anyone knows that there is a public world of enduring, three-dimensional bodies, it would be ludicrous to reply, 'The answer is "Yes"; we do know of the existence of the external world. That physiologist says we do, and he is a reputable scientist who knows what he is talking about'. It is difficult to say precisely why that is absurd—after all, the lecturer did say that we know it, and (we can suppose) he does know what he is talking about—but I think there is no doubt that that would be our reaction. Certainly the physiologist in his lecture is not responding to any challenge he sees coming his way from philosophy. No philosophical thoughts need ever have entered his head; he could say and mean exactly what he says even if there had never been any such thing as philosophy. He is simply distinguishing two groups of people on the basis of what one group knows and the other does not; he is stating what he and all the rest of us know to be a fact.

Whatever we might think about the relation between what

[9] Clarke, 'The Legacy of Skepticism', p. 756.

the lecturer says and the philosophical problem of the external world, it is clear that he cannot be accused of misusing the word 'know'. He makes a perfectly legitimate and intelligible application of the word, and once we are reminded of examples like this we see that similar remarks can be made in such relatively ordinary circumstances every day. But none of Malcolm's original three conditions are satisfied, nor does an example anything like this appear in his augmented list. When the physiologist was giving his lecture there was no question at issue about the external world and no doubt to be removed. He gave no reason for his assertion and there was no investigation in the offing that would settle the question of the existence of the external world. But violating Malcolm's conditions or not appearing in his augmented list is no proof of misuse. There are more legitimate uses of the word 'know' than the fifteen or so that are dreamt up in Malcolm's philosophy.

Moore, of course, was not lecturing on mental abormalities, and he was addressing his remarks to philosophers, so the example of the lecturing physiologist does not automatically settle the question of how we are to understand Moore. But it does show that it is possible to say, legitimately and undogmatically, what at least looks like the very same thing the philosophical sceptic doubts or denies, without settling or perhaps even touching the philosophical problem of our knowledge of the external world. That should make us more suspicious of a direct step from the understandable reaction that Moore does not really refute philosophical scepticism to the conclusion that he misuses 'know' or does not give it an everyday employment.

Consider another everyday use of 'know' not considered by Malcolm which is closer than that of the lecturing physiologist to Moore's own use. Suppose a murder has just been committed in a country house during a weekend party. The young duke is found stabbed on the far side of the large table in the hall, although the butler was with him the whole time except for a few seconds when he left to answer the telephone in the foyer where there were many people. An experienced detective and his younger assistant are among the guests and are trying to determine how it could have happened. After considerable reflection the eager assistant announces that someone must have dashed into the room and stabbed the victim and dashed out again before the butler returned from answering the telephone. 'That's the only way it could have happened' he says, 'the only thing we don't know is who did it'. 'No,' says the master detective at the scene of the crime, 'we know this table is here and is so large that no one could have come through that door and got around to this side of the table and stabbed the victim and got back out again before the butler returned'.

The master detective is not misusing the word 'know'. But when he says they know the table is there and was there a few minutes ago, there is no question at issue about the table's presence and no doubt about it to be removed. He gives no reason for his assertion, and there is no investigation that would settle the question. Nor is he doing any of the other things Malcolm lists as possible jobs for 'I know'. He is simply reminding his colleague of something he knows and appears to have overlooked or denied in his attempted explanation of the murder. That is often a valuable procedure in trying to determine what is true or what to believe. The detective knows that the reflections of his younger colleague must be wrong, since they conflict with something both of them already know to be true. He does not even need to know what thoughts led the assistant to that conclusion. Even without finding some specific flaw in his colleague's thinking, he knows it is wrong since it could be true only if the table were not there. The presence of the table is something that is known and cannot be denied in their reflections, and the detective is quite right to remind his apprentice of it. It brings the enthusiastic but misguided speculations of his colleague back down to earth.

Could Moore have been using 'know' in some such way? The technique was certainly familiar to him. In an address to the Aristotelian Society on judgements of perception like 'That is an inkstand' or 'This is a finger', for example, he acknowledges that some philosophers seem to have denied that we ever know such things to be true, and even that they are ever true, but Moore replies:

It seems to me a sufficient refutation of such views as these, simply to point to cases in which we do know such things. This, after all, you know, really is a finger: there is no doubt about it: I know it and you all know it. And I think we may safely challenge any philosopher to bring forward any argument in favour either of the proposition that we do not know it, or of the proposition that it is not true, which does not at some point, rest upon some premiss which is, beyond comparison, less certain than is the proposition which it is designed to attack. The questions whether we ever do know such things as these, and whether there are any material things, seem to me, therefore, to be questions which there is no need to take seriously; they are questions which it is quite easy to answer, with certainty, in the affirmative.[10]

Here Moore is clearly reminding his audience of something the philosophers he refers to seemed to deny. Imagine him saying it, as he did, and not just writing it[11] ('This, after all, you know, really is a finger: there is no doubt about it: I know it, and you all know it'). He thinks what he says is enough in itself to show that such views must be wrong; it is a 'sufficient refutation' as it stands. He tries to bring the philosophers back down to earth.

Moore thinks he can safely challenge philosophers in this way because he thinks nothing is more certain than that this is a finger. That is why he is confident that any argument

[10] G. E. Moore, *Philosophical Studies* (London, 1958), p. 228. I see no conflict, as M. Lazerowitz does, between Moore's saying that such questions need not be taken seriously and his continuing to write about them and even to offer a proof of an external world. Nor do I think it shows any ambivalence on Moore's part about the force of his 'refutations'. Saying over and over again that a certain thing is already known, especially when others appear to persist in denying it, does not show that one even half thinks there is a serious question about whether it is known. And the 'Proof of an External World' concentrates on the further question whether it can be *proved* that there are external things. That does not show that whether there are material things, or whether we know there are, are in any way serious questions for Moore. See M. Lazerowitz, 'Moore's Paradox' (S, 376).

[11] I think it is significant that almost all Moore's papers were invited public addresses. They were meant to be heard by an audience, and they were written specifically for particular occasions, not simply published by Moore. Even the apparent exception, 'A Defence of Common Sense', was an invited contribution to a volume in which authors were given 'an opportunity of stating authentically what they regard as the main problem of philosophy and what they have endeavoured to make central in their own speculation upon it' (J. H. Muirhead (ed.), *Contemporary British Philosophy*, First and Second Series (London, 1925), p. 10). The 'defence of common sense' was solicited, and not spontaneously offered to the philosophical world by Moore.

against it would have to rest at some point on some premiss that is less certain. This capacity to remain unruffled by apparently disturbing philosophical reasoning, and never to cast a second glance at his certainty, is characteristic of Moore's confrontations with other philosophers. Philosophers tend to regard him as dogmatic or stubborn in that respect, and to think he should take more seriously the possibility that his certainty might be ill-founded. Do we think the master detective is dogmatic or hasty in his reply to the apprentice? He knows the table is there, and so does the apprentice, and that knowledge is what assures him that any explanation of the murder must acknowledge that the table is there. He too could be confident that anyone who tried to explain the murder by denying that the table is there would have to rely at some point on something that is less certain than that is. There can be no objection to the detective's assessing the apprentice's hypothesis on the basis of how it fits in with what is already known. It is difficult to think of any other way to judge the truth or plausibility of something. The detective's remaining unruffled by the apprentice's suggestion, and his having no second thoughts about his certainty that the table is there, is not dogmatism. He would be hopeless as a detective if he could be led to deny obvious facts simply in order to have some explanation or other. Dismissing without further investigation something that conflicts with what is already known is the very heart of rationality. It is one of the things that makes him the master detective that he is.

I think Moore sees himself as following the same eminently rational procedure. He thinks that what he says conflicts with what sceptical philosophers say, and he thinks it is a 'sufficient refutation' of philosophical scepticism to point as he does to some particular thing that is known.

In lectures delivered in 1910, for example, he picks out two 'principles' accepted by Hume which he thinks together imply[12] that it is impossible for anyone to know about

[12] The two 'principles' are (1) nobody can know that something he has not directly apprehended exists unless he knows that something he has directly apprehended is a sign of its existence, and (2) nobody can know that one thing is a sign of another unless he has directly apprehended things of both

anything external to his mind. To prove that those 'principles' are false, Moore says:

> It seems to me that, in fact, there really is no stronger and better argument than the following. I *do* know that this pencil exists; but I could not know this, if Hume's principles were true; *therefore*, Hume's principles, one or both of them, are false. I think this argument really is as strong and good a one as any that could be used: and I think it really is conclusive. In other words, I think that the fact that, if Hume's principles were true, I could not know of the existence of this pencil, is a *reductio ad absurdum* of those principles.[13]

He acknowledges that a defender of Hume's views would accept that same conditional proposition and would argue from the truth of those principles to the conclusion that Moore does not know that his pencil exists. Each argument is simply the reverse of the other. Both are valid and they share a common premiss. For Moore the question of which conclusion to accept therefore comes down to the question of whether it is more certain that he knows that his pencil exists or that Hume's two 'principles' are true. Moore thinks it is obvious that it is more certain that he knows that his pencil exists. His aim is pretty clearly to refute Hume's philosophy by relying on the procedure of retaining what is known or is more certain when it conflicts with what is less certain.

The fact that 'I know that this pencil exists' is more certain than any 'premiss' which could be used to prove it false is the basis of Moore's whole strategy against sceptical philosophers:

---

kinds. Obviously it will follow from (1) and (2) that no one can know of the existence of material things only if material things cannot be directly apprehended. Moore does believe that 'nobody ever does know, by direct apprehension, of the existence of anything whatever except his own acts of consciousness and the sense-data and images he directly apprehends' (G. E. Moore, *Some Main Problems of Philosophy* (London, 1958), p. 111). I do not understand why Moore accepts that thesis. Sceptical reasoning like that of Descartes can lead one to accept it, but Moore seems immune to the force of such reasoning. Nor do I understand how Moore fails to see the sceptical *consequences* of that sense-datum thesis. Here my puzzlement extends well beyond Moore. Many philosophers appear to hold some such thesis while also believing that they know things about the world around them.

[13] *Some Main Problems*, pp. 119-20.

That is why I say that the strongest argument to prove that Hume's principles are false is the argument from a particular case, like this in which we do know of the existence of some material object. And similarly, if the object is to prove *in general* that we do know of the existence of material things, no argument which is really stronger can, I think, be brought forward to prove this than particular instances in which we do in fact know of the existence of such an object.[14]

The form of anti-sceptical argument described here in 1910 is precisely what Moore follows in his more famous 'Proof of an External World' twenty-nine years later. He never abandoned the idea of bringing forward particular things that are known to refute denials of knowledge that appear to conflict with their being known.[15]

In 'Four Forms of Scepticism' he follows the same strategy. After identifying four 'assumptions' he claims are behind several sceptical arguments of Russell's, he ends by confessing that he 'can't help asking' himself whether it is as certain that those four assumptions are true as it is that he knows that this is a pencil or that his audience is conscious:

I cannot help answering: It seems to me *more* certain that I *do* know that this is a pencil and that you are conscious, than that any single one of these four assumptions is true, let alone all four . . . I agree with Russell that (1), (2) and (3) *are* true; yet of no one even of these three do I feel *as* certain as that I do know for certain that this is a pencil. Nay more: I do not think it is *rational* to be as certain of any one of these four propositions, as of the proposition that I do know that this is a pencil. (PP, 226.)

[14] *Some Main Problems*, pp. 125–6.

[15] Moore here speaks of bringing forward particular instances in which we know of the existence of a material thing to prove that 'we know of the existence of material things'. In his reply to Ambrose he says he never intended his proof of an external world to be a refutation of 'Nobody knows that there are external things'. He takes Ambrose to task for not making the distinction, and adds 'I do not think I have ever implied that ['Nobody knows for certain that there are any material things'] could be *proved* to be false in any such simple way; e.g., by holding up one of your hands and saying "I know that this hand is a material thing; therefore at least one person knows that there is at least one material thing" ' (S, 668). But that seems to be precisely what he does say in his 1910 lecture. Either Moore is mistaken in this later disclaimer, or else he does not regard holding up his hand and saying 'I know that this hand is a material thing' as bringing forward a particular instance in which one knows of the existence of a material thing. I do not see why not. I therefore continue to treat his proof of an external world as also implying that we know there are external things.

Even Moore's acceptance of three of Russell's assumptions is not enough to persuade him that there might be something in Russell's argument. Not only is he less certain of their truth than he is that he knows that this is a pencil, he does not think it would be *rational* to believe otherwise.

The detective in his reply to the apprentice followed the eminently rational policy of rejecting the less certain because it conflicts with the more certain, or rejecting a hypothesis that conflicts with what is already known. Is Moore right in thinking that his arguments work against sceptical philosophers in the same way? It depends on the source of the philosophical conclusion. It is not always possible to reject a denial of knowledge by simply appealing to some particular thing that is known. Imagine a slightly later stage in the investigation of the murder. The apprentice, properly chastened, tries to be thorough and systematic and decides to consider everyone who could possibly have committed the murder and to eliminate them one by one. He gets from the duke's secretary a list of all those who were in the house at the time and with careful research shows conclusively and, let us suppose, correctly that the only one on the list who could possibly have done it is the butler. He then announces to the detective that he now knows that the butler did it. 'No,' the master replies, 'that list was simply given to you by the secretary; it could be that someone whose name is not on the list was in the house at the time and committed the murder. We still don't know who did it.'

This is a successful objection to the apprentice's claim to know. If he has not checked the completeness of the list, we recognize that he has been hasty and does not yet know who committed the murder. It would obviously be absurd at this point for him to try to reject what the detective said by appealing to his 'knowledge' that the butler did it. The detective said that even after all the apprentice's valuable work they still do not know who committed the murder, and the apprentice cannot reply by saying 'No. You're wrong because I know the butler did it'. In the earlier exchange the detective was quite right to reject the apprentice's claim by saying, 'No. You're wrong because we know that this table is here and was right here a few minutes ago'. That did refute the apprentice. But what might look like a formally similar reply to the detective in this later exchange would be ludicrous. It would not be a 'sufficient refutation' of the detective's denial of knowledge or a 'good and conclusive argument' against him. If what the apprentice says ('I know the butler did it') is true, what the detective says ('We still don't know who did it') is not true, but that does not provide the apprentice with a *reductio ad absurdum* of what the detective said. He cannot argue from the truth of that conditional to the conclusion that what the detective said is not true.

That is not to say that one can never appeal to one's own knowledge in just that way to refute someone who denies one's knowledge. Suppose that later still the detective and his assistant have established beyond doubt that the butler did in fact do it—they have just found a hidden camera that recorded the whole event and the film they have just watched clearly shows the butler in action. If a newspaper reporter who knows nothing about the discovery of the camera is saying into a telephone in the foyer 'It is still not known here who committed the murder' the apprentice overhearing him can easily refute him by saying 'No. I know that the butler did it'. In this case he *could* 'argue' as follows: what the reporter said implies that I do not know that the butler did it, but I do know that the butler did it, so what the reporter said is not true. That is a conclusive argument. It is 'as strong and good a one as any that could be used' to show that the uninformed reporter is wrong. But those same words in an argument of the same form do not work against the detective who denies the apprentice's knowledge.

The difference between the two cases is obviously that the detective, unlike the reporter, is denying the apprentice's knowledge by pointing out a deficiency in the way the apprentice's conclusion was reached. A certain possibility is raised which is compatible with all the apprentice's evidence for his claim and, if realized, would mean that he does not know that the butler did it. I think we recognize that even if that possibility is not in fact realized—no one whose name is not on the list was in fact in the house at that time—the apprentice still does not know in that way that the butler did it unless he has also established that the list is complete. He cannot meet the detective's challenge simply by asking whether it is more certain that the butler did it or that there is someone whose name is not on the list. The detective is not to be understood as putting forward a competing hypothesis about who committed the murder that he regards as more certain than that the butler did it. Nor is it a question of which 'hypothesis' it is rational to be more certain of. If the apprentice does not know that the list is complete his certainty that the butler did it is unwarranted. The detective's challenge obviously must be met in some other way, and that would require some understanding of the source of the conflict between what he says and what the apprentice says; the mere conflict itself is not enough to determine what a successful counter-argument will be. What succeeds against the reporter's 'It is still not known who committed the murder' does not succeed against the detective's denial expressed in those same words. What matters are the reasons for the denial in each case.

How then are we to understand Moore's typical responses to sceptical philosophers? When we see his arguments as ineffective against scepticism I think it is because we see them as parallel to the apprentice's ludicrous response to the detective's verdict that it is still not known who committed the murder. That same assertion made by the uninformed reporter is refuted by appealing to the knowledge that the butler did it, but no such appeal works against the detective who challenges the basis of that putative knowledge. I have explained the philosophical sceptic's denial of our knowledge as the outcome of an investigation into the basis of all the knowledge or certainty we think we have about the world around us. That is why I think we feel it is not a 'sufficient refutation' of that scepticism simply to bring forward 'a particular case . . . in which we do know of the existence of some material object'. The philosopher's assessment of all of our knowledge of the world around us is meant to apply to *every* particular case in which we do think we know of some material object, so no case that could be brought forward would escape that scrutiny.

The two Humean 'principles' that Moore tries to refute

(along with the sense-datum thesis that Moore accepts) do indeed imply that Moore does not know that this pencil exists. But whether he can argue that since he does know that this pencil exists, those 'principles' (along with that thesis) must be false, will depend on the source of those 'principles' (and that thesis). Descartes reached his general negative conclusion from an assessment of all of our knowledge of the world—from asking how we know what we do, and taking seriously certain general features of the senses as a source of knowledge. Hume shared that conception, and hence that conclusion, with Descartes. Perhaps that negative conclusion is not correct, or perhaps we are not driven to it by a general assessment of our sensory knowledge, but so far that has not been shown to be so. If there can be a general assessment of our knowledge of the sort the philosopher engages in, and if the most careful execution of that assessment leads to the conclusion that we never know of the existence of material objects, Moore's attempt to argue against that conclusion by appealing simply to his knowledge that this pencil exists would indeed be like the apprentice's ludicrous response to the detective. He would be trying to deny the correctness of the assessment by appealing to one of the pieces of 'knowledge' that had been called into question by that very assessment.

From the 'assumptions' said to be behind Russell's sceptical conclusion it does indeed follow that Moore does not know that this is a pencil. But if those 'assumptions' are nothing more than truths unavoidably involved in any general assessment of our knowledge of the world, Moore does not successfully refute them any more than the apprentice refutes the detective. The detective in his objection might be said to be 'assuming' (1) that it is possible that someone whose name is not on the list committed the murder, (2) that that possibility has not yet been ruled out, and (3) that that possibility must be ruled out if the apprentice is to know by his eliminative reasoning that the butler did it. From those three 'assumptions' it follows that the apprentice does not know by eliminating all the other listed subjects that the butler did it. But that does not enable the apprentice to refute those 'assumptions' simply on the grounds that they have that implication. Those 'assumptions' amount to an objection to the apprentice's claim to know. Whether Russell's 'assumptions' can be refuted in Moore's way will similarly depend on whether they are part of a negative assessment of the grounds for, among other things, Moore's assertion that he knows that this is a pencil.

It certainly seems as if Hume's 'principles' and Russell's 'assumptions' and Descartes's 'requirement' are all meant in just that way, so it is difficult to resist the conclusion that Moore's attempted refutations fail because he does not recognize that fact about the philosophers' denials of knowledge. That would be a serious deficiency in what Moore says and does. The reluctance of Ambrose and Malcolm and others to attribute such an apparent lack of philosophical understanding to Moore is what leads them to believe that he must be doing something different in his proof from what he seems to be doing.

I suggested earlier that we should not infer directly from the felt ineffectiveness of Moore's proof against philosophical scepticism that it involves some misunderstanding or misuse of words on his part. Nor should we infer on that basis alone that his assertions are dogmatic or hasty or ill-supported either. We do not regard the apprentice as dogmatic or hasty in his refutation of what the reporter said. Nor was the detective dogmatic in his original denial of the apprentice's hypothesis. There was no misuse of words in those fully effective replies, they were perfectly reasonable appeals to something that is known, and they did not require careful consideration of the reasons behind the assertions they rejected. The detective knew immediately that the apprentice's hypothesis was incorrect, however it was arrived at, and the apprentice knew without further ado that the reporter was wrong. If Moore saw his attack on philosophers' remarks in that way, he too could not be faulted for not going carefully into their reasoning.

To defend the propriety and legitimacy of Moore's assertions in this way will no doubt seem only to postpone the difficulty. It will now be puzzling how Moore could ever have come to understand philosophers' remarks in the way he does. In insisting that he knows that this pencil exists or that here is a human hand, how could he have thought he was responding to the sceptical philosopher in the way the apprentice responded to the uninformed reporter or the detective reminded his colleague of something right before their eyes? How could he have missed the fact that philosophical scepticism is not to be refuted in that way because it comes from a general challenge to all our knowledge of the world? How could he miss the parallel between the sceptical denial of our knowledge and the detective's successful undermining of the apprentice's claim to know that the butler did it? How could Moore have failed to entertain the possibility that the philosophers' denials of knowledge might be based on general considerations designed to cast doubt on the adequacy of the very reasons Moore or anyone else thinks he has got for claiming to know such things?

I would like to know the answers to those questions. I think they are all genuine questions—although largely questions about the thoughts or perceptions of G. E. Moore. It is very natural to take them as simply rhetorical questions—as exposing the absurdity of the idea that Moore could be doing exactly what he seems to be doing in his proof. But that natural reaction does rest on a certain acceptance of at least the intelligibility, if not the feasibility, of a general philosophical assessment of our knowledge of the world. If we think that Moore fails to answer a certain question or to refute a certain thesis, and that he can be expected to recognize that fact, we must also believe that there is some definite question he avoids or some intelligible thesis he fails to refute. We know that philosophers have certainly *intended* to scrutinize the grounds of all our knowledge of the world, including those particular pieces of knowledge that Moore would cite, and they have certainly thought they reached general sceptical conclusions. But intention alone is no guarantee of success, or even of a coherent project or thesis. Only if there is an intelligible general question about knowledge which, once asked, makes it impossible for Moore to answer it in the way he does will there be some deficiency in Moore's remarks against philosophers. If we find his assertions inadequate it is because we are taking it for granted that there is such a question and that we understand what it is. But if that turned out to be an illusion, if it were not really possible to subject all of our knowledge of the world all at once to the kind of assessment that would render Moore's assertions ineffective responses to it, we would be in no position to accuse Moore of having missed something or of not succeeding in doing what he seems to be doing in his 'proof' or his other claims to know things.

Even if the philosophical question and the sceptical answer to it did turn out to make perfect sense, and even if Moore does not answer it or refute philosophical scepticism, it does not follow that if he were doing and saying precisely what he appears to be doing and saying there would be nothing right in what he says or that his saying it would be of no philosophical significance. He does not have to answer a philosophical question or make what Malcolm calls a 'philosophical' employment of his words in order to reveal something of great philosophical importance. Moore says things like 'I know that here is a human hand' or 'I know that there are external things', and I think it cannot be denied that there *are* questions to which those assertions are answers and that there *are* statements about human knowledge which must be false if what Moore says is true. We cannot deny that he says something that answers *some* question or implies the falsity of *some* proposition.

Moore says his proof was meant to prove the falsity of 'There are no external things', and it must be granted that there is a way in which it does that. If there are some apples in the cupboard it is false that there are no apples in the cupboard, and the answer to the question whether there are any apples in the cupboard is 'Yes'. Apples are pieces of fruit, so it is also false that there are no pieces of fruit in the cupboard. Apples are also external things—from the existence of an apple it does not follow that someone is having or has had some experience or other—so it is also false that there are no external things. That is just how Moore sees his proof, and aside from the question of why such a 'proof' should be thought to be needed, can it be said that there is actually something wrong with it? Similarly, if Moore knows that there are external things, it is false that nobody knows that there are external things, just as it is false that nobody knows that there are external things if what the physiologist said at the beginning of his lecture is true. He said that almost everyone knows it, except those suffering from certain mental abnormalities. G. E. Moore does not suffer from those abnormalities; he is one of us who know that there are external things. But if that is so, what prevents G. E. Moore from saying it? We need not expect him to be answering the philosophical problem of the external world in saying it; we did not suppose the lecturing physiologist to be answering that question when he said what he did, but his assertion was none the worse for that.

Suppose it occurs to me to ask whether there were any apples in Sicily in the fourth century B.C. I do not know the answer to that question, but I have a good idea of how to find out. Suppose it had occurred to me instead to ask whether it is known whether there were any apples in Sicily in the fourth century B.C. If I found that historians familiar with the place and period had established that there were plenty of apples there I would have found out that it *is* known that there were apples in Sicily then. If some historians tell me 'We know there were apples in Sicily then' they are simply reporting on the state of historical knowledge; they are telling me one of the things that is known about the past. If someone then asks me whether it is known that there were apples in Sicily, I can say 'Yes, that is known'. Similarly, if I am asked whether *anything* is known about Sicily in the fourth century B.C., I can reply that among other things, it is known that there were apples there then. All these are answers to questions about our knowledge, and they are answered in the most straightforward way. It might be thought that no one could be so ignorant as not to know whether *anything at all* is known about Sicily in the fourth century B.C. Even if that is so, the answer I gave does imply that something is known about Sicily then, and therefore that the answer to that general question is 'Yes', whether anyone ever asks it or not. Moore thinks the questions whether we ever do know such things as that this is a finger, or whether there are any material things, are questions 'there is no need to take seriously' because 'it is quite easy to answer [them] with certainty, in the affirmative'. It is perhaps even easier to answer them than it is for the historian to answer my questions about the past and about what is known about the past.

The point is that there *are* general truths about human knowledge which simply follow from the fact that this or that or the other thing is known. A general question about knowledge therefore *could* be answered simply by appeal to one or more of those particular pieces of knowledge. That appears to be the way Moore understands general questions about what is known. He says astronomy gives us information about the present state and past history of different layers of rock and soil; physics and chemistry provide knowledge about the composition of different kinds of physical things. From what has been known for a long time in these and other sciences it simply follows that there are material things. If there are nine planets, there are material things (at least nine of them). That is why Moore thinks anyone who says it is not known that there are material things is simply flying in the face of what science already knows to be true. The implication is that there is no reason to take that person's denial seriously. But we do not need science to show his denial to be false; it is contradicted by what all of us know and observe in the most ordinary circumstances every day. If there are human hands, there are material things, and if someone knows there are two of them in front of him, it is known that there are material things.

That Moore understands general questions of knowledge in just this way is shown by another of his responses to Russell. Russell reports that he came to philosophy through the wish to find some reason to believe in the truth of mathematics; he thought the best chance of finding indubitable truth lay in that domain.[16] Moore takes Russell to be saying that the question whether any of the propositions of pure mathematics are true is a question for philosophers to answer. But, Moore replies:

> Surely it's the business of the mathematicians to decide whether particular mathematical propositions are true? And if so what's the

[16] B. Russell, 'Logical Atomism', in R. Marsh (ed.), *Logic and Knowledge* (London, 1956), p. 323.

> use of the philosopher discussing whether *any* mathematical propositions are true? Suppose he decides they are, can he give better reasons than the mathematicians give? Suppose he decides they aren't. He's contradicting the mathematicians. And aren't they better judges? It's admitted not to be the business of philosophers to discuss whether particular *theorems* are true. But if he insists on discussing whether *any* are, he's bound either to contradict the mathematicians, or to be doing something which seems superfluous.[17]

The same is true for sciences other than mathematics. Whether we know *anything* of a certain sort is answered in the affirmative by the fact that this or that or the other thing is known in that area.

This is what might be called an 'internal' reaction to the question what is known or whether anything is known in a certain area. By that I mean that the question is answered by actually establishing some truths in that area or by finding out what has been established by others. It is to react, in one's own case, to the question 'Do I know it?' by asking oneself 'Is it true?' or 'Should I believe it?' The answer is to be found by trying to establish the thing in question, to see whether, given what one already knows, that thing also is or must be true. I call the reaction 'internal' because it is a response from 'within' one's current knowledge; the question whether one knows a certain thing is just the question whether that thing is already included among all the things one knows, or can be included among them by finding good reason to accept that thing on the basis of other things one already knows. Given that conception of the question 'Is it known that *p*?', it seems to me that there is no good reason for denying that what Moore says about our knowledge of external things is perfectly correct. That we know of external things follows trivially from our knowing many of the things we already know.

If we have the feeling that Moore nevertheless fails to answer the philosophical question about our knowledge of external things, as we do, it is because we understand that question as requiring a certain withdrawal or detachment from the whole body of our knowledge of the world. We recognize that when I ask in that detached philosophical

[17] G. E. Moore, *Lectures on Philosophy* (London, 1966), p. 185.

way whether I know that there are external things, I am not supposed to be allowed to appeal to other things I think I know about external things in order to help me settle the question. *All* of my knowledge of the external world is supposed to have been brought into question at one fell swoop; no particular piece of it is to be available as unquestioned knowledge to help me decide whether or not another particular candidate is true. I am to focus on my relation to the whole body of beliefs which I take to be knowledge of the external world and to ask, from 'outside' it as it were, not simply whether it is true but whether and how I know it even if it is in fact true. It is no longer simply a question about what to believe, but whether and how any of the things I admittedly do believe are things that I know or can have any reason to believe. That might be called an 'external' reaction to the question whether anything is known about the external world.

The terms 'internal' and 'external' are so far nothing more than labels; they do not serve to describe unambiguously the difference between two ways of understanding questions about our knowledge. Although I think there is a difference to be captured, those terms alone do not explain what it is. It is easy to think we understand it when we do not. I have emphasized the complete generality of the philosophical question of our knowledge of the external world. Descartes was not interested in whether we know this or that particular thing about the world around us, but whether we know anything at all about it. To answer that philosophical question we cannot appeal to one thing known about the external world in order to support another; all of it is meant to be in question all at once. But whatever the special feature of the 'external' philosophical question might be, and whatever might be the explanation of Moore's failure to answer it, it cannot be simply that the philosophical question is *more general* than any question Moore answers or addresses himself to. When Moore says he knows there are human hands and therefore that there are external things he is giving an affirmative answer to a completely general question about whether anyone at all knows anything at all about the external world. It will not do, therefore, to try to characterize the philosophical or 'external' understanding of the question simply by asking 'Does *anything at all* that is believed about the external world amount to knowledge of it?' or 'Do we know, not this or that fact about the world around us, but even whether there are *any* external things *at all*?' All such general questions *can* be answered in Moore's way. No ordinary form of words alone can be guaranteed to express only the philosophical question or assertion. There will always be a way for a Moore to take it in which it does not have what we feel is its special 'philosophical' significance.

It is precisely Moore's refusal or inability to take his own or anyone else's words in that increasingly elusive 'external' or 'philosophical' way that seems to me to constitute the philosophical importance of his remarks. He steadfastly remains within the familiar, unproblematic understanding of those general questions and assertions with which the philosopher would attempt to bring all of our knowledge of the world into question. He resists, or more probably does not even feel, the pressure towards the philosophical project as it is understood by the philosophers he discusses. For Ambrose, Moore is like an ordinary man who dismisses the sceptical conclusion by simply denying it without bothering to counter the argument for it, thereby making one feel that there is something ridiculous about the sceptical conclusion. He shocks us into recognizing the contrast between what the philosopher says and ordinary life. 'Because he is himself a great philosopher,' Ambrose says, 'Moore can succeed in this, whereas the ordinary man's remarks would have no influence. For the ordinary man can so easily be lured into talking in the same way' (S, 416). That is true. It is borne out by the ease with which we feel we must go along with Descartes in his sceptical reasoning. We are 'lured' to his conclusion because it seems to be the only answer to his questions as he understands them. If Moore in his responses represents the ordinary man, he is a most extraordinary ordinary man in not being 'lured' into the traditional philosopher's understanding of his questions.

Moore does not resist the lure by simply shutting his ears to sceptical philosophers and refusing to get involved in their disputes. On the contrary. He listens to what they say, he understands the words they use, and he then answers the questions expressed in just those words on the basis of what we and they have known all along. I think what Moore says, understood as he means it, is perfectly acceptable. If it nevertheless seems completely irrelevant to the philosophical questions and does not refute the paradoxical conclusions philosophers reach, that is a very important fact about those philosophical questions and conclusions. It will now need to be explained more carefully why the philosophical questions are not answered if everything Moore says is correct. That would focus attention on what I think is the right issue: precisely how the questions and assertions of the traditional philosopher are related to the questions and assertions we express in the very same words every day without managing to raise or answer philosophical questions.

But even Homer nods, and from time to time Moore is lured further towards seeing things in the philosopher's way than I think is consistent with his total immersion in the non-'philosophical' or everyday understanding of the remarks philosophers make. That no doubt testifies even more strongly to the power of the philosophical project. No one, however firmly his feet are planted on the ground, seems able to resist it entirely. The philosopher asks not only whether it is known that there are external things but also *how* it is known, and Moore thinks he can answer the question. In everyday life, under normal circumstances, we often can say how we know a certain thing, so it would seem that there is no special difficulty in answering the question satisfactorily in Moore's way. But in this case he does not seem to me to stick closely enough to the straightforward, everyday response.

He is aware that philosophers will object to his claim to know that here is a human hand by raising the possibility that he might be dreaming, and he thinks he can meet that objection. In his lecture 'Certainty' Moore grants that if he does not know that he is not dreaming he does not know that he is standing up,[18] but he is undaunted because, as he puts it, it is 'a consideration which cuts both ways'.

[18] This is the assumption or requirement which in Descartes's reasoning seemed to lead inevitably to scepticism. I do not understand why Moore accepts it so

For, if it is true, it follows that it is also true that if I *do* know that I'm standing up, then I do know that I'm not dreaming. I can therefore just as well argue: since I do know that I'm standing up, it follows that I do know that I'm not dreaming; as my opponent can argue: since you don't know that you're not dreaming, it follows that you don't know that you're standing up. The one argument is just as good as the other, unless my opponent can give better reasons for asserting that I don't know that I'm not dreaming, than I can give for asserting that I do know that I am standing up. (PP. 247.)

Is Moore justified in his comfortable acceptance of what looks like a strong condition on our knowledge of the world? If the possibility of his dreaming is put forward by the philosopher as a criticism of Moore's claim to know that he is standing up (as it certainly is), that philosophical criticism would be parallel to the detective's criticism of his apprentice's announcement that he knows the butler did it because he has eliminated everyone else whose name is on the list. If the apprentice does not know that the list is complete he does not know in that way that the butler did it. But he could not comfortably accept that as 'a consideration which cuts both ways'. He could not say:

I can just as well argue: since I do know that the butler did it, it follows that I do know that the list is complete; as the detective can argue: since you don't know that the list is complete, it follows that you don't know that the butler did it. The one argument is just as good as the other, unless the detective can give better reasons for asserting that I don't know that the list is complete, than I can give for asserting that I do know that the butler did it.

If the apprentice did not even check the list, then for all he knows there could have been people in the house whose names are not on the list; he has to show how he knows that that possibility does not obtain. In the same way Moore would have to

uncritically. He never explains why. After a page and a half explaining that if he were dreaming he would not then know that he is standing up (what I called an 'undeniable fact about dreams'), he immediately concludes: 'I agree, therefore, with that part of the argument which asserts that if I don't know now that I'm not dreaming, it follows that I don't *know* that I'm standing up . . .' (PP, 247). Moore's 'therefore' suggests that he thinks that the epistemic requirement he here accepts follows from the 'undeniable fact about dreams' stated earlier. I do not see that it does. I argued in Chapter One that if it does follow, scepticism about the external world must be correct, since that epistemic requirement leads directly to scepticism, and if it follows from an 'undeniable fact', it must be true.

show how he knows that the dream-possibility does not obtain in his case. He cannot simply deflate the objection by reversing the philosopher's argument in the way he does.

Of course, in the earlier example, the detective might have been wrong—and in any case he could eventually be given an answer. When he pointed out that the apprentice does not know that the list is complete, the apprentice might have been in a position to answer 'No. I checked it. I also examined all the doors and windows, none of the guests reports seeing anyone else, the trustworthy doorman admitted only those on the list, the social secretary was a reliable, devoted servant of the duke . . .', and so on. He might have very good reasons for believing that the list is complete. He would thereby meet the detective's challenge and fulfil the condition for knowing by his eliminative reasoning that the butler did it. There is nothing in the detective's objection which by itself implies that it cannot be met. What is Moore to say in a similar vein about how he knows that he is not dreaming?

In his 'Proof of an External World' he thinks he has 'conclusive reasons' for asserting that he is not dreaming, 'conclusive evidence' that he is awake, although he admits that he cannot say what all that evidence is (PP, 149). But in 'Certainty' he goes so far as to admit that he would have 'the evidence of his senses' for the proposition that he is standing up only if he were not dreaming; if he were dreaming he would only be having 'an experience which is *very like* having the evidence of my senses that I am standing up' (PP, 248). He therefore could not be said simply to have 'the evidence of his senses' that he is awake, however much his present experiences resemble those he has when he is awake. By now he seems already a step or two down the slope to scepticism. Moore was apparently never satisfied with this part of his lecture.[19] He makes a feeble objection to what he believes is one of the philosopher's arguments for the conclusion that he does not know that he is not dreaming. He even concedes that if it is 'logically possible' for all his 'sensory experiences' at a certain moment to be dream-images, and to be the only experiences he is having at that

[19] See Moore's preface and also the note by C. Lewy on p. 251.

moment, he could not then know that he is not dreaming (PP, 250). He pins his remaining hopes on the possibility of remembering some things about the recent past that would enable him to know that he is not dreaming, but he is forced to admit that if that remembering itself could occur while he is dreaming he could never know that he was not dreaming and so could never know that he is standing up. But even a successful objection to an argument of the philosopher would not have been enough. Once he accepts the possibility of his dreaming as an objection to his claim to know that he is standing up, Moore must show how he knows that the possibility does not obtain. Not surprisingly, that is something he fails to do.

M. F. Burnyeat also notices and laments Moore's failure to extricate himself completely from the traditional epistemological predicament.[20] He thinks the promise of Moore's philosophy was that it would simply avoid the traditional route to scepticism by continually insisting on the certainty expressed in particular everyday instances. But any such *reductio ad absurdum* of scepticism would work, Burnyeat thinks, only if Moore could 'explain' the certainty of his examples and give 'a general rationale' that 'explains and justifies his belief that examples of knowledge . . . are the primary thing to which a philosopher should respond'.[21] Moore never does that.

My explanation of Moore's relation to the philosophical problem is different. If he had never deviated even slightly from the attitudes and assertions of the plain man, if he had always put on the philosopher's words the interpretation that can be put on those same words in everyday, non-philosophical life, he would never have taken a step down the 'philosophical' path. Although there would be no philosophical question he answered and no paradoxical philosophical assertion he managed to refute, his remarks would be none the worse for that. He would thereby represent more of a challenge to traditional philosophy, it seems to me, than if he tried to follow Burnyeat's suggestion. In fact, I do not see how trying to give a general explanation and justification

[20] M. F. Burnyeat, 'Examples in Epistemology: Socrates, Theaetetus and G. E. Moore', *Philosophy*, 1977, pp. 396–7.

[21] Burnyeat, p. 397.

of the idea that particular examples 'are the primary thing to which a philosopher should respond' could keep Moore or anyone else out of 'the traditional maze of epistemological argument'.[22]

On Burnyeat's suggestion Moore would have to know very well what the sceptical philosopher is really up to and explain to him why he cannot do it and why particular examples are the primary thing to which he should respond. On my suggestion Moore takes general questions and assertions expressed in the same words as those of the philosopher and answers or refutes them by appeal to particular examples. There is nothing wrong with that procedure as such. How else are general questions to be answered or general assertions tested? He does not go on to diagnose the philosopher's assertions or try to explain why they cannot be made; he simply denies them. On his way of understanding those words—which *is* a way of understanding them—they are simply false. Moore gives the impression of having no idea what the sceptical philosopher really wants to say or do. We feel he constantly construes the epistemologist's words only in a non-'philosophical', everyday, and therefore completely uninteresting way.

J. L. Austin, by contrast, has a quite definite view about the source of certain philosophical problems. He makes a detailed scrutiny of the expressions philosophers use in formulating their questions and doctrines about perception and the external world and tries to demonstrate that those expressions are not actually used in that way. Austin's work rests on a shrewd grasp of the traditional epistemological project; he knows only too well what the sceptical philosopher is trying to do, and he thinks he can show that it cannot be done.

It is just possible, I suppose, that Moore has that same shrewd understanding of traditional epistemology. If one thought or knew that what the philosopher wants to say is really incoherent and the result only of some identifiable confusion, one might adopt the clever policy of never speaking or responding to his remarks in the 'philosophical' way. One could deliberately strive to avoid everything but

[22] Burnyeat, p. 396.

the straightforward questions and assertions of everyday life and always reply only as a plain man, and in that way refuse to be drawn into (what one knew to be confused) philosophical dispute. That ironic policy could even extend to announcing that one had *refuted* the philosopher's views, since that would give the impression that one did not even understand anything other than the straightforward, everyday assertion made by the words the philosopher uses. If it turned out that the philosopher's views really were incoherent, one would have been correct all along in behaving as if his words cannot be understood in any other way. Behind this plan might lie the hope that philosophers would eventually catch on and realize that what they were trying to say makes no sense or cannot be said with the significance they want to give to it.

It would be very difficult to keep up this act without slipping from time to time. The ordinary man with no awareness of philosophy can easily be lured towards the 'external' perspective. A lifelong performance would take great vigilance and care. But to adopt such a clever policy would require understanding at least the aims or intentions of the philosophical project. Moore in his writing shows few signs of that. Perhaps that is because he is extremely clever and consistent in his performance, and his mask almost never slips. But the whole idea of such deception seems incompatible with the child-like honesty, directness, and lack of guile described by so many admirers of Moore. If that is so, we are left with the conclusion that Moore really did not understand the philosopher's assertions in any way other than the everyday 'internal' way he seems to have understood them.

This brings us back to the question how he could ever have come to give only that everyday interpretation to the philosopher's remarks. I have suggested that his way of taking them involves no misuse of words and is perfectly acceptable even if it does not refute philosophical scepticism. I have even conceded that there might be nothing intelligible that Moore missed; perhaps there is no comprehensible 'philosophical' way of taking the philosopher's questions and assertions. But how could Moore show no signs of acknowledging that they are even intended to be taken in a special 'external' way derived from the Cartesian project of assessing all our knowledge of the external world all at once? That is the question about the mind of G. E. Moore that I cannot answer. Moore is an extremely puzzling philosophical phenomenon.

For all my efforts to separate what Moore says and does from the sceptical philosopher's own understanding of his questions and assertions, there remains a disturbing question that I have not answered or squarely faced. I have suggested that Moore does not provide a 'sufficient refutation' of philosophical scepticism, but the possibility seems to remain that what he says is nevertheless *incompatible* with philosophical scepticism. When the detective objected that the list was not known to be complete and so the apprentice did not know who committed the murder, the apprentice did not refute him by saying 'No, you're wrong because I know that the butler did it'. But it is difficult to deny that that remark by the apprentice nevertheless *contradicts* what the detective said; they cannot both be true. It seems equally difficult to escape the idea that even if the sceptical philosopher's 'No one knows whether there are external things' is not refuted by Moore's 'I know there are external things', what Moore says nevertheless *contradicts* what the philosopher says; they cannot both be true. I have argued that there *is* a statement expressed in the philosopher's words which is incompatible with the truth of what Moore says. The present suggestion is that that statement must be the thesis of philosophical scepticism about the external world. If that is so, the relation between philosophical scepticism and the assertions Moore and all the rest of us make every day would be in one important respect as direct and straightforward as it seemed at the beginning of Descartes's argument.

That is the way Moore understands what the philosopher says. He thinks his own assertions of knowledge are true and that they obviously contradict what the sceptical philosopher says, and he concludes on that basis that the philosopher is wrong. The sceptical philosopher holds that what Moore says is no refutation of philosophical scepticism. I think the sceptical philosopher is right on that point. We seem forced to conclude either that Moore's assertions of knowledge are not true or that they do not even contradict philosophical scepticism. Descartes and other sceptical philosophers take the first alternative—no one, including Moore, knows anything about the external world. But if, as on the other alternative, the two did not conflict, it might be possible to hold that Moore does not refute philosophical scepticism even though his assertions of knowledge are nevertheless true. The price of conceding the truth of Moore's assertions, as it were, would be their lack of logical connection with the thesis of philosophical scepticism. But on that alternative philosophical scepticism would no longer imply the falsity of the knowledge-claims made by Moore and all the rest of us in everyday life. The price of philosophical scepticism's immunity, as it were, would be the corresponding immunity of all our ordinary assertions to philosophical attack. That is a price many would be eager to pay. It would mean that, however cogent and convincing the arguments for philosophical scepticism might be, they could not cast any aspersions on the knowledge we possess and seek in science and in everyday life.

Could philosophical scepticism be compatible with the truth of what we say and believe in ordinary life? I confess it is difficult for me to see how it could be so. Once one grasps the traditional epistemological project it is difficult to see the claims of everyday life as anything other than restricted in the way outlined in Chapter Two. It would then be difficult to see how philosophical scepticism could fail to be true. The chapters that follow explore other ways of trying to understand the relation between philosophical theories of knowledge and the everyday claims to knowledge which are presumably their subject-matter. Only something other than that traditional conception would enable us to avoid or defuse philosophical scepticism.

IV

Internal and External: 'Empirical' and 'Transcendental'

Moore's proof of an external world is supposed to meet a challenge he found expressed in Kant. Kant's complaint was that:

> it still remains a scandal to philosophy and to human reason in general that the existence of things outside us . . . must be accepted merely on *faith*, and that if anyone thinks good to doubt their existence, we are unable to counter his doubts by any satisfactory proof.[1]

What exactly is the relation between the scandal Kant complains of and what Moore does in his proof? If Moore really does prove what Kant says has never been proved there could not have been much of a scandal to begin with. Moore thought people had been proving the existence of things outside us for centuries in just the way he does—there is nothing for human reason to be ashamed of in that. And if there remains a scandal to philosophy it could only be that one of its greatest figures, the sage of Königsberg himself, was somehow unaware of the fact that all those proofs have been given. We know that Kant led a sheltered life and never went beyond the limits of his native town, but it is too much to believe, even of him, that he did not know that for centuries people have been doing just the sorts of things Moore had in mind.

I suggested that Moore's proof can be taken as similar in intention and achievement to the proofs we give and accept in everyday life, so in asking how his proof is related to Kant's philosophical scandal I mean to be asking how that scandal is related to the familiar procedures we

[1] *Immanuel Kant's Critique of Pure Reason*, translated by N. Kemp Smith (London, 1953), Bxl. (Hereafter cited as A—for first-edition passages—or B —for second-edition passages—translated from the pages of the original German editions.)

follow and the claims we make to know things in everyday life.

Kant is aware that human beings do not just look for misprints or go to court or perform experiments or solve murders; they also naturally seek some general understanding of how their knowledge is possible. They want to make that aspect of the human condition more intelligible to themselves. So in asking how our everyday proofs and assertions bear on Kant's philosophical scandal I am asking how that general search for an understanding of human knowledge is related to what must presumably be thought to be its subject-matter. It might look as if there is no difficulty here; I have already sketched Descartes's straightforward conception of the detached, 'external' scrutiny we can make of everything we believe or think we know about the world around us. But for Kant the relation between his philosophical project and our everyday and scientific knowledge is more indirect and more complicated than it is for Descartes. I suggested that on Descartes's conception of that relation there is no way to avoid philosophical scepticism and therefore no way to see how, or even that, our everyday knowledge is possible. Kant would agree, and for precisely that reason he develops a different conception of what a philosophical investigation of our knowledge must do and how it must proceed. He thinks it is a scandal to philosophy and to human reason in general that that has never been done, and that all past theories lead to scepticism.

What is to be investigated and explained by any such inquiry is the position we are actually in in our everyday and scientific knowledge. That is a condition of success for any adequate theory of knowledge. It means that we must not be led to deny, for example, that there is an independent world around us that we know. Of course if nothing at all existed in space, if everything that exists existed only in my own mind, Descartes's scepticism would lose its sting. It would be no limitation on my knowledge that I did not know of the existence of anything independent of me if there were nothing independent of me. But for Kant such 'dogmatic idealism' simply denies the existence of the very world we set out to understand our relation to, and that is absurd.

For Kant it would be equally unsatisfactory to say or imply that the world independent of us is unknowable or doubtful or not as reliably known as other things we know directly and unproblematically. All such views Kant calls 'idealism'—'problematic' idealism because they would leave the existence of things in space problematic for us (B274), or 'sceptical' idealism because they would leave things in space doubtful or insufficiently justified (A377). None of these forms of 'idealism' represents us as knowing of things that exist independently of us or as encountering such things in our experience. According to Kant, they therefore distort or misrepresent our actual position in the world, and so must be avoided by any theory that would explain how human knowledge of the world around us is possible. This already seems to put Kant closer to G. E. Moore than to Descartes in his attitude towards the possible consequences of philosophical reflection on human knowledge.

Kant has high standards for the success of a philosophical theory of knowledge. It must have the consequence that the proof-reader really does prove and know that there are as many as three misprints on that page, that I really do know that there is a goldfinch in the garden, and (in so far as his remarks are just like those of the rest of us) that G. E. Moore does know his hands are there and does prove on that basis that there are at least two external things. Putting it that way, it might seem that these are not really high standards at all—they seem to be nothing more than conditions that any account of our knowledge should meet. Such everyday cases of knowledge are just what a philosophical theory of knowledge should explain. But in fact very few, if any, philosophical theories of knowledge meet those conditions or explain such knowledge. We have seen that Descartes by the end of his first *Meditation* does not. And I think many more recent and more elaborate theories ultimately fail in just the same way.

For Kant they all fail because they represent our knowledge of things outside us as in some way indirect or inferential. If objects in space are never perceived directly and yet we know of them somehow indirectly, it would seem that we could know of them only by inferring their existence from something else we are directly and unproblematically aware of. Kant thinks that on any such view the existence of things in space would always be to some degree uncertain, because however certain we were we would always have to admit that the things we are directly aware of *might* be due to something other than the external world we believe to exist. We could never completely eliminate the possibility that they have a purely 'internal' source and are nothing more than a 'mere play of inner sense' (A368). External objects could not be known on such a view because it would represent their existence as 'incapable of proof' (A377).

For scepticism to be avoided, then, all accounts of our knowledge of the world as inferential or indirect must be rejected. The external things we know about must have 'a reality which does not permit of being inferred, but is immediately perceived' (A371). The position we are actually in, Kant thinks, is that:

> In order to arrive at the reality of outer objects I have just as little need to resort to inference as I have in regard to the reality of the object of my inner sense, that is, in regard to the reality of my thoughts. (A371.)

In both cases 'the immediate perception (consciousness) of [things of those kinds] is at the same time a sufficient proof of their reality' (A371). We are in a position in everyday life in which 'outer perception . . . yields immediate proof of something real in space' (A375).

I have said that 'according to Kant' this is the position we are in in everyday life, and that 'Kant thinks' that is the way things are with us, but in the light of Descartes's challenge it might look as if Kant is simply not entitled to these comfortable pronouncements about our epistemic position. But it is not really a question at this point of whether Kant or Descartes gives the right description of the state of our knowledge. Kant hopes to show that Descartes's description could not possibly be correct, and he does not oppose it merely by offering a competing alternative of his own. His remarks can be taken as expressing conditions of adequacy for any satisfactory account of our knowledge, or at the very least as a goal to be aspired to in the theory of knowledge and abandoned only as a last resort, if scepticism is finally shown to be in every way unavoidable. One important feature of Kant's requirements, then, is that they are an acknowledgement of the at-least conditional force of the traditional sceptical account. By that I mean that if Descartes were right in representing our perception of objects in the way he does he would also be right in concluding that we can know nothing about the external world. That is why Kant thinks any non-sceptical account will have to deny that we have an indirect or inferential relation to the external objects we can know about. Almost no philosophical theories of knowledge, even those since Kant, meet that condition. That is why they cannot avoid scepticism.

We can now see that Kant insists on our possession of just the kind of knowledge G. E. Moore thought he was exhibiting in his proof of an external world. Moore thought that by holding up his hands before him as he did he had proved the existence of two external things. He was as certain of the existence of his hands as he was of anything else in his experience, including his own thoughts and feelings. No inference was made or required in his perception of his hands; he simply saw them before him and knew they were there. And that was enough to prove that at least two external things exist. That is what a philosophical theory of knowledge should account for, according to Kant. It is precisely because we do prove or know such things that there is the scandal he complains of. No theory that represents our knowledge of external things as indirect or inferential could account for that knowledge; it could not show that we are in the very position Moore unquestioningly took himself to be in.

But if Kant thinks the position we are all in is just the 'common sense' position from which Moore never deviated, what do Kant and Moore disagree about? They do not disagree about whether Moore or the proof-reader actually proves what he claims to know. They both would insist on that. But that is all Moore tried to do; he did not claim anything else. And if Kant joins Moore in rejecting the scepticism implicit in the traditional Cartesian account, how can there be an issue on which Moore differs from Kant?

One difference between them is that Kant, apparently unlike Moore, regards the sceptical idealist as nevertheless 'a benefactor of human reason' (A378). His challenge, the constant threat his criticisms pose to our knowledge of the world, forces us, Kant says, 'to keep on the watch, lest we consider as a well-earned possession what we perhaps obtain only illegitimately' (A378–9). The 'possession' in question is just the position Moore took himself to be in—that of knowing with certainty of the existence of external things around him—but for Kant there is an issue of its 'legitimacy' that is not settled by the kind of proof Moore gives. That issue is raised, or brought sharply to focus, by the threat of philosophical scepticism. That is how it makes its beneficial contribution to human reason. Kant thinks the position all of us take ourselves to be in in everyday life would not be 'legitimate' or 'well-earned' if any form of philosophical scepticism were correct; we would not actually prove or know the sorts of things we think we prove and know. So scepticism must be defeated. But Kant would hold that Moore does not defeat it with his proof of an external world.

Moore was aware that many philosophers would not be satisfied with his proof. He thought they would object that he had not really proved his premisses—'Here is one hand, and here is another'—and so had not really proved his conclusion (PP, 149). Moore was right; many philosophers would object in that way. Moore thought the objection was mistaken, and it seems to me he is right on that score too. It is not in general a condition of proving something that one be able to prove one's premisses on the basis of something else. That is because it is not in general a condition of knowing something that one be able to prove it on the basis of something else. We know many things we cannot prove in that way. And things we know without proof can serve as premisses of perfectly successful proofs of something else.

It is clear, I think, that Kant is not one of those philosophers who would make this mistaken objection to Moore's proof. For him the perception of external things 'yields immediate proof of something real in space' (A376–7); we are 'immediately conscious' of external things without inference, 'on the unaided testimony' of our senses (A370). He would therefore not object that Moore could not prove the existence of external things by seeing his hands before him unless he could also prove on the basis of something else that his hands are before him or that he sees them. Seeing them is all it takes to prove it for Kant. But still Kant thinks that Moore's proof does not defeat philosophical scepticism.

For Kant we would not know the sorts of things we think we know about the world around us if sceptical or problematic idealism were true. So to show that we really are in the position Moore took himself to be in—to 'legitimize' our 'possession'—Kant thinks he must show that sceptical idealism is false. He tries to do so with a proof of his own, but not a proof like Moore's. He thinks a proof of what he wants to prove has never been given before—hence the scandal to philosophy and to human reason in general. Proving that idealism is false would prove that its opposite, realism, is true. So the issue of 'legitimacy' is to be settled by a refutation of idealism and *eo ipso* a proof of realism. But what exactly is this issue of 'legitimacy'? And if it is to be settled by a proof of realism why is it not settled by Moore's proof of the reality of things existing independently in the world around him?

The realism Kant wants to prove is a complex and powerful view. It involves more than the idea of things existing in space independently of those who perceive them and independently of the capacity of anyone to know of their existence. That is what might be called the metaphysical aspect of realism. But Kant's realism also has an epistemic aspect; it implies something about our access to such independently existing things. For Kant our perception and therefore our knowledge of external things is direct, unmediated and unproblematic. To know of the reality of outer objects we need not resort to inference; our perception of them is immediate. Any view that denied this immediacy would be a form of sceptical idealism and hence would fail as an explanation of how human knowledge is possible. That is why for Kant the only acceptable account is realism in both its metaphysical and its epistemic aspects. That is what must be established if our 'possession' is to be shown to be 'well-earned' and 'legitimate'.

Kant thinks realism has never been proved before. The unsettled issue of its 'legitimacy' is the scandal that remains to philosophy and to human reason in general. But it is not clear what the scandal of realism's never having been proved amounts to. Realism is the view that objects exist in space and we have direct perceptual access to them. But didn't Moore prove, and wouldn't Kant concede that Moore proved, the existence of things in space independent of us? And didn't Moore prove it by directly perceiving a couple of spatial objects right before his eyes? If that does not show that Kant's realism is correct it should be possible to say why not. What more is needed? Consider first the metaphysical aspect of realism. What Moore proved to be true is 'There are things existing in space independently of us'. But those are the very words used to express the metaphysical aspect of realism. Kant would accept Moore's proof, but he would not agree that it establishes the truth of the metaphysical aspect of the realism he says has never been proved. Why not? Is it possible to state the proposition Kant would say has never been proved even though Moore's proof of an external world is perfectly correct? It would seem that the only candidate is 'There are things existing in space independently of us'.

Perhaps the difference between Kant and Moore lies more in the epistemic aspect of realism. For Kant the scandal is that the existence of things outside us has had to be accepted 'merely on faith'. The epistemic aspect of realism says that we do not take the existence of external things on faith; we directly perceive them and know they exist. But if Kant allows that Moore did see his hands before him and did prove on that basis that there are external things, he cannot complain that Moore was simply taking it on faith that there are external things. That is precisely the kind of complaint Moore was trying to forestall with his robust response to what he thought was Kant's scandal. It is as if he says to Kant, 'You say the existence of external things must be accepted merely on faith. Nonsense, I'll show you I have got more than faith. I'll give you a proof—something you say has never been given'. If Kant grants that Moore does indeed give a proof and does not just make a leap of faith, what is it that Kant thinks Moore has still not done to establish realism?

It is tempting to say, and Kant would certainly say, that what needs to be proved is not simply the existence of this or that external thing, such as Moore's hands, but the existence of external things generally. But we saw in Chapter Three that Moore does prove and know the truth of a completely general proposition about external things. What he knows therefore cannot be said to be less *general* than what Kant wants to prove. Moore knows that his hands and therefore some external things exist, so what he knows is a completely general proposition. To the general question whether he knows there are any external things at all the answer must be 'Yes', if we agree with Kant that Moore does know what he claims to know.

Still, it will be felt, only if the possibility of knowing in general of the existence of external things has somehow been secured will it be possible for Moore to establish his conclusion. It is therefore natural to describe Kant's project as that of proving the very possibility of knowing or proving the existence of any external things at all. And it might look as if Moore ignores that question. This suggests that there are two different sorts of things to be proved—(a) that there are external things and (b) that it is possible in general to prove and to know in Moore's way that there are external things—and it might seem that Moore proves only the first, while Kant wants to prove the second.

But is it true that Moore, who is felt to have ignored the Kantian philosophical question, fails to answer the question of the possibility of knowledge of the world in general? If he does know what he claims to know, it seems that there is a perfectly good way in which he can be said to have settled the question of the *possibility* of knowing of the existence of external things. If I actually walk across a frozen lake I thereby also show that it is (or was) possible to walk across that lake. And if someone actually knows that some hands are before him and therefore that there are external things, he thereby also shows that it is *possible* to know such things in that way. Being actual is the best proof of being possible. So if what must be proved is both the existence of external things and the very possibility of knowing in general of the existence of external things, it cannot be said without further explanation that Moore proves only the first but not the second. If he does prove the first it follows that he proves the second. It is true that Moore himself does not actually claim to have proved the second, but we can see from his success in proving the first that he does also prove that knowledge of external things in general is possible. Kant could see it too, but he would not regard that simple proof as the one he says has never been given. The scandal of its never having been given is therefore not adequately identified simply by saying that it has never been proved that knowledge of external things in general is possible. We still have not formulated a proposition that Kant could say has never been proved even though Moore's proof of an external world is perfectly correct.

It can perhaps be felt that Moore has missed or ignored some other ingredient in the epistemic aspect of realism. He perceived his hands and proved on that basis that there are external things, but he might appear to have ignored the question whether it is possible to perceive external things directly, or whether he was actually perceiving some external things directly in that case. But again it is not easy simply to state his alleged oversight. For one thing, if he did perceive his hands directly, surely he can be said, as before, to have proved that it is possible to perceive his hands directly. So 'It is possible to perceive external things directly' cannot be something that has never been proved in Moore's way.

Furthermore, there is a way in which Moore could easily prove that he is in fact perceiving external things directly in the case he considers, and so knows of their existence without inference. He need only show that he is not perceiving his hands indirectly. To see something indirectly is to see it, for example, only on television, or around a corner by means of mirrors, or to see its reflection, as opposed to being face to face with it at arm's length in the clear light of day. One infers the existence of something from traces or evidence one finds of it, but not when one encounters the thing itself. There are many occasions in everyday life on which we can distinguish between two ways of coming to know of something by perception. It depends on the particular context which contrast we have in mind. One witness in court might be asked whether he actually saw the defendant stab the victim or only saw the victim fall with no one other than the defendant within stabbing distance of the victim; another might be asked whether he saw the stabbing directly or only watched it on television, or in a mirror. We do make such distinctions on particular occasions and it is clear that there are everyday cases of both kinds. Sometimes we perceive directly and know without inference and sometimes we do not. But in that everyday sense Moore's holding up his hands before him as he did is clearly a case of direct perception and non-inferential knowledge. And although he did not actually do so, it would be easy for Moore to prove that it is a case of that kind. He would only need to prove that no television screen or mirror or any other such device intervened between his eyes and his hands, and that he was not relying on traces or evidence but on the presence of the hands themselves. He would thereby prove in the straightforward Moorean way the truth of 'We perceive external things directly and know of their existence without inference'. But those are the very words used to express the epistemic aspect of realism. Kant would have no reason to reject this proof while nevertheless maintaining that the epistemic aspect of his realism has still not been proved. Once again we have failed to identify a proposition which we can be sure expresses Kant's realism but which Moore cannot prove in his straightforward, everyday way.

Even if we are forced to concede that there is a way in which Moore could be said to prove the truth of 'There are external things and we perceive them directly and know of their existence without inference' I think most of us (although apparently not G. E. Moore) nevertheless feel that Kant's question about realism is not and could not be settled by proofs like those I have attributed to Moore. Even without having found a form of words we can be sure will unequivocally state Kant's realism in both its metaphysical and its epistemic aspects, I think we feel the force of Kant's requirement that the realism he has in mind must be established in order for our everyday position with respect to the world around us to be shown to be a 'well-earned possession'. To make good on this feeling we must answer two questions. What exactly *is* the realist thesis Kant wants to establish; how is it even to be expressed if the words most naturally used to express it could equally express something already proved or easily provable by G. E. Moore? And second, how does Kant actually try or even hope to establish that realist thesis?

I start with the second question, since it seems the most fruitful way of approaching an answer to the first. If an understanding of the words alone does not ensure an understanding of Kant's thesis, concentrating on what might be called the 'significance' or point of those words for Kant might be a more reasonable strategy. To make any progress on either question the threat of philosophical scepticism must be brought back into the picture.

In describing the 'scandal' Kant says not only that 'the existence of things outside us . . . must be accepted merely on *faith*' but also that 'if anyone thinks good to doubt their existence we are unable to counter his doubts by any satisfactory proof'. This gives us a clue as to what Kant might have in mind, since there are at least two different ways of trying to counter someone's doubts by means of a proof, and only one of them is illustrated by Moore's proof of an external world. If someone denies or doubts something we can try to counter his doubt or denial by proving the truth of the proposition he denies or doubts. If our proof is correct he is wrong to deny what he does and we can show that there is no reason for him to doubt it. But we know that that straightforward procedure is not always successful, or at least not permanently, even when there is nothing at all wrong with the proof we give. The considerations that seem to lead so persuasively to the doubt or denial in the first place can return to re-impress us with their force, even when we have a proof to the contrary. We then can find ourselves with something like a paradox or antinomy in which our doubts have not been satisfactorily countered or our understanding increased. Someone who walks across a room thereby proves that Zeno is wrong in arguing that motion is impossible, but if I am half convinced or even tempted by each step of Zeno's argument, or do not fully understand why I shouldn't be, my knowledge that the person did cross the room will not satisfactorily counter my doubts or explain to me how motion is possible.

Another way to counter someone's doubts would be to prevent the doubts from arising by exposing them as groundless or as not warranted by the considerations that seem to lead to them. That would be to concentrate more on the source of the doubts than on the truth or falsity of their target. As applied to our knowledge of the external world this strategy would bring philosophical scepticism into the centre of the picture, since those who 'think good' to question the existence of things outside us do so on the basis of considerations like those at work in Descartes's *First Meditation.* If it could be shown that those considerations do not yield the general doubts usually drawn from them, or perhaps that no such general doubts could even be coherently formulated without already having been implicitly answered, the scandal Kant complains of would have been removed. Moore does not concentrate on the source of the doubts at all. He is content to keep crossing the room in front of the doubting Zeno, as it were, rather than looking carefully and explaining how and why he cannot get to his conclusion from true premisses. Kant thinks the sceptical argument cannot succeed, but he wants more than an assertion of the falsity of its conclusion. He wants to *prove* that the sceptical reasoning could never get to the conclusion it reaches from any premisses it could acknowledge as coherent.

Descartes arrives at his sceptical conclusion from the recognition that all our experience could be just the way it is now whether there were any external things or not. What we can know on the basis of the senses is therefore something that could be known to be true without our knowing anything at all about objects existing independently of us in space. This general gap between appearance and reality is an expression of what can be called the 'epistemic priority' of sensory experiences, perceptions, representations, or what Descartes calls 'ideas', over those independent objects that exist in space. To say that things of one sort are 'epistemically prior' or prior in the order of knowledge to things of another sort is to say that things of the first sort are knowable without any things of the second sort being known, but not *vice versa*. Things of the second sort are therefore in that sense less directly known than, or known only on the basis of, things of the first sort. That is precisely the position Descartes says we are in with respect to our knowledge of external objects. There are certain things we could know about our sensory experiences or about how things appear to us even if nothing were known about the existence of any independent objects in space. Those sensory experiences or those facts about the way things appear to us are therefore epistemically prior to facts about the external world. The external world is in that way less directly known than, or known only on the basis of, our sensory experiences.

Kant holds that any view according to which one's experiences or the appearances of things are epistemically prior to external things in this way must be rejected; it could not explain how our knowledge of objects is possible. It would be a form of idealism. The realism Kant wants to prove is the denial of all such idealist views. Proving his realism is therefore to be a matter of proving that the doctrine of the epistemic priority of sensory experiences over external objects is not, indeed could not be, correct. That is not something Moore ever seems to have concerned himself with, despite his being able to prove something correctly expressed by the words 'We perceive external things directly and know of their existence without inference'. Those same words, taken as an expression of the realism Kant is interested in, must be understood as the denial of the Cartesian doctrine of epistemic priority, and not simply as a statement of the mundane truth Moore can be admitted to have established. We will therefore understand the Kantian thesis only by understanding that Cartesian doctrine, or at least by understanding the considerations that are thought to lead to it. That is how philosophical scepticism enters the picture. Those considerations that are thought to lead to scepticism are precisely those that lead to the doctrine of the epistemic priority of 'ideas' over objects. The grounds of that doctrine must therefore be understood and appreciated if we are to make the right kind of sense of Kant's realism. The proof of that form of realism, and not the mundane proof Moore could so easily provide, is what Kant says is necessary for a satisfactory explanation of how our knowledge of the world is possible.

Kant thinks the traditional sceptical challenge shows that our everyday knowledge must be secured as a 'well-earned' and not merely an illegitimate possession. But he sees that as a philosophical demand. He does not mean that G. E. Moore or a scientist in a laboratory or a witness in a court of law must first prove the falsity of sceptical idealism before he can prove or know some fact about the world around him. Nor does the fact that there is a scandal in *philosophy* imply that the scientist or the man in the street is merely taking it on faith that there is an object before him unless he has already refuted the doctrine of the epistemic priority of sensory experiences over objects. For Kant our claims in everyday life and in science do not stand in need of any such proof. They are complete and unproblematic as they stand. But he thinks an understanding of our knowledge, an understanding of the kind we seek in philosophy of how any knowledge at all of the world around us is possible, does require that idealism be conclusively refuted. Kant rightly regards it as a scandal that philosophers have always endorsed idealist conceptions of perception and knowledge and hence have been committed to scepticism. It leaves them unable to explain our knowledge of external things as anything other than an act of faith, and hence not as knowledge or reasonable belief at all. But Kant remains fully aware of how easily one can be driven to scepticism as soon as one begins to reflect on how any knowledge of the world is possible. He shows that he is conscious of the depth required of any inquiry or proof that would once and for all block the sceptical conclusion from being drawn from such reflections.

That is something Moore seems never to have explicitly appreciated. He is fully aware that philosophers often say or imply that they do not know anything about an external world; some of his best friends are philosophers and he knows they say such things. But he responds to those philosophers as if he were reminding them that what they say is not true. For him it is as if they need or are asking for help—as if they could not quite determine how many misprints there are on a certain page, or could not quite remember whether they knew a certain thing or not. Moore is happy to help them out, to remind them of what they appear to have forgotten, or to bring them back from their abstract theorizing to the undeniable knowledge they obviously possess.

But sceptical philosophers get into their plight by seeking a general account of how our knowledge of the world is possible and then finding that certain considerations about perception and knowledge seem to lead inevitably to a negative conclusion. It is the peculiar nature of that philosophical investigation that Moore seems never to have grasped; he remains within what I called an 'internal' position with respect to his knowledge of the world. Questions about that knowledge are to be answered by appealing to other things of the same sort that are already known. The philosophical question about our knowledge of the world in general, with its corresponding threat of philosophical scepticism, appears to be a question about our knowledge that Moore could never answer in that 'internal' way. It is an 'external' question of 'legitimacy' that the proof of Kant's realism is meant to settle. (Although it must be admitted that we have still not been able to formulate in so many words precisely what question Moore missed or could never answer.)

The question philosophy must answer while avoiding the traditional sceptical account is how our knowledge of the world around us is possible. It is not enough simply to demonstrate *that* it is possible, or even that it is actual. We have seen that there is a way in which Moore can be said to have done that. What is wanted is an *explanation*, but not just any (even apparently true) explanation of how our knowledge of the world is possible will do. Moore, or someone like him, might explain our knowledge by saying that we know of things around us by seeing and touching them, for example. Kant would scarcely want to deny that. But the explanation he seeks is an explanation of how we can know things about the world in the face of those considerations that seem to lead so inevitably to philosophical scepticism.

The simple answer that says we see and touch the things around us would be unstable when presented with the sceptical challenge; it would have to give way to the verdict that we do not really see or touch those things after all. It is precisely the threat posed by philosophical scepticism that shows the need for the kind of explanation of our knowledge that Kant seeks. That is why he thinks the sceptical idealist is a 'benefactor of human reason'. And the kind of explanation Kant seeks is one that destroys or at least disarms the potential sceptical threat. Perhaps that is always the way it is when explaining how something could possibly happen. Certain considerations seem to make the thing impossible, and a 'How possible . . .?' explanation shows how the apparent obstacle to its happening is really no obstacle at all.[2] Even to understand Kant's task, then, or the problem the establishment of his realism is meant to answer, we must understand and acknowledge the apparent obstacle presented to our knowledge of the world by philosophical scepticism. Otherwise we will have nothing more than the words of the question to go on, and the perfectly intelligible interrogative sentence 'How is our knowledge of things around us possible?' is not enough in itself to give us the question Kant wants to answer.

The apparent obstacle to our knowledge comes from the doctrine of the epistemic priority of sensory experiences over independently existing objects. The directness of perception and knowledge to be guaranteed by Kant's realism is therefore to be secured by establishing, as Kant puts it, that:

> we have *experience*, and not merely imagination of outer things; and this, it would seem, cannot be achieved save by proof that even our inner experience, which for Descartes is indubitable, is possible only on the assumption of outer experience. (B275.)

What this means is that 'experience' of outer things, or 'the immediate consciousness of the existence of outer things' (B276n), is to be shown to be a condition of our having

[2] For some of the special features of this kind of explanation see W. Dray, *Laws and Explanation in History* (Oxford, 1957). I am indebted to Israel Scheffler for drawing my attention to its relevance to the traditional epistemological project.

any 'inner experience' at all, and hence of our having those sensory experiences that Descartes claims are indubitably known or more reliably known than external things in space. It is to be proved that 'inner experience in general' is possible only if 'outer experience in general' is possible (B278), where 'outer experience' is something that 'yields immediate proof of something real in space' (A375). To establish that we must have such direct access to the things around us would be to establish 'the reality of outer intuition' (Bxl) or 'the reality of outer sense' (Bxli), and thereby to show that realism is the correct account of our position in the world.

If 'inner experience in general' were shown to be possible only if 'outer experience in general' is possible in the way Kant understands it, the doctrine of the epistemic priority of sensory experiences over outer objects would have been refuted. But even though Kant means by 'outer experience' the 'immediate perception of something real in space', his realism does not imply that each and every time we have an 'outer perception' we are at that moment immediately perceiving something that exists outside us in space. We can and sometimes do make mistakes, and sometimes we cannot be sure about the reality of this or that thing. In dreams or delusions, for example, our perception is 'the product merely of the imagination' (B278). Questions can and do arise about the reality of things on particular occasions, and when they can be settled they are settled in ordinary, recognized ways.

> Whether this or that supposed experience be not purely imaginary, must be ascertained from its special determinations, and through its congruence with the criteria of all real experience. (B279.)

Kant says very little about what these 'criteria' of reality are. Beyond remarking, in effect, that we establish something's reality by fitting it coherently into the rest of reality in accordance with already-known laws of nature, he scarcely discusses the question directly. To avoid being deceived or misled by illusions, he says, we should proceed according to the rule, '*Whatever is connected with a perception according to empirical laws, is real*' (A376).[3] But he does not go

[3] The last word here is 'wirklich'. Kemp Smith translates it as 'actual'.

into detail about how we actually distinguish reality from appearance on particular occasions on which the question arises.

It might seem that his desultory treatment of this issue is a shortcoming of Kant's theory, and that anyone who wants to explain how we know of the existence of things around us should explain more carefully precisely how we can avoid error and distinguish appearance from reality. But that sort of complaint reveals a misunderstanding of the main point of Kant's realism. If, in order to know things about the world around us, we had to establish on each occasion the reality or non-illusoriness of every item we experience, Kant as a realist would obviously have to explain very carefully how, and with what warrant, we can do that. But Kant's realism explicitly denies that in each case or in general we must independently determine whether there is an external reality corresponding to the sensory experiences we know we are having. If we always had to establish such a correspondence Kant thinks we could never succeed. Problematic or sceptical idealism would then be the only answer, and reality would always be at best uncertain. So that problem as posed must be done away with. It rests on a belief in the epistemic priority of sensory experiences or perceptions over external reality, a belief that our inner experiences are more certain or more directly knowable than objects outside us in space. That is precisely what Kant's realism is meant to deny.

If 'inner experience in general' is possible only if 'outer experience in general' is possible, and if 'outer experience' is the immediate, direct perception of external things, we can know of the existence of things around us without having to determine independently in each case or in general that there is an external reality corresponding to our sensory experiences. An 'outer perception' will often be 'an immediate consciousness of the existence of . . . things outside me', so no further inference to the existence of something outside me is either required or possible in such a case. Seeing something before me will be 'an immediate proof of something real in space'. Our often having such experiences does not imply that every single 'outer perception' we ever have involves the existence of an outer thing, but it does imply that no completely general sceptical threat to our knowledge can be generated by the admitted fact that we sometimes suffer from illusions or mere plays of the imagination.

The proof of Kant's realism would therefore mean that the kind of doubt or uncertainty about reality that is sometimes appropriate and unanswerable in special circumstances cannot be extended as Descartes extends it to every case of sense perception. If it could be, there would always be an inference involved in arriving at any knowledge of the world, an inference from the character of our experiences, or from the way things appear to us, to the way things really are. That is just the doctrine of the epistemic priority of sensory experiences over outer objects. The proof of Kant's realism is meant to show that that doctrine violates one of the conditions that make any experience at all possible. According to Descartes's view we are never directly aware of any external things in our experience, and any knowledge we have of them is reached only on the basis of sensory experiences about which we can be certain. But that in turn assumes that without any perception or knowledge of outer things we could nevertheless have 'inner' experiences of the way things appear to us, and that is precisely what the thesis that 'inner experience in general' is possible only if 'outer experience in general' is possible is meant to deny. For Kant, if we have any experience at all we must be capable of direct experience of outer things that exist independently of us in space. Our access to and hence our knowledge about things in space is therefore direct and unproblematic in a way that is invulnerable to a completely general attack of the sort Descartes tries to mount. His form of problematic or sceptical idealism could not be correct if we have any experience at all.

Kant finds that Descartes's project leads to scepticism only because it does not go deeply enough, or in the right way, into the conditions of our everyday and scientific knowledge. It confines itself to what might be called the *credentials* of our everyday assertions and beliefs; it asks whether and how they can be completely certain or known. If Descartes had examined not just how our experience can support or justify our beliefs, but what makes it possible for us to have any experience at all, Kant thinks, he could never have reached his 'sceptical idealist' conclusion. Even to have the 'inner' experience Descartes's scepticism would grant us we would have to be capable of direct experience of outer things that exist independently of us. That is how the refutation of idealism shows that the sceptical conclusion violates one of the conditions that make any experience possible. Kant's investigation of those conditions is a 'dissection of the faculty of the understanding itself' (A66 = B91). It is from those conditions alone that he claims to derive the conclusion that Descartes's sceptical position is impossible; no philosophical investigation of our knowledge could possibly show that we always perceive something other than the independent objects we believe to exist around us.

Kant's realism, then, is meant to have powerful and epistemically reassuring consequences. It is time to look more closely at how he hopes to prove such a strong result. I do not want to examine the particular steps of the reasoning by which he tries to refute idealism or render harmless what he calls The Fourth Paralogism of Pure Reason. I am interested in a more basic question that would arise even if each step of those arguments were much less obscure than it is and they all added up to a convincing demonstration of Kant's conclusion.

The only way of reaching that conclusion—'the only refuge left open' (A378) for avoiding sceptical idealism and explaining how our knowledge of the world is possible—is to accept what Kant calls 'the ideality of all appearances' (A378). He thinks we can have direct awareness only of what belongs to us; what we can perceive in that way must be in some way dependent on our own sensibility and understanding after all. That is the point of the so-called 'Copernican revolution' in philosophy. We can never explain how our knowledge of the world is possible on the assumption that our perception and knowledge of things simply conform to the objects perceived or known, so we must adopt the revolutionary idea that 'objects must conform to our knowledge' (Bxvi) or to 'the constitution of our faculty of intuition' (Bxvii). To avoid sceptical idealism and thereby explain how non-inferential knowledge of things around us is possible we must view 'all our perceptions, whether we call them inner or outer, as a consciousness only of what is dependent on our sensibility', and all 'the outer objects of these perceptions . . . only as representations, of which . . . we can become immediately conscious' (A378). But to accept 'the ideality of all appearances', to view outer objects as 'representations' which are 'dependent on our sensibility', is to adopt idealism. Kant's view is that some form of idealism is required in order to explain how our knowledge of the world is possible.

He thinks the same form of idealism is also required to account for the necessary and therefore *a priori* character of our knowledge of space, as embodied in geometry. Such knowledge is not derived from experience, and yet it tells us how space must be. We also have *a priori* knowledge of necessary truths of arithmetic. Space and time, he says, must therefore be regarded as nothing more than 'forms of sensibility' and not as anything existing on their own, independently of our sensibility. And therefore all the things we perceive to exist in space or time—which exhausts all the things we perceive—must likewise be seen as having no existence independent of thought and experience. If this idealist view were not true, Kant thinks, there would be no explanation of how our knowledge of mathematics or our knowledge of the world is possible.

What this means is that 'the only refuge left open' for avoiding idealism is idealism. The refutation of idealism can succeed only if idealism is true. The things we perceive can be shown to be spatial things and to exist independently of us only if they are all appearances and are not independent of us. This will no doubt strike us as a bizarre way of refuting idealism—we avoid it by embracing it. The key to understanding Kant's philosophy is to see that there is no conflict or paradox here. The idealism that must be accepted does not contradict the realism that Kant wants to prove; in fact the truth of that idealism is the only thing that ensures the truth of that realism. It is 'the only refuge left open'.

The idealism that must be accepted is what Kant calls 'transcendental' idealism, and the realism that is the correct account of our position in the world is 'empirical' realism. Idealism and realism are incompatible views, but they do not conflict if the one is understood 'transcendentally' and the other 'empirically'. They are straightforwardly incompatible views because idealism says 'Everything we perceive is dependent upon us for its existence' and realism says 'Not everything we perceive is dependent upon us for its existence; there are independently existing objects that we perceive directly'. Those two sentences conflict; understood in the same way, they could not both be true. Kant thinks the second—his realism—can be true only if the first—his idealism—is also true. Obviously we cannot be sure we understand how that is possible simply by understanding those sentences themselves. We must see how those words could be taken or understood in different ways—the one 'transcendentally', the other 'empirically'.

The distinction is perhaps best understood as a distinction between two different ways of speaking or employing our words, or two different points of view from which things can be said.[4] I referred earlier to assertions or inquiries that remain 'internal' to our body of knowledge and those more detached, 'external' questions or claims concerned with our knowledge of the world taken as a whole. The expression 'independent of us', for example, can be used in two different ways, according to Kant. To use it 'empirically' is to pick out a class of things that can be found in experience to differ from another class of things to which that term does not truly apply. There is a significant contrast to be drawn within our experience between those things whose existence and nature are to some extent dependent on those who perceive them and those whose existence and nature are fully independent of all perceivers. Stones and trees and pencils and pieces of paper fall into the latter class, whereas pains, after-images, dreams and the like depend for their existence on the person who experiences them. That is just the point Moore insists on in the build-up to his proof. In his reply to Ambrose he points out that 'external thing' is an 'empirical' term—it does not apply to everything we can encounter in our experience—and his 'empirical'

[4] Here I am indebted to the helpful discussion of the distinction along these lines in G. Bird, *Kant's Theory of Knowledge* (London, 1962).

proof of an external world is a demonstration that there are in fact things to which the term truly applies. Taking the expression 'independent of us' 'empirically' in this way, what is being said by 'There are things independent of us that we perceive directly' is that among all the things we can perceive directly there are some that belong to the class of those things that would exist whether they were perceived or not—a class that can be distinguished within our experience from the class of things dependent upon us for their existence.

Not every empirical distinction we can understand provides us with actual instances on each side. We can distinguish between human beings who are born green all over and those who are not. But when we apply that particular distinction to all the things that fall within our experience we find that as a matter of fact nothing belongs to the former class; there are no human beings who are born green all over. So from the mere fact that we recognize and can draw an empirical distinction between two sorts of things it does not follow that there are in fact things of both sorts. For some empirical distinctions that will be true and for others it will not; it depends in each case on what sorts of things actually exist.[5] The issue is to be settled by experience. In the case of the empirical distinction between 'dependent on us' and 'independent of us', we find that it has instances on both sides. Realism (at least in its metaphysical aspect) is the view that things exist independently of us, so it is obvious that at least that part of realism, understood 'empirically', is true.

The same could perhaps be said for the epistemic aspect of realism. I have noted that we can and do distinguish within our experience between those occasions on which we come to know something through perception only indirectly (*via* television, mirrors, or inferences from traces, for example) and those on which we perceive the thing directly (for example, by seeing it at arm's length in the clear light of day). If there is an empirical distinction of this kind (or perhaps several different distinctions, depending on the

[5] This is another pitfall of the 'the paradigm-case argument' from the meaningfulness of expressions to facts of the world. See pp. 74 f. above.

context),[6] it is clear that we can and do draw it (or them) and that there are instances on both sides. Taking the expressions 'directly perceive' and 'independent of us' 'empirically' in this way, what is said by 'There are things independent of us that we perceive directly' is something like 'Among all the things we perceive at arm's length in the clear light of day and not only on television or by means of mirrors or other devices, there are some things (unlike pains, after-images, etc.) that are not dependent on us for their existence'. Can we deny such an uncontroversial empirical remark? Realism, understood 'empirically', is obviously true.

But Kant does not accept realism understood 'transcendentally'. Using the expressions 'independent of us' and 'directly perceive' 'transcendentally', he is an idealist: none of the things we directly perceive exist independently of us. Only if 'transcendental' idealism is true can 'empirical' realism be true. But what is it to be a 'transcendental' idealist, or indeed to give any expression a 'transcendental' employment? If an expression is not used to pick out a sub-class of all the things we can encounter within our experience, as an expression does when used 'empirically', how can it have any intelligible use for us?

The question is difficult to answer. We do know that for Kant what holds 'empirically' does not determine what holds 'transcendentally'. The two ways of speaking, although they use the same words, are independent of each other at least to the extent that from the fact that we are directly aware of things that are independent of us 'empirically' speaking it does not follow that we are directly aware of things that are independent of us 'transcendentally' speaking. Kant's own combination of 'empirical' realism and 'transcendental' idealism shows the failure of that inference. A 'transcendental' doctrine cannot be established or refuted

[6] If there is no single empirical distinction between 'direct' and 'indirect' perception, but only a number of different empirical contrasts, it is clear that the notion of 'direct' perception used in the statement of Kant's realism is not to be understood 'empirically'—there will be no single empirical notion that it captures. I suggest below that even if there is a single empirical distinction, the notion of 'direct' perception employed in the statement of Kant's thesis of empirical realism is not itself to be understood 'empirically'. The thesis of empirical realism is a 'transcendental' thesis.

'empirically'. That is why G. E. Moore could never establish in his way what Kant said had never been proved.

But if it cannot be established 'empirically', on the basis of sense-experience, it does not follow that a 'transcendental' doctrine must be a doctrine about some realm of entities beyond experience, a domain transcending our ordinary earth-bound sense-perception and existing somehow behind or beyond everything we humans could ever discover in perception. When Kant accepts 'transcendental' idealism he does not do so on the basis of a special non-sensory access he thinks he has got to some transcendent, supersensible domain in which it can somehow be discerned that nothing exists independently of us. 'Transcendental' for Kant does not mean the same as 'transcendent' or 'having to do with a world beyond'.[7]

That tells us something important about what the term 'transcendental' does not mean, but not much about what it does mean. A question or statement is transcendental for Kant if it has to do with the general conditions of our knowledge of objects.

> I entitle transcendental all knowledge which is occupied not so much with objects as with our knowledge of objects insofar as this knowledge is to be possible *a priori*.[8] (A11–12 = B25.)

A transcendental investigation therefore examines that part of our knowledge of objects, or that ingredient of our knowledge, that we possess quite independently of the experience from which we actually gain knowledge about the existence and nature of the things around us. Kant has no doubt that there is—in fact must be—such a part or ingredient of our knowledge of objects. He thinks there are certain sorts of things that people must know, certain things that must be 'in' that faculty of theirs he calls 'the understanding', in order for them even to be capable of having the experiences that eventually give them knowledge of the world. Those things that must be known in order for us even to gain any empirical knowledge at all, Kant thinks, cannot themselves

[7] Although it must be admitted that Kant sometimes slips and uses 'transcendental' where he should use 'transcendent'.

[8] The passage is slightly altered from Kemp Smith's translation.

be known empirically. There must therefore be an *a priori* or non-empirical ingredient in all our empirical knowledge. That ingredient is the subject-matter of a transcendental investigation, or what Kant often calls 'transcendental philosophy' (A12 = B25).

That subject-matter cannot be studied empirically. That is because any investigation of that subject-matter will be occupied with that knowledge, or those features of 'the understanding', which *must* be present for any empirical knowledge to be possible, and for Kant we cannot discover those necessary conditions of knowledge by empirical means. Experience, Kant says, can teach us 'that a thing is so and so, but not that it cannot be otherwise' (B3). Necessity is a 'sure criterion' of the *a priori*; if we know something which 'in being thought is thought as *necessary*' our knowledge of that necessity cannot be empirical but must be *a priori* (B3). So if we know that certain things must be known for any empirical knowledge of objects to be possible, our knowledge in that case cannot be empirical but must be *a priori*. The *a priori* investigation of those conditions that Kant recommends and pursues is what he calls 'transcendental philosophy'. It is in connection with that transcendental investigation of the conditions of our knowledge that idealism must be accepted—hence, 'transcendental' idealism.

Kant is optimistic about the prospects of such a study because, as he puts it:

> what here constitutes our subject-matter is not the nature of things, which is inexhaustible, but the understanding which passes judgment on the nature of things; and this understanding, again, only in respect of its *a priori* knowledge. These *a priori* possessions of the understanding, since they have not to be sought for without, cannot remain hidden from us, and in all probability are sufficiently small in extent to allow of our apprehending them in their completeness . . . (A12–13 = B26.)

Kant is sure that what does not have to be sought for 'without' cannot remain hidden from us because it is in some sense 'supplied' or 'contributed' by us to our knowledge. We can discover it by a critique of pure reason because 'reason has insight only into that which it produces after a plan of its own' (Bxiii). That is the lesson he claims to have learned from the Copernican revolution. We could know, *a priori* or independently of experience, what the necessary conditions of knowledge of objects are, only if those conditions somehow are to be found 'in', or have their 'source' 'in' us, the knowing subjects, and not in some independent conditions or states of affairs to which we might not have reliable access.

Kant's 'Copernican' point is that perception must be seen as necessarily involving thought or the understanding, and the principles of the understanding that are required even to 'constitute' objects for us must be seen as 'in us' independently of our having any experience. That alone is what makes it possible to explain how our knowledge (including our *a priori* knowledge of those very principles) is possible. If we regarded all our perceptions and beliefs as simply the results of something completely independent of us to which they might or might not conform, there would be no explaining how knowledge is possible. This shows that for Kant the view that objects conform to our knowledge or to the constitution of our faculty of perception—which is a form of idealism—is required even by the very enterprise of examining *a priori* the necessary conditions of human knowledge in general. Without that form of idealism we could never achieve the kind of knowledge of the human understanding that Kant seeks. Necessary features of the understanding that were fully independent of us could not be discovered *a priori*; and they could not be discovered empirically if they are the *necessary* features of any human understanding.

Idealism is therefore required in order to account for our knowledge in so far as that knowledge is *a priori*; that is what makes it a 'transcendental' idealism for Kant. Transcendental idealism is required not only to account for our knowledge of mathematics and our knowledge of the world around us, but also to make possible Kant's special project of a critique of pure reason and, eventually, a complete transcendental philosophy. The conception of such an *a priori* or transcendental investigation is what he sees as his most important contribution to philosophy. It is in fact a conception of the nature of philosophy itself—as a separate *a priori* discipline, distinct from all other kinds of human knowledge, not just in its detached, purely theoretical concern with human knowledge, but in its very content or subject-matter, and in its special epistemic status.

Kant's conception of that special philosophical task, with its attendant idealism, carries with it a certain conception of the distinction between the 'internal' or engaged assertions we make in everyday life and the detached 'external' conclusions we arrive at in philosophy about whether those assertions are true and how they are possible. Part of what it implies can be brought out by contrasting Kant's conception with those of Descartes and Moore.

Descartes does have the idea of a special philosophical investigation of our everyday knowledge; for him it is capable of bringing all that alleged knowledge into disrepute. That potentially threatening philosophical project is what Moore seems never to have acknowledged. He remains fully within the engaged, 'internal' everyday position. Sceptical or negative generalizations about our knowledge are refuted for him by particular cases of everyday knowledge, just as 'There are no chairs in the room' is refuted by finding a particular chair or two in the room. Descartes would hold that such ordinarily unproblematic assertions cannot be used to refute his general negative conclusion because he is assessing all our alleged knowledge of the world around us all at once, including the particular cases Moore would cite. He examines our everyday beliefs in a special way, as they are not usually examined in everyday life, free from the restrictions that human practical life normally imposes on them. What seems undeniably true within those restrictions in everyday life can be found after such an investigation to be open to doubt, in fact not to express something we know about the world around us at all.

There is in Descartes's conception of the philosophical investigation an assumption which he nevertheless shares with Moore, despite their great differences. Moore understands a philosopher's remark to the effect that no one knows anything about independently existing objects as simply a generalization of which a particular everyday assertion like 'I know there is a pencil here' would be a negative instance.

Moore thinks he can refute the philosopher's generalization because he thinks 'I know there is a pencil here' is sometimes truly asserted in everyday life, and so the philosophical conclusion 'No one knows anything about independently existing objects; we know only appearances' must be false. Descartes sees the results of his own philosophical investigation as implying that no one ever does say truly in everyday life 'I know that there is a pencil here'. That is why what Moore says can never refute Descartes's negative conclusion; what he says on those occasions is not strictly speaking true. But Descartes would grant that what Moore asserts does *conflict* with his own negative philosophical conclusion. Both Descartes and Moore agree, then, that *if* 'I know that there is a pencil here' were sometimes truly asserted in everyday life, Descartes's conclusion 'No one knows anything about independently existing objects; we know only appearances' would be false.

The special philosophical investigation is purely 'theoretical'; it is detached from the practical concerns of everyday life. But it remains sufficiently connected with everyday life so that the general conclusion it reaches about our knowledge is to be understood as in direct conflict with what is strictly speaking said or implied in those everyday knowledge-claims. I think this is one thing Kant has in mind in calling Descartes's sceptical idealism 'empirical' and in contrasting his own 'transcendental' idealism with it.

For Kant the special philosophical investigation is 'transcendental'; it uses its terms in a 'transcendental' and no longer 'empirical' way. He too would hold that Moore cannot refute the results of a philosophical investigation of our knowledge by citing particular knowledge-claims we make in everyday life. That is not simply because the philosophical investigation examines the legitimacy of the very claims Moore would cite, but more importantly because those particular claims in everyday life neither conflict with nor support any conclusion arrived at by the kind of philosophical investigation Kant has in mind. On Kant's conception it will not be true that if 'I know there is a pencil here' is sometimes truly asserted in everyday life, the philosophical conclusion 'No one knows anything about independently existing objects; we know only appearances' must be false. His own transcendental idealism says that no one knows anything about independently existing objects; we know only appearances. But when Moore or anyone else says in everyday life that he sees and knows there is a pencil there and that the pencil exists quite independently of human thought or sensibility he is not even contradicting, let alone refuting, Kant's idealist theory.

Kant agrees that on Descartes's conception of the philosophical task scepticism will always seem to be the only answer to the question of how our knowledge of the world is possible. Certainly the robust response of a Moore will be ineffectual, since the stability of the everyday knowledge Moore appeals to would have been undermined. That is to say, as I put it earlier, that Kant acknowledges the at-least conditional force of the traditional sceptical account. Unlike Moore, he is impressed by the ease with which one is driven to a sceptical conclusion when reflecting on all of human knowledge in Descartes's way. But he nevertheless rejects that sceptical conclusion. He considers its rejection a requirement on any adequate philosophical theory of knowledge. The theory he produces would guarantee in general the truth and full legitimacy of the sorts of assertions and knowledge-claims Moore and all the rest of us make in everyday life, even though in some particular cases we might be wrong or unwarranted in saying or believing what we do on the basis of the senses. But that general legitimacy or invulnerability can be secured only by adopting transcendental idealism. For Kant, everyday assertions like 'I know there is a pencil here' can be truly asserted in everyday life *only if* 'No one knows anything about independently existing objects; we know only appearances' is true. Kant therefore would not accept the conditional proposition about everyday assertions and philosophical theory that both Descartes and Moore accept. For Kant, the antecedent of that shared conditional can be true only if the consequent is false. Kant obviously has a different conception of the relation between the philosophical investigation of knowledge and the knowledge-claims of everyday life.

That Kantian conception might therefore seem to provide just what we were looking for in trying to understand Moore's proof of an external world. There the question was whether and how what Moore says could be perfectly true, legitimate, and undogmatic without settling any philosophical question or refuting any philosophical thesis. On Kant's conception of the philosophical problem of our knowledge of the world that is precisely the position Moore is in. It is also the position all the rest of us are in. Our everyday and scientific knowledge is secured as invulnerable to general sceptical attack. If anyone 'thinks good' to doubt the existence of external things in the way Descartes tries to do in his *First Meditation*, Kant is able to 'counter his doubts' with a 'satisfactory proof'. That proof is not and could not be the sort of proof Moore and the rest of us often resort to in everyday life; for Kant there is no direct inference from the truth of the sorts of things Moore says to the truth (or falsity) of any philosophical theory, including Kant's own. The proof Moore gives is perfectly rigorous and he really does know its conclusion. He establishes the truth of 'There are external things', and even of 'It is known that there are external things', but he does not thereby establish the falsity of Kant's idealist thesis, 'No one knows anything about independently existing objects; we know only appearances'. The two do not conflict.

Perhaps enough has been said by now about the point or significance of Kant's transcendental refutation of sceptical idealism. We can put off no longer the question of how well we can even understand the comfortable anti-scepticism he hopes to establish. Never mind the steps by which he tries to reach that transcendental conclusion; is that conclusion itself even intelligible to us or to him? And if it is, is it any better as an answer to the philosophical question than the sceptical idealism he is at such pains to avoid?

The philosophical task for Kant is to explain how our knowledge of external things is possible. We could know *a priori* the sorts of things we do know *a priori* which make the knowledge of external objects possible only if idealism were true, if the conditions of knowledge were 'supplied by us'. The idealism that is the only explanation of our knowledge is therefore to be understood 'transcendentally'. We can draw whatever anti-sceptical comfort there is to be drawn from that explanation only if we can understand what transcendental idealism is, or indeed what it is for any expression to have a transcendental as opposed to a merely empirical employment. That is by no means easy to understand.

It is not that we have any difficulty understanding the general idea of a study of the conditions of human knowledge—an investigation of those characteristics of human organisms that make it possible for them to come to know things about what is going on around them. But the best way to carry out such a study would seem to be by observing human beings and trying to understand how they work. It would be an empirical investigation—which is not to say that it would be uncomplicated or easy to carry out. It would involve not only the mechanisms of perception and learning but also the nature of language and language-acquisition as well as the development of thought and belief and no doubt countless other associated abilities. But Kant's concern with the conditions of our knowledge is not empirical but *a priori*. It inquires into what we must know *a priori*, or what is necessarily true of the human sensibility and understanding, if we are to know or experience anything at all. And how can we have any confidence that there *are* any such conditions or that, if there are, they can be discovered *a priori*? We will understand Kant's notion of the transcendental only when we understand his special *a priori* investigation of the conditions of our knowledge. But we have seen that the very possibility of the kind of *a priori* investigation Kant has in mind requires the truth of transcendental idealism. Only by agreeing that the conditions that make knowledge possible are 'supplied by us' can we understand how the necessary conditions of our knowledge could be discovered by *a priori* reflection alone. And now we seem to be going in a circle; to understand transcendental idealism we must understand the special nature of the investigation that endows the idealism with transcendental and not merely empirical status, and to understand how such a special kind of investigation is even possible we must see that idealism, understood transcendentally, is true.

There are other, even apparently Kantian, reasons for

finding the notion of a transcendental employment of terms difficult to understand. For Kant, human thought and discourse are possible only in application to that to which the categories apply—those general concepts under one or the other of which all intelligible aspects of our experience must fall. But the categories apply, and intelligible thought is therefore possible, only within the limits of possible experience. The concepts that enable us to make sense of our world must have an empirical application. How then could there be intelligible thought and discourse in terms whose employment is not determined by empirically ascertainable conditions we can discover to hold in our experience?

When terms like 'directly perceive' and 'independent of us' are given their familiar empirical employment we see that the sentence 'We directly perceive objects that exist independently of us' is true. Understood empirically, it says roughly that we sometimes perceive without mirrors, television, or other intermediary devices things that exist and would exist whether anyone were perceiving them or not. But when those same terms are used transcendentally, within the context of Kant's special *a priori* investigation, that sentence does not state a truth; idealism and not realism is what is said to be true. Kant's idealist thesis, 'We directly perceive only things that are dependent on us' is supposed to be the only explanation of how that mundane empirical statement of realism could be true. So the terms 'directly perceive' and 'independent of us' in Kant's idealist thesis cannot be understood to have the empirical application we are familiar with. Nor are they given some other empirical application. Their use appears to have been lifted away from the domain of possible human sense-experience altogether, and so on Kant's own principles it is difficult to see how they could be left with any intelligible employment at all.

Kant would no doubt reply that his transcendental investigation and the correspondingly transcendental employment of otherwise familiar terms simply must somehow be intelligible to us, or else we could never understand how our everyday knowledge of the world is possible. Transcendental idealism is really 'the only refuge'. If the completely general philosophical question about our knowledge of the world even makes sense to us, we must acknowledge the possibility of something like a transcendental investigation of the human understanding. Otherwise, we could never hope to find any general explanation of our epistemic position. This response certainly has its appeal, despite the obscurities of the transcendental, but it raises two serious problems that need to be faced.

First, suppose that, out of a strongly felt need to understand how our everyday knowledge is possible despite the apparent force of the sceptical challenge, we overcame our scruples against the transcendental employment of familiar terms and fell (or even leaped) into an acceptance of Kant's transcendental idealism. We might convince ourselves that there must be some such employment of our terms, some non-empirical level at which our knowledge can be discussed, if we are ever to have the right kind of understanding of human knowledge. Even granting all that, why would the 'refuge' of adopting idealism at the transcendental level then be any more attractive or satisfying to us than adopting it at the empirical level where it seemed so paradoxical and distressing? If what leads us to seek a more satisfactory explanation of our knowledge is the apparent fact that our knowledge would otherwise be restricted to things we understand to be (empirically speaking) dependent on us, why would we accept 'refuge' in the view that our knowledge is restricted to things we understand to be (transcendentally speaking) dependent on us? The thought that we can have no knowledge of things as they are independent of us is what makes scepticism so distressing. Why is that thought any less distressing when entertained in the transcendental mode rather than in the empirical mode?

Kant would reply that idealism understood empirically could not possibly be true, so the option of adopting empirical idealism is simply not open to us. Transcendental idealism alone is what guarantees that immediacy and stability of our everyday and scientific knowledge of the world that amounts to the falsity of sceptical idealism. But, and this is the second problem, there is a serious question about the strength of that guarantee, given Kant's conception of the transcendental.

The problem can be put directly by asking why Kant rejects the other alternative he mentions—transcendental realism. Why is that not a possible transcendental 'refuge'? It says that there are objects existing independently of us (transcendentally speaking). Kant thinks that theory could not be the correct explanation of our knowledge because if it were true we could never directly perceive those independently existing things and so we could never be certain of their existence.

> Transcendental realism . . . inevitably falls into difficulties, and finds itself obliged to give way to empirical idealism, in that it regards the objects of outer sense as something distinct from the senses themselves . . . On such a view as this, however clearly we may be conscious of our representation of these things, it is still far from certain that, if the representation exists, there exists also the object corresponding to it. (A371.)

Kant does not reject transcendental realism on the basis of supersensible access to some hidden, transcendent domain. He rejects it for the only sorts of reasons for which any transcendental doctrine can ever be rejected—its failure to explain how our knowledge is possible.

One puzzling aspect of that rejection is why Kant thinks transcendental realism must inevitably give way to empirical or sceptical idealism in this way. It is apparently because he believes that the only things we can ever perceive directly are things that are dependent on us. He does not hold that view as an empirical thesis, as we have seen, but he does hold that 'Everything we perceive is dependent on us' is true when understood transcendentally. He never seems to entertain the possibility that we might (transcendentally speaking) directly perceive something that is not (transcendentally speaking) dependent on us. That is probably because he cannot understand how perception is possible without the perception of a 'representation' or of something 'in us'.[9]

[9] The doctrine of the epistemic priority of representations over independent objects here seems simply to have been removed from the empirical to the

He can accept direct perception of independent things, empirically speaking, only because he does not accept it, transcendentally speaking.

Even if it is left obscure exactly why Kant thinks transcendental realism would leave independently existing objects unknowable or uncertain for us, the important point is that that is all he has got to go on in rejecting it.

> If we treat outer objects as things in themselves, it is quite impossible to understand how we could arrive at a knowledge of their reality outside us, since we have to rely merely on the representation which is in us. (A378.)

Suppose Kant is perfectly right that transcendental realism would leave our knowledge of things around us unexplained. Why does that alone disqualify that theory from being true, transcendentally speaking? Couldn't it just be transcendentally true that the things around us are unknowable? For Kant, I think, the answer to this question must be 'No', given his understanding of the very notion of 'transcendental'. 'Transcendental knowledge' is something that is part of or contributes to an explanation of our knowledge—an explanation that presents to us as intelligible the possibility of our knowing what we do through experience of the world around us. Given Kant's attachment to the idea that the things we are directly aware of in experience are one and all dependent on us, realism as a transcendental theory would have to say that, somehow corresponding to those representations, there are also independently existing things. But obviously 'judged from this point of view', we could only conclude that 'all our sensuous representations are inadequate to establish' the reality of such things (A369). The things we want to know about would have been separated from the things we are aware of in a way that would make the independent things unknowable.

The only defect in transcendental realism, then, (to put it misleadingly) is that it makes an explanation of our knowledge of the world impossible. It is misleading to put it that

transcendental level. This is perhaps further evidence of how difficult it is to avoid that doctrine completely in any serious attempt to explain in general how our knowledge of the world is possible.

way because there is no other defect (except perhaps outright contradiction) that a transcendental doctrine could have. There is no independent route to its truth or falsity; the only test of its acceptability is whether it would explain our knowledge. It is precisely because transcendental realism would lead us back to scepticism that 'sceptical idealism thus constrains us to have recourse to the only refuge left open, namely the ideality of all appearances' (A378). It constrains us to accept transcendental idealism because that is the only possible explanation left to us.

Kant quickly reminds us that the doctrine of transcendental idealism has already been established in the Transcendental Aesthetic 'independently of these consequences' (A378), but he does not mean that it has been established in some way other than a transcendental or *a priori* investigation of the conditions of the possibility of our knowledge. That is the only way a transcendental doctrine can ever be established. Transcendental idealism is 'established' in the Transcendental Aesthetic on the grounds that it is the only possible explanation of our synthetic *a priori* knowledge in geometry and arithmetic. That demonstration can perhaps be said to be independent of the considerations put forward in favour of transcendental idealism in the Fourth Paralogism or the Refutation of Idealism, but it is not a different way of arriving at transcendental idealism from the way it is arrived at in those later sections. The Transcendental Aesthetic argues that transcendental idealism is the only way we can explain our knowledge of space and time (A25 = B41). The Fourth Paralogism argues that transcendental idealism is the only way we can explain our knowledge of things around us in space and time. The same doctrine is the only explanation in both areas. But the sole consideration in favour of that doctrine in either case is that it is the only explanation of our knowledge.

But if there is no truly independent way of confirming a transcendental doctrine, if the sole ground of its acceptance is that it alone would explain how our knowledge is possible, we might begin to wonder whether the falsity of scepticism has been demonstrated quite so rigorously after all. Transcendental idealism is said to be true because otherwise our knowledge of things around us would be impossible. That seems to amount to saying that if we do not accept transcendental idealism we will not be able to explain our knowledge. But even if that is so, does it provide a proof — or even a consideration in favour—of transcendental idealism? Without some independent confirmation of transcendental idealism it would seem to be equivalent to saying: either transcendental idealism or no explanation at all. And why could this second alternative not be the case? Why *must* there be an explanation of our knowledge?

There are at least two different ways in which we might fail to have an explanation of knowledge of the world around us. First, if scepticism were true we would have no such knowledge; the correct description of our position would be one in which we know nothing of any independently existing things. Kant claims to have eliminated that possibility, at least speaking empirically, but he appears to have done so only by reinstating a transcendental version of that same description. The only explanation he thinks we can give of our position is one in which we know nothing of any independently existing things. Is this a satisfactory account of our knowledge, even at the transcendental level? I am inclined to think that if I understand the transcendental use of otherwise familiar terms at all, and therefore understand what this account says, it is not satisfactory. It still represents my knowledge as confined to things I understand to be dependent on me. I therefore find myself restricted to something I recognize to be merely subjective, with no possibility of learning anything about what is objectively the case. Fully facing the fact that there is no alternative to this explanation might reconcile me slightly to my bleak position, just as a new prisoner will reconcile himself to life behind bars, but that does not make the position itself any more satisfactory. If I understand the transcendental at all, I find it difficult to distinguish transcendental idealism, in its explanatory power, from the kind of scepticism that seemed so inevitable on Descartes's argument in the *First Meditation*. I do not mean that transcendental idealism is the same thing as empirical idealism; I mean that it is unsatisfactory as an explanation of knowledge at the transcendental level in the same way that empirical idealism is unsatisfactory at the empirical level. It would not enable me to see any of the assertions or beliefs in science or in everyday life as instances of knowledge of an independent domain.

In making such complaints I no doubt betray my lack of facility in the transcendental mode. In accepting transcendental idealism I lose nothing, Kant will say. My knowledge is not confined to things that are empirically dependent on me or merely subjective in the empirical way. I am theoretically capable of everything that the best physics, chemistry, mathematics, and other sciences can provide. And I am in a more satisfactory position than Descartes was in at the end of his *First Meditation.* At that point all putative knowledge about chairs and tables and pieces of paper (not to mention the sciences) had been brought into disrepute. Transcendental idealism reinstates it so that when someone says in everyday life 'I know that I am sitting here by the fire with a piece of paper in my hand', what he says is often literally true. Assertions and beliefs expressed in everyday life are instances of knowledge of the very thing they claim to be knowledge of; there has been no reduction in their content or in the strength of their support. Precisely that knowledge of the world around us that Descartes set out to investigate has been vindicated in just the form in which we originally supposed we possessed it. It is a legitimate possession after all.

But still, from the transcendental point of view—that is, when viewed from within the only kind of investigation that can properly explain how our knowledge is possible—everything we know in science and in everyday life has turned out to be subjective or dependent on human sensibility after all. It is not knowledge of how things really are, independently of us. When we move to the transcendental way of thinking we are left with knowledge that is too centred on us, too subjective, and in that respect not what we originally aspired to. It is rather like being told that Zeno's denial of motion is right after all, but only 'transcendentally', not 'empirically'. How satisfactory a resolution of our puzzlement would it be to be told that, although there is an obvious 'empirical' distinction between things that move and things that do not, the only explanation of our drawing that distinction as we do is that, 'transcendentally' speaking, nothing moves? If we understand that answer at all we seem simply to move the paradox or our distress to a different level without removing it.

But there could be another way in which we might lack an explanation of our knowledge of the world around us. There might simply fail to be an explanation of the kind we seek. Not because scepticism is true and there is nothing to explain, but because the general philosophical question that demands a comprehensive explanation cannot coherently arise with the significance it is thought to carry in philosophy. Kant in a way argues for a restricted version of a deflationary view of this kind. He thinks that if Descartes's question about how we can know about external things on the basis of the ideas presented to us in sense-experience could even be coherently raised in the way Descartes meant it, the sceptical answer would be the only answer available. He therefore tries to expose the question as illegitimate—to show that it violates one of the conditions of the possibility of experience, and therefore of its own intelligibility. But Kant's way of showing that there could be no explanation of the kind Descartes had in mind is to offer yet another explanation of his own. It does not explain the very thing Descartes had confusedly sought to explain, but it does purport to explain all of our knowledge of the world around us.

The dissatisfaction with transcendental idealism that I have been expressing might then be seen as another instance of what I think is a familiar pattern in the theory of knowledge. We find ourselves with questions about knowledge that lead either to an unsatisfactory sceptical conclusion or to this or that 'theory' of knowledge which on reflection turns out to offer no more genuine satisfaction than the original sceptical conclusion it was meant to avoid. After several disappointments of this kind we can come to wonder whether there could ever be a general explanation of human knowledge that remained sufficiently non-sceptical or sufficiently un-centred on the subjective element to satisfy us. Given the general questions with which they begin, and the feeling that their only prospect is either scepticism or some explanation difficult to distinguish from it, philosophers might be expected to introduce deflationary procedures at an earlier point in the argument.

I look at one specimen of that general strategy in the next chapter. It aspires to reach Kant's comfortable conclusion about our everyday and scientific knowledge without the obscure transcendental explanations thought necessary to support it. The extent to which it can avoid philosophical explanation while also eliminating scepticism will be an important measure of its advance (if any) over Kant. Kant, unlike Moore, acknowledges the appeal of scepticism and recognizes the depth any investigation would have to reach in order to yield a satisfactory non-sceptical outcome. The question is whether we can acknowledge the quest for explanation, and the depth at which it must be understood, without falling once again into scepticism or any other ultimately unsatisfactory explanation of how our knowledge of the world around us is possible.

V

Internal and External: Meaningful and Meaningless

The terms of the Kantian theory must be understood 'transcendentally' or non-empirically if that theory is to explain and guarantee the everyday and scientific knowledge that would otherwise be threatened by Descartes's sceptical argument. That makes it difficult to understand that theory and to accept its explanation and guarantee. Any view that could show how the significance or intelligibility of our terms is restricted to what Kant would call their empirical employment would avoid the obscurities of the Kantian transcendental explanation, while perhaps yielding just the kind of anti-sceptical guarantee Kant hoped to provide.

One anti-sceptical version of the idea that the significance of our terms is restricted to their empirical employment is to say that some possible sense-experience is relevant to the application or non-application of every meaningful expression or, for a meaningful sentence, that some possible sense-experience is relevant to the determination of its truth or falsity. On that view we could understand or mean something by a sentence only if it were possible for us to have some sense-experiences that count in favour of that sentence's being true, or of its being false. 'The empirical verifiability principle of meaningfulness' is the doctrine that a sentence is meaningful if and only if it is verifiable or falsifiable at least to some degree, and the confirmation or disconfirmation ultimately comes from sense-experience. It has proved impossible even to state, let alone establish, any principle along these lines that has just the consequences its supporters want to defend,[1] but the lack of an unambiguous and fairly precise statement has been no obstacle to the

[1] For an account of some of the main problems see C. G. Hempel, 'Empiricist Criteria of Cognitive Significance: Problems and Changes' in his *Aspects of Scientific Explanation* (New York, 1965).

success of important philosophical ideas in the past, and this conception of meaning is no exception.

Kant found most traditional philosophical disputes interminable and recommended a 'critique of pure reason' as the only antidote. The proper sphere of reason must be discovered and described, the limits must be drawn within which reason can proceed on a firm basis and answer the questions it poses, and then everything falling beyond those limits will be nonsense or illusion. That is also the point of the verifiability principle of meaningfulness. Any apparently well-formed indicative sentence that would not be rendered at least more likely to be true by one possible course of sense-experience rather than another is, literally, meaningless—it says nothing that could be true or false. And an apparently well-formed interrogative sentence is meaningful and asks a real question only if there is some possible sense-experience that would make one answer to it rather than another more likely to be true. Otherwise it is a mere 'pseudo-question', not a real question at all, and any alleged answer to it is no more than a 'pseudo-statement' incapable of truth or falsity.[2] The search for answers to such 'pseudo-questions' could only be based on some kind of illusion; there can be no such answers, because the questions themselves lack meaning. Despite appearances, there is quite literally nothing they ask.

Typical philosophical questions about reality are thought to fall foul of this test of meaningfulness. Any concept of reality we can understand, on this view, must be an 'empirical' concept of reality; assertions to the effect that such-and-such exists or is real must be verifiable or confirmable in experience —otherwise they would be meaningless. Now in everyday life and in science we do very often verify or confirm assertions of the existence or reality of certain sorts of things. Suppose, to take an example of Carnap's, a question has arisen as to whether a certain mountain is real or only legendary—is there such a mountain at a certain place in Africa or not? Two geographers who set off to settle the

[2] See R. Carnap, 'Pseudoproblems in Philosophy', in his *The Logical Structure of the World and Pseudoproblems in Philosophy* (London, 1967). (Hereafter cited as PsP.)

question can come to agree on what they find when they get there. If they find a mountain of a certain kind more or less where it is supposed to be, they can report that it is real, that it does exist, and is not merely legendary. In doing so, Carnap says, they are employing an 'empirical, scientific, non-metaphysical concept' of reality.[3] They are fitting the mountain into the spatio-temporal framework at a certain place, and they are claiming that it is connected with other things in that framework by known empirical laws.

But suppose these geographers are also philosophers; one of them calls himself a 'realist', the other an 'idealist'. The former declares that not only does the mountain have all the characteristics they have discovered, including its spatial dimensions and location, but it is also real—it exists independently of all experience. The latter denies this; the mountain undoubtedly has all the spatial and other characteristics they have discovered and so is not legendary, but it is not real in the way the realist has in mind either—like everything that exists, it depends for its existence on being perceived. It is clear, Carnap thinks, that 'this divergence between the two scientists does not occur in the empirical domain, for there is complete unanimity so far as the empirical facts are concerned' (PsP, 333–4). The issue between them is not one they conceive of as settleable by empirical means. According to the verifiability principle there is therefore no meaningful issue between them.

> What is true for the mountain is true for the external world in general . . . *neither the thesis of realism that the external world is real, nor that of idealism that the external world is not real can be considered scientifically meaningful.* This does not mean that the two theses are false; rather they have no meaning at all so that the question of their truth and falsity cannot even be posed. (PsP, 334.)

Kant's thesis of transcendental idealism would be eliminated as meaningless according to this test. It is meant to guarantee, and therefore to be compatible with, the empirical reality and knowability of things around us in space. But for the verificationist there is no meaningful question beyond

[3] R. Carnap, 'Empiricism, Semantics and Ontology', Supplement A of his *Meaning and Necessity*, Second Edition (Chicago, 1958), p. 207. (Hereafter cited as ESO.)

familiar empirical questions of reality to which Kant's thesis could possibly be an answer. Once he agrees that we can and do settle empirical questions using the empirical concept of reality as we do, there is no other meaningful issue of realism *vs.* idealism left unsettled. Both transcendental idealism and transcendental realism are meaningless. Kant would say that his transcendental idealism cannot be meaningless because its truth is required in order to guarantee that we can indeed settle all other meaningful questions of reality empirically; without transcendental idealism we would be stuck with scepticism. But according to the verifiability principle transcendental idealism is a 'pseudo-theory' that can explain or guarantee nothing. Its alleged explanatory powers can therefore be no reason for accepting it. But its loss is no encouragement to scepticism, since scepticism itself is also eliminated as meaningless. The possibility of our settling all meaningful questions of reality by empirical means is guaranteed by the verifiability principle of meaningfulness alone.

Philosophical scepticism about a particular area or subject-matter appears to say that we can never know anything in that area, and can never even have any more reason to believe one thing in that area rather than another. If that were true it would follow from the verifiability principle that there is nothing meaningful or intelligible in that area for us to fail to know or to lack reason to believe. Putting the point positively, we *must* be capable of knowing the truth-value of anything meaningful; or at least it must be possible to have better reason for believing that it has one truth-value than for believing that it has the other. It is meant to be a consequence of the verifiability principle, then, that it is impossible for any form of scepticism to be true. But it would be wrong to say that scepticism is therefore false, even necessarily false. If we were forever incapable of the knowledge or reasonable belief that scepticism seems to deny us, there would be nothing intelligible for us to lack knowledge of or reasonable belief in. In the putative statement of scepticism which says, 'No one can ever know whether . . .', the '. . .' would therefore be filled in with an expression that is meaningless because unverifiable. Trying to assert the thesis of scepticism would then be like trying to say (to borrow an example of Russell's) 'No one can ever know whether quadruplicity drinks procrastination'. Neither truth nor falsity is the right verdict for such a sentential expression; it has a meaningless component, so it is just as meaningless as that component.

Descartes reflected on human knowledge and reached the conclusion that no one could ever know anything about the world around him. He found that, no matter what our experience might be like, there will always be countless incompatible possibilities that are nevertheless compatible with all the evidence we could ever get. According to the verifiability principle, if Descartes were right that no possible course of sense-experience could count in favour of the truth of 'There are external things', or of its falsity, it would be literally meaningless and would say nothing at all. The corresponding interrogative sentence, 'Are there external things?', would accordingly ask nothing. It could not be a question to which one could fail to know the answer; not because it is obvious what the answer is, but because there is no meaningful answer and so no meaningful question. Carnap at one point likens the putative assertion of realism about the external world to expressions like 'This triangle is virtuous' or even 'Berlin horse blue' (PsP, 326). Those expressions do not state anything that could be true or false. They do not state anything we could know or fail to know. They do not state anything. Descartes's sentence 'There are external things' does not state anything either, if he is right that no one could ever know whether it is true.

That is not to deny that there are perfectly meaningful questions about the existence of external things that can be asked and answered empirically. The two geographers settled such a question in the case of the mountain. If they then discovered another mountain nearby they could even say 'Here is one mountain' and 'Here is another'. Called upon to describe some of the features of Africa, or of the earth, they could quite legitimately say, among other things, 'There are mountains'. That would sum up part of what they had found by their observations. There would seem to be no objection to their going further, if the occasion seemed to call for it, and announcing an even more general result. No one would deny that a mountain is an external thing. Perhaps sudden thoughts or pains or after-images are not external things, but mountains are external things if anything is. The geographers, like everyone else, could be expected to know that they are. So with all the empirical support they originally had for saying 'The mountain is real, not legendary', or 'Here is one mountain' and 'Here is another', they could also say 'There are external things'. What they say is knowable on the basis of experience, and hence not meaningless according to the verifiability principle. But that same sentence, 'There are external things', when purporting to express something Descartes thought we could never know, was declared meaningless. Obviously it is not the sequence of words alone, but the possibility of its confirmation or disconfirmation in experience, that determines whether or not an otherwise well-formed sentence is meaningful.

The geographers' imagined Moore-like performance employs only the 'empirical' concept of an external thing, and therefore an 'empirical' concept of reality or existence, as Moore himself claimed to be doing in his own proof. Therefore there is nothing in what Moore says or does that a verificationist need object to. But for that very reason nothing Moore or the geographers say or do could be relevant to Descartes's question about the external world. That question is, on verificationist grounds, literally meaningless, and the putative thesis that no one knows whether there are any external things equally meaningless for the same reason. Therefore when Moore says in the way he does that he knows there are external things, or when the geographers say it, they could not be contradicting Descartes's conclusion. To suppose that they were would be to suppose that there is a straightforward deduction from 'Here is a hand' or 'Here is a mountain' to the truth of Descartes's sentence 'There are external things', or from 'I know that here is a hand' or 'We know there are mountains' to the falsity of Descartes's sceptical conclusion 'No one knows whether there are external things'. There are sentences composed of those same words in the same order which are shown to be respectively true and false by the true assertions

Moore and the geographers make. But for that very reason those sentences cannot express what Descartes expresses by his words. According to the verifiability principle, he expresses nothing meaningful at all by his words, so what Moore and the geographers say can neither imply nor conflict with what he says. What is true and makes perfect sense cannot imply or conflict with what is nonsense.

This verificationist conception therefore provides another way of understanding how everything G. E. Moore says can be perfectly true and legitimate and undogmatic even though it refutes no philosophical thesis or settles no philosophical question at all. It is not that, as in Kant, the philosophical question properly understood turns out to be 'transcendental' and not empirical, and so nothing Moore says 'empirically' could imply or conflict with any answer to it, but rather that the question properly understood turns out to be a meaningless 'pseudo-question' and not a real question at all. Nothing empirically knowable and therefore meaningful could ever imply or conflict with any answer to that 'question' for the simple reason that any so-called 'answer' to that so-called 'question' is itself meaningless. Moore thought he was refuting what Descartes said and giving a positive answer to his question about the external world and our knowledge of it. On the Kantian conception he was doing no such thing, but there nevertheless remains a genuine question about our knowledge that cannot be answered in Moore's way or in any other empirical way. For the verificationist, Moore does not answer Descartes's question either, but there is nothing meaningful that he ignores.

This verificationist theory of meaningfulness therefore stands in direct opposition to Descartes's conception of the relation between the 'internal', engaged, empirical remarks of Moore and the rest of us in everyday life and the 'external', detached questions and theses of the philosopher. On that traditional conception what Moore ignores is the possibility of a detached philosophical assessment of the assertions and knowledge-claims we make in everyday life. The conclusion of that assessment is that none of those confident assertions are strictly speaking instances of knowledge, and so none of our knowledge-claims about the world around us are strictly speaking true. There is a direct conflict between the philosophical conclusion and our claims in everyday life. That does not in itself imply that those claims should not be made or accepted in everyday life. According to the traditional conception those everyday assertions are made and accepted within a set of tacit restrictions imposed by the practical demands of action and human communication. When those restrictions are lifted or ignored in the purely theoretical philosophical investigation it is discovered that our everyday assertions of knowledge, with the very meanings they possess in everyday life, are never strictly speaking true. There is a direct conflict between the philosophical conclusion and our claims in everyday life. We never know any of the things we quite meaningfully and intelligibly say about the world around us.

According to the verifiability principle that cannot be so. Any philosophical conclusion to the effect that we can know nothing about the world around us would put all talk of the world around us beyond the limits of the meaningful. If the sceptical philosopher even so much as allows that the things we say about the world around us in everyday life are meaningful at all, his 'external', detached philosophical assessment cannot be correct in declaring them unknowable. The verifiability principle guarantees that the truth or falsity of those everyday remarks must be knowable. The traditional conception must be wrong.

It is not surprising to find the verifiability principle in conflict in this way with what I have called the traditional conception of our position in everyday life. On that conception as I described it what I ask about when I ask whether there is a mountain more than five thousand metres high in Africa is something that holds or fails to hold quite independently of anyone's ever being able to know or reasonably believe or justifiably assert that there is a mountain that high there, or that there is not. But according to the verifiability principle what I am asking about is meaningful and therefore could possibly be true only if it is possible for someone to know or to have some reason to believe that there is a mountain there, or that there is not. That principle goes directly against any conception of objectivity which does not include within it the possibility of our knowing or having good reason to believe what the objective facts are. Any conception of objectivity that includes and therefore guarantees the possibility of knowledge obviously makes scepticism about the objective facts impossible.

It follows that according to the verifiability principle we cannot even be said to have a belief in the external world of the sort the traditional philosopher attributes to us. Of course we can all be said to believe or assent to the truth of 'There are external things' when that is understood as an obvious and uncontroversial consequence of 'There are mountains' or 'Here is a human hand'. But that is not the way Carnap thinks the sceptical philosopher understands it in his investigation into our belief in the external world. The sceptical conclusion is supposed to show that it is a belief which can find no confirmation or disconfirmation in experience. According to the verifiability principle, therefore, 'there is no such belief or assertion or assumption' (ESO, 208). Carnap does not discover that we have no such belief by taking an inventory of all the things human beings believe and finding that that belief is not among them; he deduces from his verifiability principle that what people would believe if they believed what the philosopher says they believe is meaningless. There is nothing that could be true or false that we could be said to believe. But if we do not even have such a belief there is nothing for the traditional philosopher to assess, nothing whose credentials can be examined. The justification he seeks is therefore nothing more than a will-o'-the-wisp, and the eventual statement of his scepticism nothing more than a pseudo-statement.

This apparently harsh verdict on the traditional epistemological enterprise is nevertheless based on a deeper and more sympathetic understanding of its true nature than G. E. Moore ever seems to have expressed. Carnap and his fellow verificationists understand the traditional problem of the external world well enough to see that it cannot be settled in Moore's way, and in fact that it cannot be settled at all, and so is meaningless. Although he officially declares it an unintelligible 'pseudo-problem', Carnap could be said to understand the problem only too well. He finds himself in a position to assert positively that it has no meaning. He makes that discovery by following the traditional philosopher's argument and seeing that for him no possible experience could make a belief in the existence of the external world any more warranted than a belief in its non-existence. Moore made no such discovery about the sceptical argument.

Carnap shows more than an understanding of what the traditional epistemologist is up to; he is fully in sympathy and even total agreement with the philosopher's sceptical conclusion—or at least with what it would be if it were intelligible. If that were not so, he could never reach his verdict that it is meaningless. The only reason Carnap has got for declaring the sceptical conclusion meaningless is that the philosopher's 'statement' of the existence of the external world is neither confirmable nor disconfirmable in experience. But the sceptical philosopher has precisely that same reason for declaring the truth of scepticism—all possible experience is equally compatible with the existence and with the non-existence of the external world. That is why we can never know by experience whether there is an external world or not. Carnap's grounds for the charge of meaninglessness are therefore the same as the sceptical philosopher's grounds for his scepticism. Carnap cannot arrive at his destructive conclusion unless he accepts what might be called the 'conditional correctness' of scepticism: *if* the traditional philosopher did manage to raise a meaningful question about our knowledge of the world, his sceptical answer to it would be correct. Only if that conditional is true will the problem be meaningless according to the verifiability principle; if a non-sceptical answer were even possible the statement of the existence of the external world would be empirically meaningful after all.

Another way to describe the overlap between verificationism and scepticism is to say that both parties agree that if we do have a belief in the external world of the sort the philosopher attributes to us, it is right to conclude that scepticism is true. That belief could never be confirmed or disconfirmed. It is for precisely that reason that Carnap denies that we have any such belief. But that differs from scepticism only by adding to it the verifiability principle of meaningfulness.

What puts the verificationist in a position to wield his powerful principle is nothing more nor less than the conditional correctness of scepticism. The empirical undecidability of the issue is essential. But the empirical undecidability of our belief in an external world is the only thing the sceptical philosopher insists on. It is also the only thing Carnap insists on, along with a little help from the verifiability principle, when he declares that the sceptical philosopher is wrong to suppose that we have any such belief in the first place.

The verifiability principle is meant to have devastating effects on the practice of philosophy and on our understanding of it. It would condemn as meaningless many questions and theories of traditional philosophy. Used for purely negative purposes, it would simply expose each meaningless philosophical problem that came along, and leave it at that. To pursue such a deflationary strategy would not require that one take a stand on, or even have any conception of, the source and nature of philosophical problems. Discovering that a problem was empirically unresolvable would be enough to dismiss it. Just as G. E. Moore tried simply to answer the philosophical questions, the cautious, destructive verificationist could simply eliminate them, while betraying no more curiosity than Moore did about what sorts of questions they are or what might really lie behind them.

The best verificationists do not confine themselves to such a policy of non-committal counter-punching. They are more philosophical than Moore. They see that the verificationist doctrine itself must be grounded in a sound positive philosophy, and they typically offer an explanation of the unsoundness of the traditional philosopher's procedures. Distinguishing legitimate, respectable philosophizing from the empty illusions of the tradition is part of the important task of finding a place for philosophy on the intellectual map.

Carnap, for example, does not merely expose traditional philosophical problems as empirically meaningless. He not only suggests in addition a positive account of their nature and source, but also—perhaps because of that—offers in effect what he takes to be the correct description of our everyday position in relation to the things we know about, and an explanation of how that knowledge is possible. It differs from the traditional conception, but is designed to make intelligible the very thing scepticism so obviously fails to explain. We found reason to doubt whether Kant's positive theory ultimately represents a real advance over the scepticism it was meant to supplant. It remains to be seen whether Carnap's account is any more satisfactory than traditional scepticism and the Kantian theory.

Carnap finds that philosophical questions appear to differ from questions typically asked in everyday life or in science in being more general. Philosophical questions of existence or reality tend to be concerned not with this or that particular thing or type of thing, but with all things or all types of things within a certain domain. Moore too saw the philosopher's questions as general; that is why he thought they could be settled one way or the other by citing the particular facts he thought could not be denied. And we have seen that there is a way in which completely general propositions are established by what Moore knew. But for Carnap those general propositions of Moore's and the questions to which they are answers are not philosophical; they are not 'external' questions of the sort philosophy has tried to answer. When the two geographers said they knew there were external things they did not answer what Carnap calls 'the external question of the reality of the thing world itself' (ESO, 207). That question is raised, he says, 'neither by the man in the street nor by scientists, but only by philosophers' (ESO, 207). What sort of question is it, and what makes it philosophical?

It cannot be that the question or its answer is philosophical simply because it is completely general. 'There are external things' as said by the geographers is completely general, but it does not answer the philosophical question about external things. Nor can it be simply that it is asked or asserted by a philosopher. G. E. Moore is a philosopher who said 'There are external things', but according to Carnap he did not thereby manage to answer any philosophical question. Rather the question or statement becomes philosophical for Carnap only when its generality is understood in a certain way. The 'empirical concept of reality' as applied to the geographers' mountain raised no such problem.

> To recognize something as a real thing or event means to succeed in incorporating it into the system of things at a particular space-time position so that it fits together with the other things recognized as real, according to the rules of the framework . . . . To be real in the scientific sense means to be an element of the system; hence this concept cannot be meaningfully applied to the system itself. (ESO 207.)

The question of the reality of the whole system of external things is the question Carnap thinks is raised only by philosophers. He thinks it cannot be meaningfully raised. Why does he think that? From the fact that 'to be real in the scientific sense means to be an element of the system' he concludes that '*hence*' the concept of reality cannot be applied to the whole system. What is he relying on in making that inference? It might look as if it is simply the complete generality of the question that he has in mind, because it might look as if he denies that the general sentence 'There are external things' is meaningful. He says that 'the thesis of the reality of the thing world . . . cannot be formulated in the thing language or, it seems, in any other theoretical language' (ESO, 208). This might make it look as if Carnap thinks the philosopher is asking or saying something the mere formulation of which goes beyond the expressive resources of the very language in which he tries to say it, and that that is why he fails to raise a meaningful question or to assert a meaningful proposition.

Quine appears to interpret Carnap as holding some such view. He finds in Carnap's distinction between 'external' philosophical questions and 'internal' scientific questions a distinction between what he calls 'category' and 'sub-class' questions of existence. For Quine that amounts to nothing more than a distinction between two ways of formalizing the language in which the things in question are talked about. In a formalized language with only one style of bound variable extending over the whole domain of things, the question 'Are there so-and-so's?' will be an 'external' or 'category' question, but when there is one kind of variable for one sort of thing and another for another, a question asked of the so-and-so's of one of those kinds will be an 'internal' or 'sub-class' question that does not encompass all the things that can be said to be. Understood in this way, the distinction is really a distinction between two different ways of writing sentences about what there is. The choice of notation is what determines how the different sorts of questions about the existence of so-and-so's are to be classified.

A crucial difference between Quine and Carnap is Quine's belief that philosophy differs from other truth-seeking enterprises like geography or physics or mathematics 'only in breadth of categories'.[4] His understanding of Carnap's 'external–internal' distinction seems to be an expression of just that belief. He finds that the 'external' or 'category' questions of the philosopher differ only in their generality from the 'sub-class' questions entertained by the more specialized sciences, but they are to be answered in essentially the same ways. We can move to the most general 'category' questions or assertions simply by letting one style of variable range over things of all kinds. I will look more closely at Quine's 'empirical' conception of philosophy, and in particular his treatment of the philosophical problem of the external world, in the next chapter. For the moment it is enough to say that Carnap in drawing the 'external–internal' distinction as he does must have something else in mind.

Carnap would allow that there is a perfectly meaningful question to which the perfectly meaningful general sentence 'There are external things' is the uncontroversial answer. It is precisely because it is meaningful and uncontroversial that it is not to be confused with an 'external' philosophical question about external things. Carnap distinguishes a number of different 'languages' or 'systems', and in almost every case he considers he explicitly states that there is an 'internal' general statement like 'There are numbers', 'There are propositions', 'There are properties', 'There are space-time points', etc. They are meaningful and obviously true sentences, but they do not state answers to what a philosopher asks when he asks the 'external' question whether there are numbers, propositions, properties, etc. So what prevents the philosophical question from being meaningful cannot be simply that it goes beyond the expressive resources

[4] W. V. Quine, *Word and Object* (Cambridge, Mass., 1960), p. 275.

of the terminology in which it is formulated. There is a question expressed in that terminology which is perfectly meaningful and answerable.

For example, we have a linguistic framework in which we talk about and prove things about numbers. Within that framework the statement 'There are numbers' follows from the 'internal' (in this case analytic) statement that five is a number. The 'internal' statement 'There are numbers' therefore 'does not say more than that the . . . system is not empty' (ESO, 209). But philosophers who ask in general whether there are numbers are presumably not asking whether five is a number or whether there is a number between four and six. In the system of numbers that we have, from the fact that five is a number or that there is a number between four and six, it follows that there are numbers. Similarly, for Carnap the question 'Are there space-time points?' 'may be meant as an internal question; then the affirmative answer is, of course, analytic and trivial' (ESO, 213). It is analytic because the particular assertions of the existence of points from which it follows are, like number-statements, themselves analytic. But in other 'systems' the affirmative answer to the 'internal' question is equally obvious and trivial although it is 'empirical' and not analytic. For example, the 'internal' assertion 'There is an *f* such that *f* is a colour, and . . .' is 'of an empirical, factual nature' (ESO, 212). But the general 'internal' statement 'There are colours' follows from it, so that statement too is 'empirical' and 'factual', however obviously true. The same thing holds for 'There are external things', taken 'internally' to the 'system' of physical things, although Carnap does not explicitly say so. It follows trivially and uncontroversially from the geographers' discovery, as well as from the premisses of Moore's proof.

'External' questions of the kind Carnap thinks only philosophers ask do not have uncontroversial answers. Different philosophers who ask whether there are numbers 'offer lengthy arguments on either side' (ESO, 209), thereby showing that they do not have the internal question in mind. And when the question turns to the reality of things 'the controversy goes on for centuries without ever being solved'.

That is because it 'cannot be solved'—'it is framed in a wrong way' (ESO, 207).

The 'external' or philosophical question about the world of things is distinguished from its 'internal' counterpart and identified as philosophical precisely on the grounds of its undecidability and ill-formedness. It is not that it is grammatically or syntactically ill-formed; its syntactically identical 'internal' counterpart is perfectly meaningful and answerable. The only reason Carnap gives for saying that the 'external' question about the whole system of things is framed 'in a wrong way' is simply that it is an empirically unanswerable question.[5] The philosophical assertion of 'realism' as an answer to that 'question' is also meaningless and neither true nor false. There is no possible empirical way to establish its truth, or its falsity.

When Carnap says that 'the thesis of the reality of the thing world . . . cannot be formulated in the thing language or, it seems, in any other theoretical language', then, he is not saying simply that 'There are external things' is not a meaningful sentence, or that it cannot be formulated in the thing language, or that it is neither true nor false and so cannot express the answer to a perfectly meaningful 'theoretical' question. He means that that same sentence, taken as an answer to the 'external' philosophical question of the reality of the world of things, or taken as an assertion of the philosophical thesis of 'realism', is meaningless and therefore could not be an answer to any meaningful theoretical question. To say that there is no 'theoretical language' in which it can be formulated is to say that in no language could it express something that is either true or false. And that is simply because, as Carnap understands it, no possible sense-experience is relevant to the determination of its truth or falsity.

'Theoretical' questions are here being distinguished from 'practical' questions; questions whose answers are truths are

[5] He points out that 'the non-cognitive character of the questions which we have called here external questions' was emphasized by the Vienna Circle, and in explaining their rejection of 'both the thesis of the reality of the external world and the thesis of its irreality as pseudo-statements' he explicitly refers to his own *Pseudoproblems in Philosophy* and to Schlick's 'Positivism and Realism' (ESO, 215). In those works an appeal to the verifiability principle of meaningfulness is the only argument used to show that those 'theses' are meaningless.

distinguished from problems whose solutions are actions. An 'external' question as asked by a philosopher about the whole system of things is misconstrued as a 'theoretical' question with a right or wrong answer. For Carnap it is really 'a practical question, a matter of practical decision concerning the structure of our language. We have to make the choice whether or not to accept and use the forms of expression in the framework in question' (ESO, 207). That kind of choice obviously could not be settled by the 'internal' assertions of Moore or the geographers, however legitimate those assertions might be. It is not a theoretical question that can be decided by investigation and discovery at all; it is a matter of decision.

The practical solution might be influenced by theoretical knowledge; we might try to determine how efficient or fruitful the adoption of a certain form of language would be. But discovering what the effects of adopting it are likely to be is one thing, and adopting it or deciding to adopt it is quite another. Even if the decision is strongly justified by its predicted effects, it remains true that what is thereby justified is our adoption or use of something, not a truth or set of truths about the things that the adopted language enables us to speak of. The language of things has undoubtedly proved useful and fruitful, but for Carnap:

> . . . it would be wrong to describe this situation by saying 'The fact of the efficiency of the thing language is confirming evidence for the reality of the thing world'; we should rather say instead: 'This fact makes it advisable to accept the thing language.' (ESO, 208.)

This is not an objection in general to the idea of confirming a hypothesis on grounds of its greater fruitfulness or simplicity. Carnap is pointing out that in this case there simply is no hypothesis or thesis to be justified in that way or in any other way. The verifiability principle implies that there is no such proposition and that we therefore have no such belief.

This positive conception of 'external' philosophical questions as 'practical' and not 'theoretical' goes well beyond a simple appeal to the verifiability principle of meaningfulness. We have already seen that if the philosophical questions are empirically unanswerable, that principle implies that they are not 'theoretical'—they do not have answers that are true or false. That in turn implies that scepticism is meaningless. But Carnap holds in addition that what seems to the traditional philosopher to be a 'theoretical' question is really a 'practical' question about the choice of linguistic framework. That thesis about 'external' questions does not follow from the verifiability principle alone. It is part of a general theory of knowledge according to which the meaninglessness of the traditional pursuit would be revealed and a non-sceptical answer would be given to the question how our knowledge is possible. We can try to understand that theory by comparing it with the misguided traditional conception it is meant to replace.

For Carnap there are two essential ingredients in our knowledge of things around us: the experience on which it is based and the linguistic framework in terms of which we understand that experience. The language of external things, in fact any language, is a set of 'rules for forming statements and for testing, accepting or rejecting them' (ESO, 208). Once we are equipped with some rules for saying things and for testing and accepting or rejecting what we say, we are in a position to find that some of the things we say about the world around us are supported by our experience and some are not. Without the statements that our acceptance of the language of things enables us to formulate, we would have nothing that experience could either confirm or disconfirm for us.

So far there is nothing in this for the traditional philosopher to object to. He too would insist that we must have terms for talking about the things around us, and ways of supporting and assessing what is thereby said, if we are to be capable of knowing anything about the world. But Carnap finds that the traditional philosopher misunderstands the relation between the linguistic framework of external things and the truths he can express and know about external things from 'within' that framework. In granting that a linguistic framework is needed for seeking and expressing knowledge of the things around us, the traditional philosopher appears to think the framework is needed only for expressing something that is objectively true or false quite independently of the adoption of that framework. That is what enables him to ask whether the world really is the way we take it to be, even after all our everyday and scientific procedures for gaining knowledge have been scrupulously followed. That is in effect to ask whether the language of external things is the right one to accept, whether it can be known to represent accurately the way things independently are.

That for Carnap is nonsense. Any talk of the objective facts or of the way things are is either 'internal' to some linguistic framework and so cannot serve to justify our possession of that framework, or it is 'external' to all frameworks and therefore meaningless. The only 'theoretical' questions we can meaningfully ask about a whole linguistic framework are what its rules and principles are, and what would be the likely effects of our following them. That leaves only the 'practical' issue of adopting the framework or not. To ask whether adopting it would put us in a better position to say and know things that are true independently of our adoption of it is to ask a meaningless 'external' question about the things only the framework alone enables us to talk about. That is where the traditional philosopher goes wrong, according to Carnap; there are no independent facts or truths which could make the choice of a framework the right (or the wrong) one. The issue of adopting a linguistic framework or not is always a matter of degree. It is a question of how fruitful and efficient the framework in question will be for the purposes at hand.

As a historical or psychological hypothesis the idea of our actually choosing or adopting the kind of language we use to talk about the world around us sounds far-fetched, to say the least. It is more realistic to say that we simply grew up learning about the world around us; there was no decision or choice involved. Carnap concedes that 'we all have accepted the thing language early in our lives as a matter of course' (ESO, 207). But for him that is not to be understood as our having accepted as true a certain 'external' thesis about the world of things; we have simply accepted or adopted a certain language. There was no 'deliberate choice' or explicit convention.

> Nevertheless, we may regard it as a matter of decision in this sense: we are free to continue using the thing language or not; in the latter case we could restrict ourselves to a language of sense-data and other 'phenomenal' entities, or construct an alternative to the customary thing language with another structure, or finally we could refrain from speaking. (ESO, 207.)

It is the complete 'freedom' we continue to enjoy with respect to the linguistic framework of external things, and not any historical discovery about childhood language-learning, that reveals the purely 'practical' or conventional character of the question whether to adopt that framework. It is a matter of decision, and not a question that can be settled by any objective facts about external things.

It is not easy to understand the kind of 'freedom' that is essential to Carnap's account. He says we are free to remain silent, but no traditional philosopher would deny that possibility. It can be granted that we might have said or believed nothing about the world around us; we might never have had the language of things, or we might come to have it no longer. The kind of 'freedom' Carnap has in mind is not established merely by the fact that there are many different linguistic frameworks, either. When he says 'we are free to continue using the thing language or not' he does not just mean that there are also other languages we can use as well—the 'systems' of natural numbers, or propositions, or space-time points, for example. The traditional philosopher would allow that we can talk of other things than the external physical objects we take to be around us.

Carnap speaks of 'an alternative to the thing language with another structure', and he means a genuine *alternative* to the thing language, not just a different language. What is an 'alternative' language in that sense? It must be a language that would enable us to do whatever we now do with the thing language we have got. But is even that enough? Carnap suggests that 'a language of sense-data and other "phenomenal" entities' is an alternative to the language of external things. There is obviously a way in which the sceptical philosopher would not deny that. He claims to have discovered that, strictly speaking, sense-data or other 'phenomenal' entities are the only things we can be empirically justified in talking about and having beliefs about. That is precisely why the problem of our knowledge of the external world arises as it does; it seems impossible to go beyond such 'data' to a reasonable belief in independent, external things. If we want to confine ourselves to what we can know or have reason to believe, we should confine ourselves to the 'phenomenal' alternative to our customary ways of speaking of independent objects around us. The 'phenomenal' language is a better alternative than the thing language for asserting things we know or have reason to believe. But on the traditional view that does not imply that there are no objective facts about external things; it means only that, since we can never know what is true or false of the things around us, we must restrict ourselves to 'phenomena' if we want to express any knowledge or reasonable beliefs. That is not Carnap's sense of 'alternative'.

For Carnap the language of sense-data is not just a language we might adopt if we realize we are unjustified in stating most of the things we now express in the thing language. He wants to oppose the view that in choosing an alternative language over the thing language we would be missing something or leaving unsaid or unknown countless things that remain true independently of our adopting that language for stating them. The language of sense-data is a genuine alternative to the language of external things in the required sense only if it is in some way or other an alternative means of achieving the same purpose. We must not think of the statements expressible in the two different systems as potential competitors in the task of stating what is true independently of the adoption of this or that framework. There is no such meaningful task; there are no 'external' truths for the statements 'internal' to a particular framework to capture or fail to capture. Statements 'internal' to one framework do not conflict with those 'internal' to another. Like the frameworks in which they belong, they are genuine alternatives and not competitors whose relative merits can be assessed on a theoretical or true-false basis.

This idea of a statement in one framework being an alternative to—and not just different from or a competitor of—another in another framework is essential to Carnap's conception of alternative linguistic frameworks. Without it we could still ask which of several frameworks best enables us to state the truth, or which is best for finding out about the objective world. If we thought of them as merely instrumental in this way to the search for objective truth we could simultaneously adopt all frameworks that do not conflict. There would be no need to choose among alternatives. The relation of 'being an alternative to' must therefore be understood not in terms of truth or falsity at all, but in connection with some goal or purpose for which linguistic frameworks are adopted.

It is no doubt too much to expect that we can specify very precisely the goal or goals relative to which linguistic frameworks are to be reckoned as genuine alternatives. But even with something as vague as the goal of 'making sense of our experience' we run into difficulties in understanding Carnap's view. The language of sense-data, the language of things, and alternatives to the language of things with different structures are all presumably different ways of making sense of our experience, and we are free to choose among them for that purpose. But the very description of that common goal appears committed to something called 'us' and something that happens to us, called 'experience'. That we exist and have experience cannot be simply a truth 'internal' to the thing language or to the 'phenomenal' language or to some other particular language that might be expected to lead to that goal, since it is something that presumably remains true whichever of the various alternatives is chosen. If not, the different languages would not be genuine alternatives subserving the same common goal; they would merely be different. Is the truth about 'us' and our 'experience' something that is common to all those alternative frameworks, with a common 'internal' statement in each? If not, where does it belong? It cannot be 'external' to all linguistic frameworks, since it would then be meaningless. But if it is 'internal' to one or more frameworks, what would be the effect of our abandoning those frameworks to which it belongs in favour of an alternative which lacks it altogether?

These are questions Carnap does not answer—perhaps not

surprisingly—but even leaving them aside it remains difficult to grasp his positive theory. He thinks the traditional philosopher misunderstands the relationship between the linguistic framework of external things and the truths expressed and known 'within' that framework, but what exactly is his own non-sceptical account of that relationship? He opposes the view that there are truths that hold quite independently of our adoption of this or that framework, and that suggests that for Carnap statements about external things would not be true or false if we had not adopted the thing language. Aside from the problem, recently broached, of what linguistic framework that thesis itself belongs to, there is now the problem of understanding exactly what it says, or of finding some reason to accept it.

What does it mean to say that the statements we make about external things in the 'linguistic framework' of external things would not be true or false if we had not adopted that framework? Take the truth that there are mountains in Africa. It is presumably a statement 'internal' to the language of things. Not only is it true, we also know it is. It expresses part of our knowledge of the world of things. Equipped with the rules for forming sentences about external things, and for testing, accepting, or rejecting them, human beings have had the appropriate experiences and have thereby confirmed that statement. So much is Carnap's theory of knowledge. What does it mean to say in addition that that is not a truth that holds independently of our adopting the language of things? Let us grant that under some circumstances we might not have adopted the language of things, and even that we could now decide to reject that language and no longer speak that way. Does it follow from Carnap's view that under those circumstances the statement we can now make and understand about mountains in Africa would no longer be true? No doubt that statement would never have been made if no one had had a language in which to talk about external things, and no doubt it would never be made again if no one from now on were ever to speak or think in that way. But that is not what I am asking. I am asking whether it is Carnap's view that that statement we can now make and understand about mountains in Africa would no longer be true if we abandoned the thing language, or would not have been true if we had never adopted it.

If that does follow from Carnap's view it is difficult to see how his view could possibly be right. To say that it would not have been true that there are mountains in Africa if we had not adopted the language of things, or that it would not be true if we were to abandon that language, seems to amount to the absurd idea that whether there are mountains in Africa or not depends on how we choose to speak or think. That would be idealism of truly heroic proportions. It is absurd because we already know enough about mountains to know that they are not affected one way or the other by how human beings decide to speak or think. The mountains were there (or were not) long before human beings or any other perceiving or thinking subjects appeared on the scene. That too is something we know 'within' the language of things. Taken as a statement 'internal' to the language of things, Carnap's thesis is obviously false. It conflicts with a great deal of what we already take ourselves to know about the things around us. Considered 'empirically', it is a form of idealism that simply flies in the face of the known facts.

It is no doubt misguided to take Carnap's thesis 'empirically' or 'internally', as itself something said 'within' the language of things. But it must be 'internal' to some framework or other, or else it is meaningless. In any case, it is a view about the relation between the adoption of a linguistic framework and the statements expressible 'within' that framework, and if it implies that those 'internal' statements would be neither true nor false if the framework in question had not been adopted, it still looks like an unacceptable idealism, whether 'empirical' or not. It still seems to imply that the mountains in Africa are in some way dependent on human choice or human forms of speech or thought. And of course it is not just a matter of mountains in Africa, or even of external things generally. The truth-values of all 'internal' statements in any 'system' would be dependent on human choice or human speech or thought in the same way. So the things we say about numbers, or propositions, or space-time points, or whatever it might be, would not be true if we had not decided to speak that way.

It is worth stressing just how important this apparently unavoidably idealist thesis is for a view like Carnap's. If it does not follow from his view that truths 'internal' to the language of things would be neither true nor false if that framework had not been adopted, his account cannot be distinguished from the traditional sceptical conception it was meant to supplant. He would then be leaving room for the possibility that truths about things remain true even if we abandon the thing language, and would have been true independently of our having adopted it. And that in turn would allow (as on the traditional view) that our adoption of a linguistic framework is necessary only to provide us with some means of formulating and eventually coming to know what is or is not true independently of our adoption of that framework. That is precisely what renders intelligible what Carnap would call a 'theoretical' question about the adequacy or acceptability of the thing language as a whole. It would make sense to ask whether the particular means we have chosen do or do not enable us to know the way things objectively are.

The unintelligibility of any such 'theoretical' question about the thing language as a whole is the heart of Carnap's opposition to the traditional conception. It is easy to see why. The idea that the way things objectively are is completely independent of us and our language, and that we seek knowledge of those independent facts, is what lies behind the traditional philosophical investigation of our knowledge. It is what makes possible the conclusion that even when our best procedures are followed as carefully and as thoroughly as we can humanly manage, things might still be other than we believe them to be, and so we can never know.

Carnap accepts what I have called the conditional correctness of scepticism: if the traditional philosopher did succeed in raising a meaningful question about our knowledge of the world, his sceptical conclusion would be correct—we could never know. If Carnap did not deny that the assertions we now make 'within' the thing language would remain true or false quite independently of our adopting that language, his account would be as tolerant of the sceptical question as is the traditional conception of our relation to the things around us. That denial is therefore essential to Carnap's position despite its obscurity and its apparent commitment to some form of idealism.

Kant also accepts what I have called the conditional correctness of scepticism. He too sees that if Descartes's description of our experience and its relation to the things around us were correct, we could never know whether there are external things. Kant is aware of the depth and scope required of any investigation that could satisfactorily refute that conception of Descartes's. It would have to discover the very conditions of our being able to think of an external world—indeed of our even being able to think at all—and only out of those conditions could the impossibility of 'empirical' or sceptical idealism be derived. But we saw that for Kant the only way that derivation can succeed and thereby explain our knowledge is by establishing the truth of idealism. If we did not take refuge in idealism, and did not accept the 'Copernican' point that objects must conform to our knowledge or to the constitution of our understanding and sensibility, we could never explain how our knowledge is possible.

What might be called the 'pre-Copernican' idea that our perception and knowledge simply conform or fail to conform to objects is what Kant thinks makes an explanation of knowledge impossible. That is why 'outer things' cannot be regarded as things in themselves independent of us, and why idealism rather than realism must be accepted in the philosophical explanation of our knowledge. Carnap's thesis that the truths we come to know once we have adopted a particular linguistic framework are not to be understood as true independently of our adoption of that framework is another version of that same Kantian or 'Copernican' idea. And it is held for the same reason. If we could think of those statements as independently true or false whether we had adopted a particular framework in which to express them or not, there would be no explaining how knowledge of them is possible. A potential gap would have been opened between the most we can establish 'within' the framework and what is objectively true independently of it. Carnap's account of our knowledge is in that respect fully Kantian, and it seems to inherit all the obscurity and the idealism of the Kantian view as well. Perhaps it is not 'empirical' idealism, 'internal' to the framework of our knowledge of the things around us, but it is idealism or non-realism nevertheless. If not, there would be no explaining how knowledge is possible.

In fact, Carnap's account parallels Kant's theory in almost every other respect. For both philosophers there can be a kind of detachment or stepping back from our beliefs about external things. We can engage in a philosophical scrutiny of our everyday beliefs taken all together. But that philosophical investigation of those beliefs is not a mere assessment of their credentials—an examination of how well, if at all, they are supported by experience. It is concerned rather with the conditions that make those beliefs even so much as possible, with how we can even think intelligibly about things around us in space. Out of those conditions alone both Kant and Carnap claim to derive the consequence that Descartes's sceptical conclusion can never be reached. The verifiability principle is held to express a condition of intelligible thought, and it leads directly to the impossibility of scepticism. But in order to explain how our knowledge is possible and how the traditional philosopher is wrongly led into scepticism, Carnap also provides a theory of knowledge that would explain why intelligibility requires verifiability. His notion of alternative linguistic frameworks denies the possibility of 'external' theoretical grounds on which such frameworks could be judged adequate or inadequate. The parallel Kantian explanation is transcendental idealism; if we allowed that the things we sought to know were fully independent of our ways of perceiving and knowing them, scepticism would be inevitable. Transcendental idealism is difficult to square with an empirical verifiability principle of meaning. Does Carnap's own positive theory fare any better in that respect?

It is a question of the status of Carnap's own theory. The theory is meant to explain the very thing Kant's transcendental idealism is meant to explain—the possibility of our empirical knowledge—but without itself overstepping the limits of intelligibility as, on verificationist grounds, Kant's transcendental idealism appears to do. Kant's theory is *a priori*, but for the verificationist the only truths that can be known *a priori* are analytic, true solely by virtue of the meanings of their terms. That is not a rejection of the Kantian idea of philosophy as a separate *a priori* discipline investigating the concepts and principles employed in the sciences and in everyday life, but it is a denial that we can discover by *a priori* means any truths that are not already included in or guaranteed by the meanings of those concepts and principles themselves. Philosophy on this view is 'conceptual analysis'. For the verificationist Kant goes wrong not in his conception of philosophy as *a priori*, or in his idea that the impossibility of scepticism can be established and explained on purely *a priori* grounds, but only in his conception of the scope and nature of *a priori* knowledge itself. Kant thought transcendental idealism had to be true even for the *a priori* investigation he had in mind to be possible, but he did not think his *a priori* investigations led only to analytic truths. Carnap would condemn transcendental idealism as meaningless, but in order to leave room for his own theory he would have to show that everything he relies on in his own philosophical investigation of the possibility of knowledge is itself analytic, true solely by virtue of the meanings of its terms. Can that be said of Carnap's thesis that no statements about external things are true or false independently of our adoption of the thing language? What concepts is it an analysis of? What framework do those concepts belong to? And is that thesis, whether analytic or not, itself 'internal' to some particular framework? And whether it is or not, isn't it as much an expression of idealism as Kant's transcendental idealism is?

These are all difficulties we face in trying to understand Carnap's positive theory of alternative linguistic frameworks. I will not pursue them further, because by now we might begin to wonder whether they are really difficulties that stand in the way of understanding and accepting the verifiability principle itself. Even if Carnap's theory is no improvement on Kant's obscure idealist explanation of our knowledge of the world, and even if it makes no advance over the scepticism or idealism that seems inevitable on the traditional account, that might show that the basic mistake is to try to provide any competing theory at all to what the traditional philosopher offers. A purely negative or deflationary use of the verifiability principle would simply eliminate the traditional problem as meaningless. If that succeeded, no more would be needed to undermine the threat of scepticism, and we would be wise to resist any temptation we might feel to offer an acceptable positive answer to what would after all have been eliminated as a meaningless pseudo-question.

But even such a purely negative anti-philosophical strategy, for all its austerity, still comes up against the formidable problem of the status or acceptability of the verifiability principle itself. Kant saw the acceptance of transcendental idealism as the only way of getting a proof of the impossibility of Descartes's scepticism. The verifiability principle leads directly to that anti-sceptical result, but that will give us reason to abandon Descartes's scepticism as meaningless only if we have good reason to accept the verifiability principle as stating a necessary condition of any meaningful sentence or any intelligible thought. Whether the principle can be taken in that way depends on how it is established. Trying to establish it in the appropriate way can be expected to lead one well beyond the austere deflationary strategy of simply applying a principle to weed out what it says are the lush excrescences of meaningless philosophical speculation.

The principle is meant to distinguish the meaningful from the meaningless, and that might suggest that it will be acceptable as long as it draws that distinction correctly: if everything that satisfies the conditions stated in the principle is in fact meaningful and everything that fails to satisfy them meaningless. Judging the acceptability of the principle would then be a matter of seeing how well it captures a distinction we already know how to draw. The only effective test would be whether sentences we already regard as meaningful and as meaningless get classified in what we regard as the right way. But even if the principle proved extensionally or descriptively adequate in this way as far as we had tested it at any given time, and therefore seemed quite likely to draw the distinction between the meaningful and the meaningless everywhere just as we do, it would never put us in a position to rule out as meaningless something we already and quite independently think we find intelligible. Taken as a statement of the conditions we actually rely on in drawing the distinction as we do, the principle would have to answer to our independent judgements of meaningfulness, and could not be used as a weapon to deprive us of something we are fairly sure we already understand.

This answerability of the principle to our prior judgements was to a certain extent acknowledged by those who tried hardest to formulate a satisfactory principle of meaningfulness. Like the framers of immigration laws, they already knew what they wanted to exclude, and the task was to find an acceptably-worded principle that would be sure to exclude everything undesirable but no more. Early drafts were rejected when they were seen to admit the obviously unacceptable (e.g. statements about the Absolute) or to make it impossible for the obviously respectable (e.g. general laws of nature) ever to be admitted. No fully satisfactory law was ever framed. But even if it had been it would have to have been shown to be more than a principle which happens to capture a distinction we all know how to draw, and certainly more than a device that would separate what logical positivists approve of from what they would like to exclude from serious intellectual concern.

Behind any truly deflationary use of the verifiability principle there would have to be at least the outlines of a conception or theory of how intelligible thought is possible, and only in the articulation and defence of that conception or theory could the basis be found for eliminating as meaningless philosophical problems which otherwise seem intelligible enough. Explaining and defending such a theory would not be simply a matter of applying a powerful destructive instrument to a meaningless philosophical problem. It would require the sort of thing that Kant, for all his obscurity and idealism, tried to provide. It would have to be explained why the verifiability principle is correct, why the possibility of empirical confirmation is required for any intelligible thought. I am not at the moment suggesting that that cannot be done, but I do suggest that doing it would be indistinguishable from explaining how thought and knowledge about the world around us are possible. That is just what the traditional epistemologist tries to explain.

The original defenders of the verifiability principle based their acceptance, first, on the idea that a sentence is meaningful only if it has 'factual content' or expresses a state of affairs, and second, on the claim that understanding a sentence is a matter of knowing what state of affairs would obtain if it were true or would fail to obtain if it were false.[6] So far there is nothing uniquely congenial to verificationism in that. What gives those reflections a verificationist twist is the further idea that we cannot even understand something that we could never know to be true or know to be false or at least have more reason to accept than to reject. Empirical confirmability was taken, largely without argument, as the criterion of the meaningful, and the problem of formulating an acceptable principle of meaningfulness became the problem of formulating an acceptable definition of empirical confirmability. Even as an attempt to pick out the empirically confirmable sentences from all other expressions we can formulate, the programme failed. But if that definitional task had succeeded we would still need an additional argument to show that the empirically confirmable so defined is co-extensive with the meaningful, and to explain why that is so. Discussion of the verifiability principle never got to that crucial question. It got stalled at an earlier step—at the definition of 'empirically confirmable' itself.

As with most such programmes in philosophy, what is interesting and important is not that it failed but why. In this case the difficulty arose from those sentences and those methods of confirmation that in any way involve 'theory' or 'inferred entities' as opposed to being simple reports of direct observation.[7] If our only source of empirical knowledge were simple enumerative induction on generalizations framed solely in predicates definable in unquestionably 'sensory' terms, perhaps success would have been in sight. But our terms and our reasoning do not always (perhaps

[6] e.g., see Carnap's sketch of 'The Meaning Criterion' (PsP, 325-8).

[7] In addition to Hempel's classic 'Empiricist Criteria of Cognitive Significance' see also 'The Theoretician's Dilemma: A Study in the Logic of Theory Construction' in his *Aspects of Scientific Explanation.*

ever) follow such a simple pattern; they are not so strictly tied to what on that conception is called 'sensory experience'. The history of the failure of logical positivism is not my main concern. What is important for present purposes is that verificationists could have succeeded only if they could have explained how we can and do confirm our beliefs in experience, and hence how we can come to know things about the world around us. That is what an adequate definition of empirical confirmability would have provided. But if that had been done there would be no need to go on to fashion an instrument with which to eliminate philosophical scepticism as meaningless. We would already have a positive non-sceptical explanation of how our knowledge of the word is possible—a positive philosophical theory of knowledge that would explain just what the traditional epistemologist wanted to explain.

This brings out an important and little-recognized fact about the relation between the verifiability theory of meaningfulness and the traditional problem of our knowledge of the external world. It is customary to see only a rather one-sided contest between them—the principle implies that the sceptical answer to the problem is meaningless, so the problem itself is meaningless if it inevitably leads to a sceptical answer. But in fact the traditional philosopher concerned to understand our knowledge of the world around us and the verificationist seeking a principle to limit the range of meaningful sentences to the empirically confirmable are both faced with precisely the same task: to explain how our beliefs can be empirically confirmed, or how our experience can give us more reason to believe one thing rather than another. In carrying out this common task, the sceptical philosopher and the verificationist differ as to whether anything fulfilling the verificationist's standards for empirical confirmation really does amount to a case of confirmation or not. This is a dispute about what our standards actually are, how they are to be inferred from our practices in everyday life and in science, and whether anything actually fulfils them. Neither side is automatically in a better position than the other for answering those questions. It is a shared problem.

To take our familiar example, the sentence 'I am sitting by the fire with a piece of paper in my hand' would seem on ordinary standards to be easily confirmable or disconfirmable simply by looking around me and seeing what I find. That is what we go on in everyday life. But if, as the traditional sceptical philosopher maintains, what we normally accept as confirmation in everyday life does not fulfil all the conditions we ourselves on reflection can see to be strictly required for empirical confirmation, a definition of confirmation that simply codifies those unreflective everyday procedures will be inadequate. If, strictly speaking, I must know that I am not dreaming if I am to know that that simple sentence is true, then when I have not ruled out or even considered that possibility (as I will not have done in everyday life), its looking and feeling to me just as if I were sitting by the fire with a piece of paper in my hand gives me no more reason to believe that I am really sitting there than to believe that I am not. On the traditional conception, what is normally accepted as positive confirmation is, strictly speaking, no confirmation at all. No statements about the world around us would be confirmable or disconfirmable to any degree. The verifiability principle implies that if that were true no statements about the external world would be meaningful and so scepticism itself would be incoherent. But that in itself is no argument against the traditional conception of our standards of confirmation. The conflict between the two views arises in the very attempt even to formulate the verifiability principle, in the attempt to define empirical confirmability. An adequate verifiability principle would imply that there could be no meaningful difficulty of the sort the traditional philosopher raises. But no such principle can be appealed to simply to eliminate what is in effect an objection to the crucial notion of confirmation used in the formulation of that very principle.

This stand-off shows that a definition and defence of a notion of empirical confirmability that actually applies to the sentences we utter and accept about the world around us would have to explain how and why what I am calling the traditional conception of our everyday practices of confirmation is misguided. The sceptical arguments cannot be finally dismissed until their underlying conception of the relation between the 'internal', engaged assertions of everyday life and the 'external', detached assessment we make of them in philosophy has been exposed as incoherent. On that conception we are for various practical reasons normally satisfied with less than what we can see to be the full conditions of knowledge or reasonable belief, and we can be brought to see that those full conditions are never satisfied in everyday life. Any successful theory of empirical confirmability would therefore have to show what is wrong with that conception—why what ordinarily passes for confirmation really is confirmation after all.[8] Until that had been done, the traditional conception would stand as a constant challenge to any proposed definition.

My efforts to even the scales between verificationism and the traditional epistemological enterprise might be felt to impose unreasonable demands on the verificationist without requiring comparable thoroughness and precision on the part of the traditional sceptical philosopher. I have argued that a thoroughly successful definition and defence of an applicable notion of empirical confirmation would require a solution to the same problem that faces the traditional epistemologist. Only then could an empirical verifiability principle of meaningfulness be precisely formulated. But even if such a principle has not been precisely and definitively stated, and even if many unsolved problems remain, it can seem that verificationism might nevertheless be on the right track. Whatever the difficulties of final formulation might be, we might have enough of an intuitive idea of empirical confirmation to see that in some form or another a verifiability

[8] This requirement was partly honoured in attempts to solve the problem of justifying 'induction'. What was to be explained was how getting more of what is normally regarded as 'positive evidence' does indeed give us more reason to believe a hypothesis. It is interesting to note that verificationists who grappled with the problem of induction were not content simply to appeal to their principle to eliminate the whole problem as meaningless—although that follows from the verifiability principle, just as the meaninglessness of the problem of the external world does. More of an attempt was made to expose in some detail the 'illegitimate' assumptions behind Hume's sceptical argument about 'induction' than was made in the parallel case of Descartes's argument about the external world.

principle of meaningfulness might well be true. Surely we should not demand a definitive statement of the idea before we can even begin to assess its plausibility and to reflect on its implications.

In this particular case an insistence on the details of precise formulation seems especially beside the point, since the problem of the external world as traditionally conceived is obviously empirically undecidable on any conception of empirical confirmability one might choose. That is precisely what the difficulty of our knowing anything about the world around us amounts to—the impossibility of our getting any empirical evidence that would render a belief about the world around us any more reasonable than its opposite. That common ground must be shared by the sceptic and the verificationist. So it will seem unreasonable to demand that the verifiability principle must be carefully and precisely stated before it can be used to undermine scepticism. Even the sceptical philosopher himself insists on the impossibility of empirical confirmation or disconfirmation of everything we say or believe about the world around us. As long as verifiability in some form or other is linked with meaningfulness, all our talk about the world around us will be condemned as meaningless if the sceptic is right that we can never know or have any reason to believe anything about the world.

I think this puts the issue on the proper footing. We can leave to one side large questions about the feasibility of a 'rational reconstruction' of all human knowledge and simply reflect on the plausibility of the idea that meaningfulness is directly linked to verifiability. But how are we to assess in these rough-and-ready terms the plausibility of verificationism? It seems to me that we cannot do it independently of assessing the plausibility of the sceptical arguments it is intended to dismiss. G. E. Moore thought he simply knew the sceptical conclusion was false, just as the detective knew his apprentice's original suggestion was wrong, and there was then no real need to look carefully into the reasoning that produced it. But someone who is as convinced of the truth of the verifiability principle as Moore was of the existence of his hands cannot equally easily decline to look carefully into the source of the (to him spurious) plausibility of the sceptical arguments. Even if verificationism is true we still need an explanation of how and why the traditional philosophical investigation goes wrong.

I do not mean we need such an explanation only to satisfy pedantic curiosity or to account for the fact that many people have found those arguments convincing. I mean that we need an intelligible diagnosis of how and why scepticism goes wrong even in order finally to accept the verifiability principle. The conclusion of Descartes's reflections as I presented them is said to be meaningless by the verifiability principle, but it certainly does not *seem* meaningless. Whatever our reactions to it might be, and however intolerable we find it, I think we do not initially find ourselves dismissing it as literally without meaning. We seem to understand it well enough to see what would be the case if it were true. Of course that initial appearance of intelligibility might turn out on reflection to be illusory. But it might also turn out not to be illusory. In trying to decide the issue whether the sceptical conclusion is intelligible or not, our original response to the reasoning that leads up to it is a large part of what we have to go on. We cannot simply dismiss our response in the face of a certain principle which perhaps on other grounds seems plausible enough and conflicts with it.

The point is that for anyone who finds the sceptical argument at all persuasive its very persuasiveness provides just as strong an argument against accepting the verifiability principle as that principle can provide against the meaningfulness of the sceptical conclusion. Scepticism says no one ever has any reason to believe anything about the world around us. Verificationism says that no statements about the world around us would therefore be meaningful. But that amounts just as much to a *reductio ad absurdum* of the verifiability principle as to a rejection of scepticism about the external world. Any theory of meaningfulness that implies that such obviously intelligible sentences as 'There are mountains in Africa', 'I am sitting by the fire with a piece of paper in my hand', and 'Here is a human hand' mean nothing would clearly be unacceptable. Of course the verifiability principle implies that those sentences are meaningless only when it is conjoined with the traditional epistemological investigation that concludes that they can never be known. But unless we saw how and why that sceptical argument is unacceptable we would have excellent reason for not accepting the verifiability principle. Our reflection on the link between meaningfulness and verifiability would have come up against the obvious counter-example of scepticism about the external world.

To forestall that kind of objection, we would have to see how and why the verifiability principle has nothing to fear from the sceptical argument. That would require an explanation of how the general sceptical conclusion can be meaningless (as the principle implies) even though particular everyday assertions and knowledge-claims about the world around us are perfectly meaningful on verifiability grounds. It cannot be simply because the meaningful assertions are particular and the sceptical conclusions general. The force of Descartes's conclusion comes from our inclination to take what he says about the particular case he considers as representative of all of our putative knowledge of the world. We know that verificationists are rightly suspicious of that generalizing move. For Carnap, assertions about reality made 'within' the framework of things cannot be meaningfully made about the whole system. But whatever blocks that step is not simply the complete generality of those allegedly meaningless assertions. 'There are external things' and 'We know there are external things' are general sentences, and they are perfectly meaningful as long as they are taken 'internally', as following trivially from particular assertions or knowledge-claims about the world around us. It is only when they are taken 'externally' that they become meaningless on verifiability grounds, so what needs to be explained is the impossibility of the move from the 'internal' to the 'external', and not that from the particular to the general. That would require an explanation of why the traditional conception of the relation between 'internal' and 'external' questions and assertions cannot be correct. That is just what I think must be explained if scepticism is to be avoided.

Descartes's conclusion might be rejected on verificationist grounds by arguing that even the particular case he considers is meaningless from the outset, since 'I am sitting by the fire with a piece of paper in my hand' is treated as unverifiable. It would then have to be explained why the verifiability principle does not imply that all particular verdicts in everyday life are equally meaningless. 'I do not know whether sitting in a draught can cause a cold' or 'The airplane spotter does not know whether that plane is an F' are not supposed to be meaningless on verifiability grounds, and indeed the sentence 'I do not know whether or not I am sitting by the fire with a piece of paper in my hand' is not supposed to be meaningless either. It might sometimes be true. If the verifiability principle condemns it as meaningless as used by Descartes on that particular occasion there must be some way in which his use of it on that occasion deviates from the way it is used when it is used meaningfully. Without some understanding of that difference the verificationist will simply be in the position of knowing that *something* has gone wrong in Descartes's reasoning, but his only warrant for the suspicion of meaninglessness will be the verifiability principle itself. Once again it would be more plausible to reject that principle than to agree that Descartes's sentence never means anything. If Descartes is in effect treating even that particular case, as it were, 'externally' from the outset, and not as one would treat such a question in a particular 'internal' case, some account of the difference between them must be given. The traditional sceptical philosopher has his own account of that difference and of why only the detached 'external' verdict gives us the truth about our position. The verifiability principle will remain implausible until it is understood why that traditional conception of the 'internal' and the 'external' cannot be correct.

So there appears to be no verificationist short-cut to a dismissal of philosophical scepticism. If, as the verificationist would agree, it cannot be answered or refuted directly in experience as Moore tried to do, the only way the question itself can be exposed as meaningless without also condemning everything else as meaningless is to carefully dismantle the traditional conception of the problem and to explain how and why the move from meaningful 'internal' to meaningless 'external' assertions cannot be made. When that had been done it would not matter, as far as the fate of scepticism is concerned, whether the verifiability principle of meaningfulness were true or not. We would already see that the Cartesian sceptical conclusion is unreachable, and perhaps we would even understand why. But as long as that sceptical conclusion continues to look reachable, perhaps even reasonable, we will have precisely that same reason for rejecting the verifiability principle of meaning.

VI

Naturalized Epistemology

The traditional Cartesian examination aims at an assessment of all our knowledge of the world all at once, and it takes the form of a judgement on that knowledge made from what looks like a detached 'external' position. I have tried to show that on the traditional conception of the philosophical enterprise and its relation to the knowledge-claims we make in science and in everyday life there is no substance in the familiar charge that scepticism violates or distorts the meanings of the very words used to express it. And I have tried to suggest how, once we become familiar with the prospect from that lofty, detached philosophical standpoint, it becomes difficult to see how anything but scepticism could be the proper verdict on our putative knowledge of the world. Scepticism can come to seem inevitable, not just invulnerable against a certain line of attack.

When we try to explain all our knowledge of the world as Descartes does we try to understand how the things we believe in science and in everyday life are connected with and warranted by the bases or grounds on which we come to believe them. All possible evidence is ultimately sensory; our knowledge of the world is empirical. But it cannot be denied that any particular course of sensory experience could fail to give us reliable information as to how things are; the world can be different from the way it is perceived to be. Within the special context of the traditional epistemological project this otherwise apparently harmless truism seems to have disastrous consequences. If all our knowledge of the world around us is in question all at once we cannot then help ourselves to some independently reliable information about the world, as we usually do, to settle the question whether our present course of experience is or is not on this occasion a reliable guide to the way things are. Once we have granted that the grounds or bases of all our beliefs about the world are restricted to what we can get through the senses, and we have distinguished in general between everything we get through the senses and what is or is not true of the external world around us, there will be no eliminating the possibility that the external world is completely different from what we perceive it and believe it to be. The dream-possibility as it is deployed in Descartes's argument is a dramatic illustration of the point. If it must be eliminated for knowledge of the world to be possible, and it cannot be eliminated on the basis of sensory experience alone, sensory knowledge of the world is impossible.

We then appear to ourselves to be in the position of someone limited to the television screens in a locked room. If we really imagine him fully restricted to the images he can see, with no independent information about whether or not those images are generated in the normal way by the states of affairs they unquestionably represent, I think we must conclude that he knows nothing of the world outside the room. Of course it would be difficult if not impossible to contrive an actual case like this. Unless the victim had been raised in the room since birth he would already possess at least some reliable information about the outside world when he began his confinement. But from those television screens alone, with no such independent information, he could never know. If our information in everyday life were similarly restricted to what we get through the senses, so that it was always an additional step to any conclusion about the world beyond them, our knowledge would be similarly restricted to what is directly available to us and could never extend to the external world beyond.

The apparent inevitability of this conclusion can make it look as if what must be avoided is the idea that our sense-experience can be understood in that Cartesian way—as providing us only with information that leaves it open whether the world around us is this way rather than that. That is how it looked to Kant; a completely general distinction between what we get through the senses and what is or is not true of the external world would cut us off forever from knowledge of the world around us. But perhaps that general distinction has fatal sceptical consequences only within the context of the traditional philosopher's conception of the epistemological task. Perhaps it is only when it is put to work from a detached 'external' viewpoint that the distinction between what we are given through the senses and what is true of the external world can be seen to make knowledge impossible. If so, scepticism might be avoided and our knowledge of the world made intelligble without abandoning a general distinction between 'the sensory given' and what is true of the external world. It would be a matter of avoiding or exposing as illusory that detached 'external' standpoint from which our epistemic position has traditionally seemed so impoverished.

W. V. Quine's 'naturalized epistemology' rests on the denial of any such 'external' position. Science and everyday knowledge and the languages and thought processes in which they are pursued and expressed are to be seen as natural phenomena and studied and described and explained scientifically like any other part of the natural world. That is just the empirical study of how knowledge is possible from which Kant's special *a priori* investigation was distinguished. But epistemology or the theory of knowledge is nothing more than the study of what knowledge is and how it comes to be. And for Quine there is no reason to suppose that the study of human knowledge or language or thought requires a fundamentally different sort of investigation from the study of physics or animal behaviour or mathematics. All attempts to find out about ourselves and the world must be made from within the conceptual and scientific resources we have already developed for finding out about anything. Even those questions traditionally regarded as especially philosophical can only be pursued from within what we now take to be our knowledge or our best hypotheses as to how things are. We have no alternative. Whatever the proper role of the philosopher might be, then, it cannot require an investigation of the world or of science or of our conceptual resources by someone who even momentarily stands outside them.

There is no such cosmic exile. He cannot study and revise the fundamental conceptual scheme of science and commonsense without having some conceptual scheme, the same or another no less in need of philosophical scrutiny, in which to work.[1]

There is no special detached position from which a philosopher might conduct such inquiries.

Science, even at the most abstract reaches of theoretical physics, proceeds always 'from within'. Hypotheses and theories are evaluated and accepted or rejected in the light of what is already known or can somehow be discovered. Scientists, then, are like sailors who must repair or rebuild their ship while staying afloat on it in the open sea. There is no dry-dock in which they can lay a new keel and start again from new foundations; nor can they simply abandon ship and choose another of more efficient design. There is no other. This metaphor of Neurath's is Quine's favourite image for the scientific enterprise, and for him 'the philosopher and the scientist are in the same boat' (WO, 3). The philosopher too is concerned with reality, with how things are, but his investigations are simply more general than geography or physics or mathematics. To determine what particular kinds of physical objects there are is the task of the natural scientist. Whether there are even prime numbers, for example, is a question for the mathematician. But the acceptance of the realm of physical objects itself, or of numbers or classes, is a question that typically falls to the philosopher. But such questions differ from the others only in 'breadth of categories' (WO, 275). Philosophy is simply a more general attempt to discover the truth and advance our understanding of the world and our place in it 'from within'.

It is Carnap's view that philosophical questions that appear to be about reality or what there is are really 'practical' questions to be resolved by the adoption of this or that linguistic framework for talking about reality. Philosophy deals with words or linguistic frameworks for understanding reality, not with reality itself. It is a 'second-order' or 'metascientific' investigation. We saw that any such view would apparently have to countenance an inquiry or activity that takes place 'outside' mathematics or physics or the framework of ordinary spatial things; its questions would be

[1] W. V.Quine, *Word and Object*, pp. 275–6. (Hereafter cited as WO.)

'external' to all such frameworks. We found difficulty in understanding the 'externality' of Carnap's questions and in accepting the associated idealist thesis that no facts hold or fail to hold independently of our adopting this or that linguistic framework. And there was the further difficulty of identifying the linguistic framework, if any, to which that thesis itself belongs. Quine's conception of philosophy as continuous with the rest of science would avoid all those obscurities.

He does not deny that ontological questions traditionally regarded as philosophical seem to be more about words or about our conceptual framework than about extra-linguistic reality. They also seem to be governed more by pragmatic considerations of convenience, simplicity and overall conceptual economy than by current matters of observable fact. As we move from asking whether there are mountains in Africa or unicorns anywhere to asking whether there are numbers or propositions or physical objects we seem to move to a different sort of question. Carnap thought it was the kind of question that cannot be settled by observation or theoretical considerations at all.

Carnap's conclusion ought to be resisted, according to Quine. It is true that in philosophy it is usually more profitable to talk about the terms and frameworks we use to understand reality than to talk directly about reality itself. For Quine that is simply because progress on ontological philosophical issues is more likely if the participants engage in 'semantic ascent' and discuss the theoretical efficacy of their terms by mentioning them in the 'formal mode' rather than simply using them in the 'material mode' to talk directly about what does or does not exist. Such direct use obscures the theoretical character of ontological disputes. But semantic ascent from the 'material' to the 'formal' mode is possible everywhere; it does not apply uniquely to philosophy or even to the most abstract levels of discourse. Nor does the possibility of 'semantic ascent' show that assertions or questions that mention words rather than using them to talk directly about reality are really only about words or linguistic frameworks and not about the reality they are used to describe. For example, what we regard as the empirically known contingent truth that there are wombats in Tasmania can be paraphrased in the 'formal mode' as ' "Wombat" is true of some creatures in Tasmania', but that does not transform it into an assertion solely about language and not about extra-linguistic reality (WO, 272).

On Quine's view, Carnap's conception of philosophical questions as linguistic and as resolvable only on pragmatic and never on factual grounds arises partly from a misreading of the significance of semantic ascent.

> For it is not as though considerations of systematic efficacy, broadly pragmatic considerations, were operative only when we make a semantic ascent and talk of theory, and factual considerations of the behavior of objects in the world were operative only when we avoid semantic ascent and talk within the theory. Considerations of systematic efficacy are equally essential in both cases; it is just that in the one case we voice them and in the other we are tacitly guided by them. (WO, 274.)

This is not a rejection of Carnap's stress on pragmatic considerations such as convenience or simplicity of theory to philosophical questions; it is rather a reminder of the importance of such factors to all investigations into what is the case, and hence a denial of the distinction Carnap would draw between philosophy and everything else.

Kant also would distinguish between philosophy and everything else, and Quine's 'naturalizing' of philosophy obviously stands equally opposed to the Kantian idea of a special *a priori* philosophical investigation, and indeed to the belief that there is any *a priori* knowledge at all. But Kant's and Carnap's views, for all their obscurities, were meant to explain how traditional scepticism about the external world is to be avoided. They both acknowledge what I called the conditional correctness of scepticism: if the traditional philosopher had managed to raise a meaningful theoretical question about the external world his sceptical answer to it would be correct. Quine rejects the Kantian and Carnapian accounts of philosophical problems and insists on the 'scientific' or 'theoretical' character of the question about external physical objects and our knowledge of them. Does he thereby avoid the scepticism that Kant and Carnap (and Descartes for that matter) would argue is then inevitable? Does Quine's naturalized or scientific epistemology give a satisfactory answer to the very question Kant and Carnap despaired of answering directly and so developed a special philosophical theory to explain away? Does Quine even try to answer that very question? It is not easy to say.

Many things he says about his conception of epistemology make it sound as if it is meant to answer the very question the traditional philosopher found himself faced with. 'Given only the evidence of our senses', Quine asks, 'how do we arrive at our theory of the world'?[2] The problem arises because 'we know external things only mediately through our senses'; 'physical things generally, however remote, become known to us only through the effects which they help to induce at our sensory surfaces' (WO, 1). Here we have what looks like a completely general problem—how do we come to know anything at all about external physical things?—which is to be answered by an explanation of how what we get through the senses provides us with the knowledge we want to explain. Relative to what we claim to know about the world around us, Quine says, our sensory 'input' is 'meager'. That is what gives rise to the problem—to explain how the human animal could have arrived at 'a description of the three-dimensional external world and its history'[3] from 'the sensory information that could reach him' (RR, 2) at his sensory surfaces. This sounds in many respects just like the problem Descartes leaves us with at the end of his first Meditation: how, on the basis of what we are immediately aware of in perception, can we ever come to know things about the world around us?

The object of Quine's study is the relation between those sensory stimuli and the knowledge to which they eventually give rise, or 'the relation between the meager input and the torrential output' (EN, 83). But since that relation is itself part of the world around us it is to be studied like any other natural phenomenon. We can observe and experiment with

[2] W. V. Quine, *The Roots of Reference* (La Salle, Illinois, 1974), p. 1. (Hereafter cited as RR.)

[3] W. V. Quine, 'Epistemology Naturalized', in his *Ontological Relativity and Other Essays* (New York, 1969), p. 83. (Hereafter cited as EN.)

human beings while making use of any parts of current natural science that we think might be helpful. The question is how our science or our knowledge of the world has come to be, and the answer is to be found by pursuing that very science whose origins we seek to understand. There is no alternative. Epistemology for Quine must be seen as part of natural science—'naturalized epistemology' is the only epistemology there can be.

One respect in which Quine's conception of his philosophical task seems to resemble that of the traditional epistemologist is his completely general distinction between everything we can get through the senses on the one hand and what is or is not true of the external world on the other. That distinction is essential to the formulation of the problem Quine thinks a naturalized epistemology should answer, just as it is to the traditional problem of the external world. But for Quine the distinction is itself derived from scientific investigation and reflection.

> we can investigate the world, and man as part of it, and thus find out what cues he could have of what goes on around him. Subtracting his cues from his world view, we get man's net contribution as the difference. This difference marks the extent of man's conceptual sovereignty—the domain within which he can revise theory while saving the data. (WO, 5.)

We find by investigation that the 'data' that can be 'saved' are 'meager' relative to the scope of man's 'conceptual sovereignty'. We thereby discover the extent to which all of science is man's 'free creation' or even, in Eddington's phrase, 'a put-up job' (RR, 3–4). By 'science' here Quine means everything we take to be true, including all truths about the external world. What we find when we study man's position in the world is how all those things he believes about the world go far beyond the 'information' or 'data' he gets through his senses.

> It is a matter of scientific fact, or theory, that our only avenue of information about external objects is through the irritation of our sensory surfaces by forces emanating from those objects. There is thus a wide gap between our data and our knowledge of the external world, and it takes bold inference to bridge it.[4]

[4] W. V. Quine, "The Natural Theory of Knowledge', unpublished, 1979, p. 2.

The same gap between 'our data' and 'our knowledge of the external world' that gives rise to the traditional problem seems to be present here, but for Quine the fact that our theory of the world far outstrips its 'sensory or stimulatory background' (WO, 3) is itself a deliverance of science, part of that very theory of the world. So much the better, it would seem, for that distinction, and for the epistemological enterprise itself. The problem a naturalized epistemology must answer is thrown up by the very science whose origins it is meant to explain.

Once we see the epistemological problem in this way, a certain kind of answer to it naturally suggests itself. Of course we do not have all the details of a solution, or even a clear idea in every case of what to do in order to discover them. The scientific study of perception, learning, language-acquisition, and the development and transmission of human knowledge is bound to continue in directions and with methods we cannot at the moment clearly foresee. But for Quine the general outlines of the story are clear enough to give us a very abstract and schematic, but nevertheless illuminating, account of human knowledge. At the level of generality appropriate to philosophy we can explain how human knowledge of the external world is possible.

Our knowledge of external things in general is to be understood in just the way any piece of theoretical knowledge is to be understood relative to the 'data' on which it is based. In order to explain some of the things that happen to ordinary perceivable things, a physicist might invent or appeal to a theory committed to unperceived or even unperceivable objects as a way of introducing greater simplicity and economy of basic principles into his total account of the physical world. The truths he introduces and accepts about molecules, for example, or other extraordinary objects, will not be uniquely determined by all the truths he knows or even can imagine about the ordinary perceivable objects whose behaviour his wider theory is meant to explain. There could be many different possible theories, even perhaps equally simple theories, that could be used to imply and therefore to account for the same set of truths about ordinary perceivable things. He is not forced by those 'data' alone to introduce molecules as a simplifying explanatory device. But the theory he does introduce or appeal to is accepted and retained because it does its job. Relative to those truths about ordinary things, the existence of the molecules is therefore a 'hypothesis' or 'posit'; it does not follow from those truths alone, but it is asserted by a theory which, with other facts and theories, can be shown to imply those ordinary observable truths.

For Quine the existence of physical objects in general is to be understood as a 'hypothesis' or 'posit' in just the same way. It is not a 'hypothesis' or theory relative to a set of truths about ordinary perceivable things, of course—such truths already imply the existence of physical objects. Rather all statements even about ordinary physical things are to be understood as 'hypotheses' or theoretical statements relative to what we get through the senses. They are all 'far in excess of any available data' (WO, 22). Science tells us that the only information that reaches us through the senses is provided by irritations at our sensory surfaces, but all the truths we believe about the physical world around us 'are less than determined by our sensory irritations' (WO, 22), just as the physicist's assertions about molecules are less than determined by observable truths about ordinary physical things. And in the case of our beliefs about the physical world in general it is not simply a matter of our limited experience. The underdetermination would remain 'even if we include all past, present, and future irritations of all the far-flung surfaces of mankind' (WO, 22). The theory or 'hypothesis' of physical objects remains far in excess of all such data. Seen in relation to our sensory surface irritations it is therefore just like the theory or hypothesis of molecules seen in relation to truths about ordinary perceivable things. The only important difference for Quine is that:

> the physicist audibly posits [molecules] for recognized reasons, whereas the hypothesis of ordinary things is shrouded in prehistory. Though for the archaic and unconscious hypothesis of ordinary physical objects we can no more speak of a motive than of motives for being human or mammalian, yet in point of function and survival value it and the hypothesis of molecules are alike. (WO, 22.)

If we can understand how a physicist can come to know there are molecules we can also understand in the same way how we can come to know there are any physical objects at all.

What is the 'function and survival value' that the two sorts of hypotheses are said to share? Precisely that of providing a simpler and more economical total 'theory' while accounting for the 'data' on which that 'theory' is based. Since it is 'underdetermined' by all the 'data', the choice of theory is not uniquely determined, but Quine has long found that the 'hypothesis' of physical objects has succeeded in the task for which, however unconsciously, it was designed. It 'has proved more efficacious than other myths as a device for working a manageable structure into the flux of experience';[5] it gives us 'the smoothest and most adequate overall account of the world' (WO, 4). The origin of the physical object theory is 'shrouded in prehistory' in that it is embodied in the languages spoken by human beings from time immemorial. In acquiring the language of our community each of us gradually becomes master of the mechanisms of objective reference by means of which external physical things can be spoken of, and the irritations we inevitably undergo at our sensory surfaces then dispose us to believe and assert things about an objective physical world. Thus do we come to know of external things.

The scientific character of this sketch of an explanation—or the scientific character of the study of the relation between our sensory impacts and our subsequent theory of the world—is the key to understanding a fully naturalized epistemology. Not only does the problem or task of the enterprise arise from within science, its solution is to be sought and found there too. Given his quite general philosophical purposes, Quine himself is more concerned with recommending and sketching the outlines of a naturalized epistemology than with carrying it out in detail. Beyond mentioning the 'two dimensional optical projections and various impacts of air waves on the eardrums and some gaseous reactions in the nasal passages and a few kindred

[5] W. V. Quine, 'Two Dogmas of Empiricism', in his *From a Logical Point of View* (Cambridge, Mass., 1953), p. 44.

odds and ends' (RR, 2) we get through the senses, he scarcely goes into the physiological or psychological facts. But the project he recommends is nevertheless a scientific project which 'may be pursued at one or more removes from the laboratory, one or another level of speculativity' (RR, 3). His own speculations on the subject tend to concentrate on language-acquisition, and that is an observable phenomenon in the world, however abstractly we might think about it. We know that a child acquiring a language from his elders has nothing but the bombardments of his sensory surfaces to go on, and he ends up speaking, as they do, of objective physical things. A genetic understanding of how that competence comes about could then provide us with an understanding of the relation between our sensory impacts and our theory of the world. That, for Quine, would be to understand the relation between 'observation' and 'scientific theory'.[6] That is why he regards the theory of language as vital to the theory of knowledge.

Quine's emphasis on the empirical, scientific character of the problem of our knowledge of the external world makes it look as if his project or question is not the same as the problem that exercised the traditional philosopher. It is true that for Quine the problem arises because there are many possibilities compatible with everything the senses provide. Since we could adopt any one of several different theories based on the same 'data', the problem is to explain how we know that there are external objects, how we know that the 'physical object theory' is the right one. Quine says we arrive at that theory, or at any rate that we continue to believe it, on grounds analogous to those on which any scientist accepts a theory that goes beyond his evidence. 'The last arbiter is so-called scientific method, however amorphous' (WO, 23). But could we hope to answer the traditional philosopher's question about the external world simply by emulating even the best scientific procedures? Scientists explicitly engaged in theory construction do not normally even consider, let alone justifiably rule out, the kinds of possibilities brought up in generating

[6] W. V. Quine, 'The Nature of Natural Knowledge', in S. Guttenplan (ed.), *Mind and Language* (Oxford, 1975), p. 74. (Hereafter cited as NNK.)

the traditional problem. An experimenter does not establish that he is not dreaming when he puts a certain chemical theory to a test. If we ordinary non-scientific mortals arrive at our view of the external world by inference of the same general kind, we will not consider or try to eliminate such bizarre possibilities either. So much is borne out by Quine's account of the genesis of our theory of the world. Nowhere in his story does he explain how we eliminate the possibility that our sensory data are merely the products of a dream or of an evil demon or of some other source incompatible with the physical object 'hypothesis'. That suggests that whatever Quine's naturalized epistemology is meant to do it could not answer the very question that proved so difficult to the traditional epistemologist. The justified elimination of possibilities incompatible with knowledge of the physical world is precisely what was in question in the traditional problem.

Another apparent difference is that Quine's question about our knowledge is to be answered by making use of any scientific information we happen to possess or can discover, whereas the traditional epistemologist's question was meant to put all that alleged information into jeopardy and hence to render it unavailable for such explanatory purposes. Any question empirical science can answer could not be the traditional philosopher's question. That is not to say there can be no such thing as a science of human knowledge, but only that any such 'internal' investigation, however feasible, could never be expected to answer the traditional question. That is precisely Carnap's reaction. He agrees that there can be an empirical scientific study of human beings and of how they come to know the things they do, and he would have no objection to Quine's naturalized epistemology so conceived. But precisely because of its empirical, resolvable character, the question could not be the same as the traditional philosophical question. That question is philosophical and meaningless for Carnap because no evidence could help to settle it. No one 'theory' is made more credible than any other on the information said to be available to us.

Quine sometimes seems to acknowledge the traditional question and to agree that the sceptical answer to it is correct.

He finds empiricist philosophers of the past concerned with the relation between sensory data and beliefs about the external world in two different ways. There is the 'conceptual' question of whether statements about external physical objects can be fully expressed or reformulated without loss in purely 'sensory' terms, and there is the 'doctrinal' question of whether our knowledge of external physical things can be adequately justified on the basis of purely 'sensory' knowledge (EN, 69–70). On this 'doctrinal' question of justification he finds us no farther along today than where Hume left us. 'The Humean predicament is the human predicament' (EN, 72). By that he presumably means that our beliefs about bodies are not justified by our sensory data.

There are apparently two reasons for this despairing verdict. The first is that all general statements or statements about the future (and also presumably the past), even if they could be expressed in purely 'sensory' terms, could not be known with certainty on the basis of present sense-experiences. They go beyond what is true of actual impressions. The other reason, at least for Hume, was that any justification our sense experiences could give to statements that go beyond them would have to come from the reliability of inductive or non-demonstrative inference. Any such inference would take us from what has been experienced to what has not, and the principle of an inference of that kind could not itself be a report only of actual sense-experiences. Even if we could explain 'scientifically' why we make the kinds of inferences we do, it would not follow that we had answered the traditional 'doctrinal' question of whether the conclusions of our inferences are justified by their premisses. That is because the scientific information we appeal to in our explanation would itself have been arrived at by just such an inference.

Quine at times seems to grant the vicious circularity in any 'scientific' attempt to justify inductive inference in that way. He thinks the Darwinian theory of natural selection, for example, might help explain why induction works so well for those of us survivors who reason inductively; we are descendants of those with well-adapted 'similarity standards'. But that biological explanation could not justify induction. 'This would be circular,' Quine concedes, 'since biological knowledge depends upon induction' (NNK, 70). The same strictures against circularity determined the traditional project. If all our knowedge of the external world is in question all at once, no part of that putative knowledge can be appealed to to help explain how we know the rest; all of our knowledge is to be justified on the 'sensory' basis alone. Quine grants that:

> a surrender of the epistemological burden to psychology is a move that was disallowed in earlier times as circular reasoning. If the epistemologist's goal is validation of the grounds of empirical science, he defeats his purpose by using psychology or other empirical science in the validation. (EN, 75-6.)

Quine's own naturalized epistemology is precisely 'a surrender of the epistemological burden to psychology' (and to any other sciences that might help us understand human knowledge). If that does not defeat Quine's purpose, although it would defeat the traditional epistemologist's purpose, is that because the question Quine asks and answers is different from the traditional question? What then is the relation between them?

At times he suggests that the questions are different. The 'doctrinal' issue of justifying our knowledge of physical bodies in purely 'sensory' terms, he suggests, should be abandoned as a vain hope. We can then concentrate on the manageable scientific project of understanding the relation between 'observation' and 'science', between the 'meager input' at our sensory surfaces and the 'torrential output' that embodies our theory of the world. Because the traditional epistemologist was bent on validating or justifying our knowledge of the world, he insisted on isolating certain objects of awareness in sense-perception. He wanted to identify the indubitable information we could be said to acquire in perception so that he could pose more sharply and more precisely the question of how that information could ever justify our richer beliefs about an external world. But once the project of justification is abandoned, Quine thinks, we can sidestep the issue of awareness and simply try to explain how our torrential theoretical output arises from those events that take place at our sensory surfaces. And in seeking or providing that explanation we are obviously free to use any scientific information we happen to have or are lucky enough to get. An understanding of the relation between two sorts of events in the observable physical world is now our scientific goal, not the hopeless extra-scientific project of somehow supporting our rich theory of nature on the basis of some strange entities that we find we are, strictly speaking, aware of in perception.

This now makes it look as if Quine is simply changing the subject, or recommending a different subject from the one that interested the traditional epistemologist. That would leave open the possibility, sometimes apparently endorsed by Quine, that scepticism is and remains the only answer to the traditional question, and that nothing he says in his naturalized epistemology affects that answer one way or the other. But this accommodation Quine also wants to resist.

In *The Roots of Reference* he denies that the 'liberated epistemologist' who now marches under the banner of empirical psychology has changed the traditional subject; his 'is an enlightened persistence rather in the original epistemological problem' (RR, 3). The enlightenment comes from recognizing something the traditional philosopher missed. He thought the appeal to any or all of empirical science to explain how our empirical science of the world is possible would be circular reasoning, so no validation or justification of our knowledge of the world could come out of such an appeal. But we can now see, according to Quine, that 'this fear of circularity is a case of needless logical timidity, even granted the project of substantiating our knowledge of the external world' (RR, 2). A liberated naturalized epistemology appears capable of giving us what the timid traditional philosophy despaired of finding. This new understanding of epistemology is 'enlightened':

> in recognizing that the skeptical challenge springs from science itself, and that in coping with it we are free to use scientific knowledge. The old epistemologist failed to recognize the strength of his position. (RR, 3.)

What the traditional epistemologist failed to recognize, according to Quine, was that the challenge he raised against our knowledge of the world came from that very knowledge itself. The reasons he had for finding knowledge problematic or doubting its reliability were scientific reasons. If he had recognized the real source of his doubts he would have recognized the strength of his position and the fact that he can use science in answering the doubts he has raised.

Here we return to the important point, mentioned earlier, that the problem the theory of knowledge must answer is thrown up by that very knowledge whose origins or possibility it is meant to explain. The theory of knowledge for Quine as for the tradition has its origin in doubt and the threat of scepticism.

> Doubt prompts the theory of knowledge, yes; but knowledge, also, was what prompted the doubt. Scepticism is an offshoot of science. (NNK, 67.)

The 'strength of his position' that Quine is pointing out to the traditional epistemologist is the availability of scientific knowledge for answering his question. However difficult or complicated the investigation might prove to be, it is a scientific pursuit like any other, so we are in no worse position for explaining our knowledge of the world than for explaining any other natural phenomenon.

Quine thinks the confusion centered on the issue of awareness. Older epistemologists thought the facts about the meagreness of our sensory data were discovered by direct introspection or perhaps by simply attending carefully to what is given in perception. But in fact the reasons for finding our data meagre and hence knowledge problematic came from science itself. Knowledge of the world and of how what we perceive can deviate from it were needed as a springboard for the scepticism epistemology then tried to avoid. The suggestion is that because the traditional epistemologist failed to recognize this important fact—that 'sceptical doubts' are really 'scientific doubts'—he failed to recognize that he was in the strong position of being able to use his science to answer those doubts and explain how scientific knowledge is possible.

This is both a diagnosis of the traditional philosopher's quandary and a defence of Quine's scientific epistemology as 'an enlightened persistence in the old epistemological problem'. Not only is naturalized epistemology all we can have; it is all we need or ever needed. Having stressed the fact that the posing of the epistemological problem depends on accepting certain results of natural science, Quine immediately concludes, 'Epistemology is best looked upon, then, as an enterprise within natural science' (NNK, 68). He is not simply saying here that epistemology is best looked upon as an enterprise within natural science, as he might do if he were tired of the interminable disputes of philosophers and thought it better (or 'best') to concentrate on psychology or physiology instead. His 'then' indicates that his scientific conception of epistemology is meant to be supported by what has just been said. What has just been said is that 'sceptical doubts are scientific doubts', that the epistemological problem arises within science itself.

The inference is even more strongly suggested by Quine's talk of the 'crucial logical point' he thinks the traditional epistemologist missed.

> The crucial logical point is that the epistemologist is confronting a challenge to natural science that arises from within natural science. The challenge runs as follows . . . [Here is a description of our meagre sensory irritations] . . . How, the challenge proceeds, could one hope to find out about that external world from such meager traces? In short, if our science were true, how could we know it? Clearly, in confronting this challenge, the epistemologist may make free use of all scientific theory. (RR, 2.)

The traditional epistemologist did not think it was clear that he could make free use of scientific theory; he thought it was clear that he could not. But if the 'logical point' about the scientific origins of his challenge to science is the only thing he missed, the implication is that ('clearly') scientific knowledge can be used in meeting that challenge precisely *because* the challenge arises within science itself.

Many philosophers have been tempted by an even stronger conclusion from the scientific origins of the epistemologist's doubts. Those doubts are typically based on the possibility of illusion. But if, as Quine says, 'the concept of illusion itself rested on science, since the quality of illusion consisted simply in deviation from external scientific reality' (RR, 3), it might look as if we can conclude immediately that no completely general sceptical doubt about all our knowledge can ever be reached. For Quine, 'illusions are illusions only relative to a prior acceptance of genuine bodies with which to contrast them', and 'bodies have to be posited before there can be a motive, however tenuous, for acquiescing in a non-committal world of the immediate given' (NNK, 67). This easily seems to lead to the conclusion that since some knowledge of science is needed even to understand what an illusion is, it is impossible for an appeal to the possibility of illusion to undermine all our scientific knowledge all at once. It would pull out from under us the very support we originally needed to get that undermining project going in the first place. Whatever got undermined or thrown into doubt, it would seem, could therefore not be all of our science all at once. Or so the argument would run.

I have mentioned arguments of this general type earlier. They are one species of the criticism that the sceptical epistemologist could reach his general conclusion only by distorting the meanings of its terms or by violating the conditions necessary for those terms to mean what they do. The argument would see the dependence of what Quine here calls 'the concept of illusion' on some unquestioned knowledge of external reality as part of the meaning, or a condition of the meaningfulness, of the notion of illusion. In Chapter Two I expressed some general doubts about the prospects of success along these lines. But whatever the argument based on meaning or meaningfulness might be, it is clear that Quine is not making it. His view of language and his rejection of the philosophical use of synonymy or analyticity leave him in no position to appeal to what is or is not included in the meaning of a particular term. It is one of the merits of Quine's views about language that they do not support such dubious argumentation. But if he does not think the scientific origins of the epistemologist's doubts lead the sceptic to outright contradiction or self-refutation, why does he think that because 'sceptical doubts are scientific doubts' the epistemologist is 'clearly' free to use empirical science in answering them?

The question is made more difficult by Quine's explicit disavowal:

> I am not accusing the sceptic of begging the question; he is quite within his rights in assuming science in order to refute science; this, if carried out, would be a straightforward argument by *reductio ad absurdum*. I am only making the point that sceptical doubts are scientific doubts. (NNK, 68.)

This is an important concession, and amounts to a very powerful point in the traditional philosopher's defence. If there is nothing logically peculiar or self-defeating in starting with some scientific knowledge and ending up by rejecting or doubting it all, what becomes of 'the crucial logical point' that the traditional epistemologist is said to have missed? If the 'only' point Quine is making is that 'sceptical doubts are scientific doubts', does it follow that epistemology, 'then', is part of natural science, and that 'clearly' the epistemologist may make free use of all scientific theory? Once it is granted that the sceptic might be arguing by *reductio ad absurdum*, I think it does not follow.

The *reductio ad absurdum* would presumably run something like this. Either science is true and gives us knowledge or it does not. If it is not true, nothing we believe about the physical world amounts to knowledge. But if it does give us knowledge, we can see from what it tells us about the meagre impacts at our sensory surfaces during perception that we can never tell whether the external world really is the way we perceive it to be. But if that is so, we can know nothing about the physical world. So once again nothing we believe about the physical world amounts to knowledge. On either possibility we know nothing about the physical world.

I do not suggest that this is itself the sceptical argument. The discovery of the meagreness of our sensory data and the impossibility of their supporting our beliefs about the world would be reached on the second horn of the *reductio*'s dilemma only after fairly elaborate reflections of the kind I outlined in Chapter One. The present question is only whether someone whose sceptical reasoning is understood as falling within this general *reductio* pattern would then be in a position to use part or all of his scientific knowledge of the world to show how knowledge is possible after all. It seems to me clear that he would not. That is why Quine's concession that the sceptic can be understood as arguing by *reductio ad absurdum* seems to me to count so strongly in favour of the traditional philosopher's understanding of his question. If I am right, the fact that 'sceptical doubts are scientific doubts' does not put the epistemologist who raises such doubts in the stronger position of being free to use scientific knowledge of the world in his effort to answer those doubts and explain how knowledge is possible.

Suppose we ask, as Descartes does, whether we know anything about the world around us, and how any such knowledge is possible. And suppose we ask this question and find an answer to it difficult because of certain things we take at the outset to be true about the physical world and about the processes of perception which give us the only access we have to it. If we then reasoned as Descartes reasons and arrived by *reductio ad absurdum* at the conclusion that we know nothing of the physical world, and we found ourselves dissatisfied with that conclusion, clearly we could not go blithely on to satisfy ourselves and explain how knowledge is nevertheless possible by appealing to those very beliefs about the physical world that we have just consigned to the realm of what is not known. By our own arguments, despite their scientific origin, we would find ourselves precluded from using as independently reliable any part of what we had previously accepted as knowledge of the world around us. The scientific origin of our original question or doubts would therefore do nothing to show that the answer to our question or the resolution of our doubts can be found in an empirical study of human knowledge as an observable phenomenon in the physical world.

This says nothing about the independent desirability or feasibility of an empirical study of the psychology and physiology of perception, learning, and language-acquisition. Nothing I have said about traditional epistemology is meant to cast any aspersions on that. What is in question is only the relation between Quine's project and the traditional epistemological enterprise. Nor would I cast aspersions on the confident everyday assertions of G. E. Moore. In fact I tried to remove philosophically-motivated aspersions cast by others. In that case too the only question was the relevance of Moore's assertions to what we recognize to be the traditional project. On views like those of Carnap and Kant, what Moore says is perfectly legitimate and unassailable, but it does nothing to settle the philosophical issue one way or the other. The results of an independently-pursued scientific explanation of knowledge would be in the same boat. They would be 'scientific' versions of Moore's 'common sense' remarks. But if we feel that the philosophical question is not and could not be answered directly in Moore's simple way (as I think we do), we should also find that it cannot be answered by apparently more scientific assertions to the same effect. The scientific story is not more true or more highly confirmed or more clearly based on experience than what Moore says; it is just more complicated. For Quine 'science is self-conscious common sense' (WO, 3).

Quine does not accept the Kantian or Carnapian conception of the philosophical enterprise, so their appeal to the isolation of the philosophical from the scientific is not open to him. He rejects the possibility of an 'external' position from which all of our knowledge of the world can be seen whole; for him philosophy is continuous with science. Descartes and other traditional philosophers could accept that continuity—at least they understand their philosophical assessment of our knowledge to have the sceptical consequence that what we thought was scientific knowledge of the world is not really knowledge at all. We have no more reason to believe it than to disbelieve it. That is something no philosophical investigation could show, according to Carnap and Kant. But for Descartes science and our common-sense view of the world can come under general philosophical attack, and if the argument can be seen in Quine's way as a *reductio ad absurdum*, that attack will be seen as coming 'from within'. Even if the doubts that lead to the eventual rejection of our science of the world are themselves 'scientific doubts', we reach a final position in which nothing about the external world counts as knowledge or reliable belief, including the very beliefs that helped generate the doubts in the first place. Given the possibility of a *reductio*, Quine's repudiation of an 'external' detached position for the assessment of knowledge would not in itself guarantee the impossibility of epistemological scepticism. A sceptical challenge 'from within' would be possible, and the knowledge thereby repudiated could not be appealed to to meet the challenge.

What then is wrong with scepticism according to Quine? How can it be avoided? It once looked as if recognition of 'the crucial logical point' that 'sceptical doubts are scientific doubts' would be enough to 'liberate' the traditional philosopher from his gloomy sceptical conclusion. But if that alone does not legitimize a 'scientific' answer to what remains a real question, the problem is still with us.

In the face of that apparent problem Quine is content to stress his 'naturalism', the idea that in his reflections on knowledge he is:

> reasoning within the overall scientific system rather than somehow above or beyond it. The same applies to my statement . . . that 'I am not accusing the sceptic of begging the question; he is quite within his rights in assuming science in order to refute science.' The skeptic repudiates science because it is vulnerable to illusion on its own showing; and my only criticism of the skeptic is that he is over-reacting.[7]

Scepticism about the external world is not incoherent on Quine's view. He defends the sceptic's right to put it forward ('quite within his rights'). He criticizes it only as a form of extremism.

What is the sceptic's over-reaction, according to Quine? It might look as if it is the panicky response of rejecting science completely and never making use of it again simply because 'it is vulnerable to illusion on its own showing'. That *would* be an over-reaction, like getting rid of my car or never trusting it to start again simply because it failed once in freezing weather on a high mountain. But I argued that the sceptical reasoning does not turn directly on the simple fact that illusions sometimes occur. That alone does not imply that we know nothing about the world around us. The

[7] W. V. Quine, 'Reply to Stroud', *Midwest Studies in Philosophy*, vol. VI, 1981, p. 475.

sceptical conclusion comes only with the realization that everything we get through the senses is compatible with countless different 'hypotheses' about what is the case beyond those sensory data, so there is no way of telling which of the many different possibilities actually obtains. If that is the position we are in, it is no over-reaction to conclude that we can know nothing about the world around us. That would be the only reasonable reaction to such a plight. If on the basis of what I see I cannot tell whether the bird in the garden is a goldfinch or a goldcrest or a canary it is far from an over-reaction to conclude that I do not know it is a goldfinch.

But Quine suggests that the sceptic is over-reacting because we do not at the moment actually have good reason to reject science on the sceptic's grounds. He grants that:

> Experience might, tomorrow, take a turn that would justify the sceptic's doubts about external objects. Our success in predicting observations might fall off sharply, and concomitantly with this we might begin to be somewhat successful in basing predictions upon dreams or reveries. At that point we might reasonably doubt our theory of nature in even its broadest outlines. But our doubts would still be immanent, and of a piece with the scientific endeavor.[8]

This suggests that the sceptical 'theory' is not yet as well-confirmed as some other views. Perhaps it will become so, but for the moment it lacks sufficient justification.

What Quine calls scepticism here is a far cry from the position reached at the end of Descartes's *First Meditation*. In invoking the dream-possibility and arguing that there is no way we can eliminate it, Descartes is not suggesting that we should base our predictions on dreams or reveries rather than on what we are pleased to call scientific observation and experiment. And in repudiating science as a source of knowledge of the world he is not announcing that our success in 'predicting observations' is going to fall off if we keep reasoning and theorizing scientifically as we have been doing, and that we should look to our dreams instead. Quine speaks of future experience as perhaps justifying the sceptic's doubts about external objects, as if those doubts are not sufficiently justified at the moment. But whether scepticism is the correct

[8] 'Reply to Stroud', p. 475.

answer to the epistemological question is not something to be settled by further observation or experimentation. If the question is posed correctly—as Quine himself poses it—we already know that whatever future experience might be like, it can only give us more of what will remain laughably meagre sensory data relative to our rich set of beliefs about the world around us. We will always be faced with the question of whether we have any more reason for adopting the physical object 'hypothesis' rather than any one of a hundred others that equally go beyond all possible data.

The sceptical view that is a response to that question does not itself take a stand on what is actually the case beyond the data—on which one of the many 'theories' we should adopt—so we do not need to wait for further evidence to see whether the sceptical view becomes more, or less, worthy of our acceptance. If we are restricted to data which far underdetermine what we believe, the sceptical doubts are justified today—in fact, they were justified in that same way in the 1630s. It is not a question of more experience. Scepticism does not say that current science is not knowledge of the world but something else (say, reveries) really is instead. It simply says that none of the competing 'hypotheses' about what is true beyond the data can be known to be true; in fact, that we can have no more reason for believing any one of them rather than others on the basis of the only sensory data we can ever have. If our data are so inevitably restricted in relation to what we claim to know on the basis of them, the conclusion that we can know nothing beyond the data is no over-reaction at all.

Kant and Carnap, in different ways, both see the sceptical potential in the traditional question. That is why they concentrate on the question itself and on how something must go wrong in the way it gets raised. Quine eschews such purely 'philosophical' or diagnostic activities. He finds sufficient reassurance in the idea that the epistemologist, like everyone else, must operate from within the accumulating body of theory we find ourselves constantly assessing, revising, expanding, and trimming as we are carried along by it. We rebuild and repair our ship on the open sea. But if the sceptic can be seen as arguing by *reductio* to the conclusion that all of that science nevertheless provides no knowledge of the world, the consolations of naturalism alone will not be enough. It would leave us with no way of ensuring that the greater part of our ship, insofar as it represents what we know or have reason to believe, cannot be, or perhaps already has been, abandoned. It would provide the traditional epistemologist in our midst with the possibility of sawing all around that meagre portion of the ship that represents our sensory data, and setting the rest of it adrift, rudderless on the open sea. Certainly there is no guarantee against such sabotage merely in the thought that the saboteur must be aboard ship from the beginning of the journey, or even that he would have to stand with at least one foot on that huge, dispensable portion in order to cut it loose from the ship of knowledge in the first place.

Quine's naturalistic study of knowledge proceeds in terms of a general distinction between what we get through the senses and everything we believe about the physical world on the basis of those data. I would now like to argue that that conception of knowledge and of the epistemological task not only tolerates scepticism, as I have just been suggesting, but is actually committed to it. It would make it impossible for us to understand, even on its own terms, how our knowledge of the external world in general is possible. I must emphasize that I do not mean that there is anything wrong with the scientific study of human knowledge. It is the particular conception of the task that Quine relies on that I want to examine. It is not just a matter of finding out whatever we can about human knowledge by any respectable means; the specific task for Quine is to understand how our knowledge is possible by understanding how the 'meager input' at our sensory surfaces gives rise to the 'torrential output' in the form of sentences we accept as true about the external physical world.

Let us begin by asking how, in the most ordinary or even scientific contexts, we explain someone's knowledge, or explain how it is possible. For Quine it is a straightforward matter of scientific observation and explanation. We study:

> a natural phenomenon, viz., a physical human subject. This human subject is accorded a certain experimentally controlled input—certain

patterns of irradiation in assorted frequencies, for instance—and in the fullness of time the subject delivers as output a description of the three-dimensional external world and its history. (EN, 82-3.)

There is nothing problematic in this sort of investigation. As an observer or experimenter, I can observe a human being and observe his environment while also observing the 'output' he produces in the form of utterances I understand to be about the world around him. Given what I know about his surroundings and what (according to Quine) science tells me about the processes of perception, I can try to explain how the 'torrential output' to which I have access is related to, or produced by, the 'meager input' I know he is receiving at his sensory surfaces. Because I know how 'meager' those 'inputs' are, I know that what he says about the world is grossly underdetermined by his sensory impacts—indeed, on Quine's view by all the sensory impacts he and everyone else will ever have (WO, 22).[9] In that sense I can see his talk of physical objects as a 'hypothesis' relative to his 'data'. Nothing he says about the physical world follows from truths about what is happening at his sensory surfaces. Relative to those sensory impacts, physical objects are for him 'posits', something he 'projects' from his 'data' (EN, 83).

In calling his conception of the physical world a 'posit' or 'projection' beyond his 'data' I do not in this normal context imply that he does not know anything about the physical world or that his beliefs about it are not true or not reasonable. Since I am in a position to see whether what the person says about the world around him is true, I can determine whether his belief on a particular occasion is a *mere* posit or projection—something he believes and asserts, but

[9] To say that truths about the physical world are 'far in excess of any available data' or are 'less than determined by our surface irritations' could mean that (i) truths about the physical world do not follow from the fact that certain surface irritations are occurring, or that (ii) truths about the physical world do not follow from the 'data' or 'information' supplied by those surface irritations. On the first interpretation, not *all* truths about the physical world would be underdetermined by the sensory impacts, since the truth 'Impacts I_1, I_2, . . . occurred at sensory surfaces S_1, S_2, . . .' is not underdetermined by those impacts, and it is a truth about the physical world. I give more reasons below for thinking that Quine is to be understood in the second way, despite his explicit repudiation of the notion of 'awareness' or 'data'.

with no basis in fact. If I find, in a particular case or in general, that what he says is true of the world around him, I can still hold that his beliefs go well beyond his sensory impacts and in that sense are 'projections', even though they do not go beyond or in any other way misrepresent what is actually the case right before his eyes. If he says 'There is a tree' in a situation in which I find there is a tree before him, I know that what he says is true. If I were to explain his knowledge of the world in that situation I would at least have to explain how he came to get things right in that situation. In the normal case that is of course not difficult to do. I as an observer of the subject of my study can tell whether he gets things right or not because I can know both what he is saying about the world around him and what is true in the world he is saying it about. That is why my granting that the subject's beliefs about the world are 'hypotheses' or 'posits' relative to the meagre impacts at his sensory surfaces does not in itself imply that he knows nothing of the world or that I cannot explain how his knowledge is possible.

Sometimes when I am observing another human subject I can see that what he says or believes about the world around him is not true; there is no tree or anything else before him, despite his confident assertion that there is. In that case I see immediately that he does not know there is a tree before him, he only believes there is. I might then say that he is *merely* projecting, that his belief in the tree is a mere posit, and is not true. I might go on to try to explain how and why he comes to have that false belief, but of course that would not be an explanation of how he knows there is a tree there, or of how his knowledge is possible, or of how he comes to get things right. In that case I would know that he does not get things right, he does not know there is a tree there. Since I see that his belief is false and he does not know, my explanation does not explain his knowledge, nor does it explain how he comes to have a true belief. Not every explanation of a subject's beliefs is therefore an explanation of knowledge, or even of true belief.

What then is required for us to explain someone's knowledge or even true belief in the kind of experimental situation

Quine envisages? I think the two kinds of cases considered so far show that the truth of what the person believes must play an essential role. But although the truth of the subject's beliefs is always relevant to whether he knows, it is not enough. Even if I can explain how and why the person comes to believe what he does, I will not necessarily thereby have explained how he comes to know it, or how he comes to have a true belief, even if his belief is in fact true and I as the observer know that it is. That is because it is possible for someone to have a true belief and yet lack knowledge—it might have been a coincidence or a lucky guess or a belief held for reasons unconnected with the truth of what is believed. A subject in such a position would lack knowledge, despite the truth of his belief, so no explanation of his belief would be an explanation of his knowledge.

This important condition of success for the kind of explanation even a fully naturalized epistemology should provide is not a consequence of imposing unreasonable standards of strictness or certainty on the notion of knowledge. Any explanation of the desired kind must at least explain how the subject comes to get things right, how he comes to have a true belief, whatever else (if anything) beyond that minimal condition the notion of knowledge is thought to imply.[10] Of course, I might be able to explain how a person comes to believe what he does, and I might also be able to explain how or why the state of affairs he believes in actually came about, but that in itself would not be an explanation of true belief of the kind any theory of knowledge should provide. Suppose someone believes there are exactly one thousand four hundred and seventeen beans in a certain jar, and suppose I as a student of human behaviour can explain how he came to have that belief. He did not count the beans, he did not see them being put into

[10] Some philosophers hold that knowledge requires nothing more than a true belief that p that is partly caused or maintained or explained by the truth of p. Even on such a view an explanation of someone's knowledge would have to explain how the person comes to get things right. For some examples of views along these lines see A. Goldman, 'A Causal Theory of Knowing', *The Journal of Philosophy*, 1967; P. Unger, 'Experience and Factual Knowledge', *The Journal of Philosophy*, 1968, and 'An Analysis of Factual Knowledge', *The Journal of Philosophy*, 1967; F. Dretske, 'Conclusive Reasons', *Australasian Journal of Philosophy*, 1971; R. Nozick, *Philosophical Explanations*, ch. III.

the jar, no one connected with the filling of the jar told him how many beans there are, but he became convinced that there are just that number, and I know how he got that belief. Suppose I also happen to know that there are in fact exactly that number of beans in the jar, perhaps because I put them there myself, and I can explain how and why exactly that number of beans got there. Now those two explanations together—the explanation of the person's belief and the explanation of the jar's containing just that number of beans—might be said to provide me with an explanation of how he comes to have a true belief, or of how what he believes came to be true, but it will not be an explanation of how that person came to get things right. It will not be the kind of explanation of a true belief that must be involved in any explanation of human knowledge.

The kind of explanation that is required for explaining someone's knowledge involves something more. It will not be enough if it does not trace a connection between the truth of what is believed and its being believed. My combined explanation of the truth of the person's belief about the beans in the jar failed to do that. It leaves the truth of the belief an accident or coincidence. It is no accident that the person believes what he does—I have a fully satisfying explanation of that—and it is no accident that there are just that many beans in the jar—that too I can explain. But simply accepting both explanations does not provide me with an intelligible connection between the truth of the belief and its being a belief of his. In the kind of experimental situation Quine is imagining, then, I can explain the subject's knowledge in the right way only if I know that the world around him is as he says it is, and that its being that way is partly responsible for his saying or believing it to be that way. Only then would I be doing more than explaining the origin of a belief that happens to be true. An appeal to its truth would play an essential role in the explanation of the origin of the belief.

I am not raising a difficulty for the scientific, experimental study of human knowledge. It is obvious that we can and do observe human beings in interaction with their environment, that we can and do regard them as knowing things about that environment, and that we can and do explain how they come to know those things. I have only been concerned to stress one of the conditions of our understanding how that knowledge comes about. We must be able to establish some connection between the truth of what they believe and their believing it. Knowing only what they believe, or even that what they believe happens to be true, would not be enough.

The point is confirmed by reflection on another position it is possible to find ourselves in when we are observing another person. So far I have imagined a case in which I know what the subject's beliefs are and I know whether or not they are true. If I know they are true, and I can explain how they come to stand in the proper relation to the facts they are about, I can understand how the person knows what he does. If they are not true, I can see that he lacks knowledge. But sometimes I might not be able to tell whether the beliefs I am interested in are true or not. I might be able to observe the subject of my study and determine what his sensory impacts are, and I might know what beliefs are expressed in that part of his 'torrential output' now of interest to me, but for some reason I might be unable to see or get any other information about the states of affairs he believes to hold. Perhaps some barrier obstructs my view, so I cannot at the moment tell, for example, whether there is a tree before him or not. In such a situation I would be restricted to what is happening in the subject himself and to his 'output', but I would know nothing about the world he is describing.

This of course is no position from which to conduct scientific research into this or any other subject's knowledge, and there is no suggestion that it is our normal position. If some barrier prevents me from checking on the truth of his beliefs I should simply remove the barrier, or wait until it goes away, or change my position, or at the very least study those beliefs of his on which I *can* check without difficulty. I do not mention this possibility to suggest any difficulties for the empirical study of man.

The point is that in this untypical and unusually restricted position I could not establish whether the subject knows something about the world he is describing or not. I would know what he believes, and I would perhaps know what impacts at his sensory surfaces led him to believe it, but since I would not have access to the part of the world those beliefs are about there would simply be no telling whether they amount to knowledge or not. I could not compare what he says with the world he says it about, as I can in the normal unobstructed observational position, so I could not explain the relation or lack of relation between them. Given only what I would have access to in this unusually restricted position, I could see his beliefs as 'projections' from his 'data', so I could say 'He projects (or posits or puts it forward) that . . .', but I could not say 'He correctly believes that . . .' or 'He knows that . . .'. I could not see those beliefs as anything more than a *mere* projection or posit on his part. That is not to say that I would be in a position to say that they are nothing more than a mere projection and that they are not really true. I couldn't tell that either. It is just that I would not be in a position to see them as more than that.

Even if I could somehow explain in that position how the subject's 'meager sensory input' has led him to make and adopt the 'construction' or 'projection' I know he has made (and it is not clear how I could do even that)[11] that explanation would not be an explanation of his knowledge or of how

[11] The problem is that if we had no information about the world beyond the subject's sensory surfaces we could 'explain' his 'output' by tracing its genesis only as far as his sensory surfaces. We could not go further and explain why his sensory surfaces are stimulated in just the ways they are. That would be at best a very limited 'explanation' of how our subject 'posits' bodies and 'projects' his physics from his 'data'. Furthermore, we could never explain how he came to speak as he does, and therefore how he came to believe what he does. Language-learning is to be explained by showing how the subject comes to behave linguistically in ways that conform to the general practices prevalent in his linguistic community, and we would know nothing about that community since it is beyond his sensory surfaces. Why he says things in the particular form in which he says them cannot be explained by his sensory impacts alone. Englishmen and Frenchmen often get the same impacts. Worse still, without some independent information about the world the subject's utterances are about, we could not even understand those utterances and thereby identify his beliefs about the world. So even to suppose that we have access to the subject's 'output' presupposes that we know things about the world he is talking about—even if, on a particular occasion of utterance, we might lack such information. This unusually restricted position with respect to another person's knowledge is therefore not one we could find ourselves in quite generally. This point is stressed by Donald Davidson in his theory of 'radical interpretation'.

he comes to have a true belief. I am simply not in a position to see his beliefs as knowledge, or as true. To explain how his knowledge or true belief is possible I must know what his beliefs are, and I must know what is the case in the world they are about. And I must gain my knowledge about the world independently of knowing simply what the subject's beliefs are; that he believes there is a tree before him is not enough for me to know whether that belief is true. Only if I had that independent information could I compare his belief with the world it is about and ascertain whether or not it is true.

So far I have discussed some conditions of success in the experimental study of particular cases of another person's knowledge in observable circumstances. That study as Quine conceives of it proceeds in terms of a distinction between a person's 'meager' sensory 'data' and everything he believes to be true about the external physical world on the basis of them. Even if there is nothing problematic about that distinction when applied in particular cases, we are still faced with the completely general question of how any human knowledge of the external physical world is possible at all. An explanation in terms of 'meager input' and 'torrential output' would help me explain how anyone at all ever comes to know anything about the external physical world only if I could see that that same kind of explanation can be applied quite generally to all other people and also to myself. We have perhaps by now learned to be at least suspicious of such generalizing moves in philosophy. We need to look carefully at the extension of what seems to work in particular cases to a general conclusion about all of human knowledge. If it turned out that I could successfully apply that distinction on some occasions to some other people only because I did not simultaneously apply it to all, or if I could apply it to everyone else only because I did not simultaneously apply it to myself, I could not employ that distinction to understand with complete generality how our knowledge of the world is possible. Let us grant for the moment that I can understand in Quine's way how other people's knowledge is possible. That leaves the question whether I can understand in that way how my own knowledge of the external physical world is possible.

There might seem to be no difficulty here. Quine explains how we are to achieve the required generality:

> We are studying how the human subject of our study posits bodies and projects his physics from his data, and we appreciate that our position in the world is just like his. Our very epistemological enterprise, therefore, and the psychology wherein it is a component chapter, and the whole of natural science wherein psychology is a component book—all this is our own construction or projection from stimulations like those we were meting out to our epistemological subject. (EN, 83.)

The position we find another human subject in, on Quine's view, is that of 'positing' bodies or 'projecting' all of physics from the 'meager' sensory data to which he is restricted in his contact with the world he believes to exist. If each of us, in thinking of himself, must 'appreciate that our position in the world is just like his', each of us will have to appreciate that we too are restricted to 'meager' sensory data, and that all of our beliefs about the physical world around us go far beyond, or are grossly underdetermined by, those data.

I think we cannot perform that act of 'appreciation'—we cannot see all our own beliefs about the world as a 'construction or projection from stimulations'—while still explaining how our own, or anyone else's, knowledge of the world is possible. I do not mean simply that I cannot see all my own beliefs about the physical world as 'posits' or 'projections' which go beyond the 'meager' data at my sensory surfaces. Perhaps I can manage to see my position that way. It certainly seems possible to see another person as in just that position. Nor do I mean that an explanation of how someone else's knowledge is possible cannot be understood to apply to my own knowledge as well. I am a human being like everyone else, so what is true in general of others is also true of me, including the ways we come to know things about the world around us. But I do deny that I can do both things at once. I think I cannot see all my own beliefs about the physical world as a 'construction or projection from stimulations' and at the same time explain how I can know anything about the world around me. Even if I can see others' beliefs in that way and still explain their knowledge of the world in those terms, as it seems I can, what I want to argue is that I cannot explain how my own knowledge is possible if I regard all my beliefs about the world around me as 'posits' or 'projections' that go beyond my 'meager' sensory data. And if I cannot understand in that way how my own knowledge is possible, I cannot understand in that way how any other person's knowledge is possible either. Or, putting it another way, I can understand others' knowledge as a 'projection' from 'meager' sensory 'data' only on the condition that I do not understand *all* human knowledge of the world in that way. That is what I will now try to show.

What happens when I try to take up the view that all my beliefs about the external physical world amount to a 'construction or projection' from 'meager' sensory 'data'? I know what all my beliefs about the world are, but I do not have any independent access to the world those beliefs are about on the basis of which I could determine whether or not they are true. In the normal case in which I am studying another person in interaction with the world, I can do that. I know what his beliefs are, and I can know, independently of the fact that he has those beliefs, what is the case in the world those beliefs are about. That is what enables me to explain how his knowledge is possible in that situation. In my own case, if I regard all my beliefs about the world as 'posits' or 'projections' from sensory data, I would not be in that position. I would find myself with a set of beliefs or dispositions to assert things about a physical world, but I would have no independent access to the world those beliefs are about.

Of course, I could try to do what is normally regarded as finding out whether my beliefs about the world are true. I could do what we call looking at the world around me, or perhaps listening or reaching out and touching, or even measuring or doing experiments in order to see whether my beliefs are true or not. But as long as I retained the idea that *all* my beliefs about the physical world are a 'construction or projection from stimulations' which they far transcend (as I must do if I am to perform Quine's act of 'appreciation'), I would have to regard myself as getting no closer to knowing whether or not my beliefs about the world are true. After 'looking at the world' (or experimenting on it) I would at best find myself with a set of stronger, or perhaps altered, beliefs or dispositions to assert things about a physical world. I would know what those reinforced or newly-acquired beliefs are, but I would have to regard them in turn as simply further elements of my 'construction or projection' from my recently-increased, but still extremely meagre, 'input'. Those 'confirmations' or 'verifications' or 'experiments' could not be seen as giving me any independent information about the world against which the truth of the earlier beliefs had been checked. They would just give me more of the same. And what I would still not know is whether any part of my 'construction or projection' is true.

I am not simply making the point that it is impossible to check our beliefs against the world they are about. In fact I think that in the normal case that *is* possible—at any rate, I see nothing wrong with describing our verification or testing procedures in that way. If I say or believe that a certain book is in a certain position in the next room, and I then go into that room to find out whether I am right in what I say or believe, I see nothing wrong with saying that I checked my belief against the facts, or even that I compared my assertion or belief with the way things are. I think such things happen every day, and that they can be described in those ways. My present point is that I could not check my beliefs about the physical world against the facts of the world in that way *if* I at the same time regarded *all* my beliefs about the physical world as nothing more than a 'construction or projection from stimulations' in the way Quine intends. I would have no independent information about that world that I could use as a test or a check.

We saw that in studying another person it is possible to find ourselves at least temporarily barred from information about the world that person's beliefs are about. In that rather unusual if nevertheless possible position, independent access to the facts is denied me, so I cannot regard the person's beliefs as knowledge or explain how his knowledge or even true belief is possible. I would know enough to enable me to say 'He projects (or posits or puts it forward) that . . .', but I would have no way of going on to the stronger verdict 'He correctly believes that . . .' or 'He knows that . . .'. I would be in no better position with respect to my own beliefs about the physical world if I followed Quine's proposal of regarding all my beliefs as a 'construction or projection from stimulations'. I could see myself as believing or 'projecting' or 'positing' various things about a physical world, but I could not see myself as having knowledge or even true beliefs about such a world, so I could not give an explanation that explains my knowledge or explains how I came to get things right.

This is not to deny that I could think it is possible that I have true beliefs, in the sense that nothing prevents my beliefs from being true. And if I think true belief amounts to knowledge if the state of affairs believed in is connected in the right way with my belief, I might also think it is possible that my beliefs amount to knowledge, since I find no contradiction in the thought that my beliefs are connected in that way with the world they are about. It is to be expected that I would have these thoughts, since if I believe something I will also think it is not impossible that it is true, and if I claim to know something, I will think it is not impossible that I know it. But even if my beliefs did happen to be true or did happen to be connected with the states of affairs they are about, I still could not explain or understand my true belief or knowledge in the way a theory of knowledge should explain it. I could never show that what I believe is in fact true or explain how or why it does amount to knowledge, as long as I retain the idea that all my beliefs about the world are a 'construction or projection' from 'meager' impacts at my sensory surfaces.

In fact, if we take completely seriously this talk of sensory surfaces, we can see that applying Quine's proposal to oneself would leave each of us in an even worse position than the one I have described so far, and worse with respect to ourselves than even the unusually restricted situation we can find ourselves in when we lack knowledge about another person's environment. Quine's epistemological problem is to explain the relation between the 'meager input' at one's sensory surfaces and one's 'torrential output' in the form of a body of beliefs or assertions about a physical world. But strictly speaking, my belief that I suffer impacts at my sensory surfaces, and indeed that I even have sensory surfaces at all, are themselves beliefs of mine about an external physical world. Even my 'scientific' belief that my beliefs about the physical world are 'projections' from impacts at my sensory surfaces is itself a belief about the physical world. If I am to see that 'discovery' too as nothing more than a 'projection' from my 'data', what attitude do I now take to the very problem a naturalized epistemology is supposed to answer? In trying to study another person while lacking access to his environment, I at least can know what is happening at his sensory surfaces and what his beliefs about the world are. I cannot fully answer the question about the relation between his 'meager input' and his 'torrential output' in that position, but I do have some independent information about at least part of the physical world; I know what his 'impacts' are. But in my own case, following Quine's proposal, I would not even have that. The unquestioned information about part of the physical world that enables me at least to ask the question about another person would have to be seen in my own case as nothing more than a further part of an elaborate 'projection' of a physical world that I somehow have been led to 'construct' and believe. I would see all my beliefs about my sensory surfaces as just more of my 'torrential output'. I would have lost independent access to anything physical whose role in producing my 'output' I can ever hope to investigate or explain.

Trying to follow Quine's proposal and apply his conception of knowledge to myself, then, I would be left in an even worse position than that of an observer barred only from information about the truth of his subject's belief. Perhaps the closest parallel to it in a third-person case would be that of finding myself alone in total darkness and silence and suddenly hearing the words 'There is a tree' coming from somewhere. Obviously there is simply no telling in that situation whether those words express knowledge, or even truth, so there would be no possibility of explaining, with only that sort of information, how in that case knowledge or even true belief is possible. I would have nothing but that bit of 'output' to work with. But that is the position I would always be in with respect to my own beliefs about the physical world if I 'appreciated' that all my beliefs about the physical world are 'projections' from 'meager' sensory data.

I would have nothing but my own 'output'. That for me would be no better than whistling in the dark.

While I continue to regard all my beliefs about the physical world as 'projections', and so remain within this very restricted position, I might nevertheless come to wonder how some of the things I believe in are related to or connected with my believing and asserting the things I do. I believe in impacts at my sensory surfaces, for example, and I believe that my sensory 'input' is meagre and my scientific 'output' torrential. Natural curiosity, not to mention the 'reasons that always prompted epistemology' (EN, 83), might then lead me to seek some explanation of how that torrential 'output' could be generated on such a slender basis. In an effort to understand this puzzling relation between some of the things I believe I might appeal to other beliefs of mine—for example, about psychology or physiology or language-acquisition, or any other part of science that I think might help. But as long as I remember that all the 'science' I am appealing to itself just amounts to more and more 'projections' from my 'data', I will appreciate that telling myself that complex story about 'input' and 'output' is just a matter of expressing more and more of my elaborate 'construction or projection' of a physical world. I could not see my efforts as providing me with an explanation that itself is something I know or have reason to believe, as opposed to a complicated story I fully accept and find myself disposed to tell myself from time to time.

The requirement that we see all our beliefs about the physical world as 'projections' has disastrous consequences for the theory of knowledge. I think we tend to overlook them or deny them because (not surprisingly) we do not usually manage to fulfil the requirement completely, even in our thoughts. We unwittingly take *some* things as unquestionably true about the physical world, and not merely as 'projections', even while we are trying to think of human knowledge in Quine's way. But if we accept with complete generality the idea of human knowledge as a combination of a subjective and an objective factor, and we see the objective contribution of the world as small relative to the total set of beliefs we hold about the world, we must see the subjective factor (the contribution of the knowing subject) as largely determining our total set of beliefs about the world. Countless 'hypotheses' or 'theories' could be 'projected' from those same slender 'data', so if we happen to accept one such 'theory' over others it cannot be because of any objective superiority it enjoys over possible or actual competitors. Every consistent 'theory' compatible with those same meagre 'data' is in that sense a competitor of the 'theory' we now accept, so our continued adherence to our present 'theory' could be explained only by appeal to some feature or other of the knowing subjects rather than of the world they claim to know. And that is precisely what the traditional epistemologist has always seen as undermining our knowledge of the external world. The possibility that our belief in an external world is nothing more than a mere 'projection' on our part, nothing more than something we accept because of certain things true about us and not about the independent world we believe in, is the very thing that had to be shown not to obtain if we were to understand how our belief in an external world amounts to knowledge or even something we have reason to believe.

It is Quine's idea that depriving the would-be philosopher of a vantage-point outside our knowledge of the world would be enough to eliminate the prospect of a totally sceptical outcome to reflections on knowledge. That would leave naturalized, scientific epistemology as the only epistemology there could be. There is wisdom in that strategy, but I have argued that it will not succeed as long as all our knowledge of the world is seen as a 'projection' from meagre sensory data that grossly underdetermine it. I thereby echo Kant's idea that a completely general distinction between everything we get through the senses, on the one hand, and what is or is not true of the external world, on the other, would cut us off forever from knowledge of the world around us. That general epistemic distinction is fatal to the naturalizing project. It has the effect of casting us out of our own knowledge of the world, as it were, and leaving us with no independent reason to suppose that any of our 'projections' are true. It appears to provide just the kind of place an epistemic exile could resort to when he discovers the poverty of his position with respect to knowledge of the world. If there is to be no such exile, there should be no such place.

But for Quine the very distinction that I say leads to difficulty is itself a deliverance of science. 'It is a matter of scientific fact, or theory', he says, 'that our only avenue of information about external objects is through the irritation of our sensory surfaces by forces emanating from those objects'. And 'science itself teaches that . . . the only information that can reach our sensory surfaces from external objects must be limited to two-dimensional optical projections' and the like (RR, 2). If that is indeed what 'science tells us' (NNK, 68), how could that general distinction have the consequences I draw from it? In arguing that we cannot understand all our knowledge of the world as a 'torrential' 'construction or projection' from 'meager' sensory 'data' in that way, am I not simply flying in the face of the scientific facts?

I don't think so. Nothing I have said implies that we cannot observe a person in interaction with his environment and isolate from everything else certain events that are occurring at his sensory surfaces. We know, and he might know, a great many other things about what is going on in the world around him beyond those events. In fact it is extremely unlikely that he himself will have any idea of what those events at his sensory surfaces are like. But there are such events, and if we know enough about physiology, and about him, we can pick them out from all the rest. And of course this holds quite generally. Whenever any of us is in interaction with his environment there are events occurring at his sensory surfaces. No doubt such events should be reckoned as part of what causes us to get the beliefs about the world around us that we do. It seems obvious that if our sensory surfaces were not stimulated we would never come to believe anything about the world around us. Science (in Quine's all-encompassing sense) does 'tell us', as Quine puts it, 'that there is no clairvoyance' (RR, 2). There are causal chains of events leading from objects around us to events deep in our brains, and the events at our sensory surfaces occur as parts of such chains.

There could be no objection to studying those events and seeing what they lead to, and what their effects lead to in turn, and so on.

Quine sometimes describes his project of naturalized epistemology in this way, especially when he is emphasizing how it would avoid the traditional worries about circularity and epistemic priority. The traditional epistemologist was concerned to isolate something that we are directly aware of in perception, and that led to disputes between 'sense-data' theorists and Gestalt psychologists about what sort of mental item is present to consciousness in perception. Quine would avoid the issue by 'talking directly of physical input at the sense receptors' (RR, 4). Since 'reception is flagrantly physical' (RR, 4), 'it is simply the stimulations of our sensory receptors that are best looked upon as the input to our cognitive mechanism' (EN, 84). There is then no talk of awareness and no need for the notion of epistemic priority that was essential to the traditional question.

> Now that we are permitted to appeal to physical stimulation, the problem dissolves; A is epistemologically prior to B if A is causally nearer than B to the sensory receptors. Or, what is in some ways better, just talk explicitly in terms of causal proximity to sensory receptors and drop the talk of epistemological priority. (EN, 85.)

A naturalized epistemology so understood would study the relation between our 'input' and our eventually coming to believe what we do about the world around us by studying how those events at our sensory surfaces cause other events closer to 'our cognitive mechanism' and eventually cause our beliefs about the world around us. More strictly, it would study the ways in which events at our sensory surfaces cause those events which are comings-to-believe-something about the world around us. But whatever such an investigation managed to discover and explain, it would not provide an explanation of how our 'meager sensory data' give rise to a 'torrential output' about the world that is grossly underdetermined by those data. It would not show by what 'bold inference' we manage to 'bridge' the 'wide gap between our data and our knowledge of the external world'. That is because it makes no sense to say that between one event and another in the same causal chain there is a 'gap' that is to be 'bridged' by 'inference'. There is just one event which leads to another, and then to another, and so on. It makes no sense to say of one event (e.g., an impact at a sensory surface) that it 'underdetermines' another event (e.g. a coming-to-believe-something) that occurs later in the series. Of course it is true that all the events that occur in the interval between the earlier and the later event are also needed to bring about the later event, so in that sense the impact alone does not cause the believing, but that kind of causal insufficiency is not what Quine means by 'underdetermination'.

He means that the 'data' do not *imply* the 'torrential output'; they do not logically determine what the 'output' will be; many different 'outputs' are logically compatible with those same 'meager' 'data'. Just as '*truths* about molecules' are underdetermined by '*truths* that can be said in common-sense terms about ordinary things', so the '*truths* that can be said in common-sense terms about ordinary things' are 'less than determined by our surface irritations' (WO, 22, my italics). It is the truth or falsity of the content of the 'output' that Quine says is not 'determined' by the data or the sensory impacts; the relation of 'underdetermination' holds between one set of truths and another. The sensory impacts or irritations (along with the intervening events) *cause* the event that is the coming-to-believe or coming-to-be-disposed-to-assert the 'output', but that is not the kind of 'underdetermination' Quine has in mind in posing his epistemological question. He asks how knowledge is possible, given that 'the only *information* that can reach our sensory surfaces from external objects' (RR, 2, my italics) is 'meager' in relation to what we come to believe about those objects as a result of receiving that sensory 'information'. That gap is just what gives rise to Quine's epistemological problem. That is why in answering it we will learn 'how evidence relates to theory, and in what ways one's theory of nature transcends any available evidence' (EN, 83).

The 'impact' itself, the event, is not 'meager' in relation to another event that is 'torrential'. Something happens at a sensory surface, and then a coming-to-believe-something-about-the-world occurs. The relation between those two events is simply that the former causes the latter (along with the help of those in between). But 'underdetermination' speaks of a relation between something that is 'meager' relative to something else that is 'torrential'; the latter 'transcends' the former. If we think only about the events involved—the events at the sensory surface and the events closer to 'our cognitive mechanism' that result in our believing what we do—and we drop all talk of 'meagerness', 'underdetermination', 'torrential output', and so on, what becomes of Quine's question about our knowledge of the world around us? We are left with questions about a series of physical events, and perhaps with questions about how those events bring it about that we believe what we do about the world around us. But in trying to answer those questions we will not be pursuing in an 'enlightened' scientific way a study of the relation between 'observation' and 'scientific theory', or of the 'ways one's theory of nature transcends any available evidence', or of 'the domain within which [man] can revise theory while saving the data'. We will be studying the connection between one kind of event and another.

I think the question Quine poses in terms of the 'underdetermination' of the 'torrential output' by the 'meager input' makes essential use of a notion of epistemic priority. It is because the 'information' we get at 'input' does not uniquely determine the truth of what we assert as 'output' that we must explain how we get from the one to the other. We could know everything included in our 'evidence' without knowing any of the things asserted in our 'theory'. If 'input' were not understood as 'evidence' or 'data' or 'information' in this way, to say that it 'underdetermines' thc 'output' would make no sense, or not the kind of sense Quine says it makes. But if the 'input' is to be understood in that way, our 'data' must be understood as something we are in some sense aware of, after all. They could be described as 'evidence' or 'information' only if that were so. Quine explicitly denies that he thinks of impacts at our sensory surfaces in that way; he wants to avoid all questions of awareness. But he can do so only by avoiding all talk of the 'meagerness' of our 'input' relative to our 'torrential output' as well.

It might seem that once again we simply come up against the deliverances of science. 'It was science itself', Quine says, 'that demonstrated the limitedness of the evidence for science' (RR, 3). Has science demonstrated that? Quine does not specify what scientific results he has in mind here. It could not be the simple fact that we would not believe or know anything about the world around us unless we received impacts at our sensory surfaces. That says nothing about the 'evidence' we might have for our beliefs about the world, so it says nothing about 'the limitedness of the evidence'. Still, as things are, it is true that there is no clairvoyance. The indispensability of causal interaction between the world and active sensory surfaces seems undeniable. What I have meant to deny, with Kant, is that we can regard all our beliefs about the world as 'projections' or as 'theoretical' relative to some 'data' or bits of 'evidence' epistemically prior to them, while at the same time explaining how our knowledge of the world is possible. I do not see what actual, or even possible, scientific findings I could be in conflict with in saying that. Quine's project of naturalized epistemology has the interest and the apparent connection with traditional epistemology that it has only because it contains and depends on just such a bi-partite conception of human knowledge of the world. That is what I have argued cannot succeed in explaining how knowledge is possible. But without that conception, 'naturalized epistemology' as Quine describes it would be nothing but the causal explanation of various physiological events.

The 'nothing but' is not a disparaging expression. It would be absurd to disparage the scientific study of human beings, or of anything else. My aim is only to distinguish 'naturalized epistemology', understood as physiology, from the 'enlightened persistence . . . in the original epistemological problem' (RR, 3) that Quine claims for his own project. It was also absurd to disparage the lecturer in Chapter Three who said that most of us know there is an enduring world, or even to disparage G. E. Moore who said that he knew there are external things. I have wanted only to point out that those remarks do not answer or even address themselves to the philosophical problem of the external world.

The same is true of the physiological study of causal chains of events leading inwards from our sensory receptors. It is only Quine's project conceived in terms of 'data', 'evidence', 'theory' and 'output' that I want to say (with Kant) can never explain how human knowledge of the world is possible.

VII

Coda: The Quest for a Diagnosis

It was clear from Descartes's reflections that the epistemic priority of ideas or appearances or perceptions over external physical objects has fatal consequences. Once some such distinction is in place, we will inevitably find ourselves cut off forever from sensory knowledge of the world around us. The discovery that we are indeed in that position is the outcome of Descartes's general assessment of his knowledge of the world. There is no trouble in the thought that sometimes we do not know what is happening in the world around us and are certain only about how things appear. Only when knowledge or certainty confined to appearances is generalized into an account of our relation to the external world in general do we reach the philosophical doctrine of epistemic priority and its attendant scepticism. That is just the conclusion Descartes draws. From the particular case he considers he finds that we can never know anything about the world around us.

I have been trying to focus attention on what I think we need in order to come to terms with Descartes's reasoning. We need a firm understanding of how his assessment of his knowledge in the particular case he considers does not fully correspond to the familiar assessments of knowledge we know how to make in everyday life or, if it does, why he cannot draw the general sceptical conclusion from it. If it does correspond, and if the case he considers is representative of our knowledge of the world in general, then scepticism is correct.

The question of the correspondence between the two sorts of assessments is more complicated than it might seem; I have tried to identify some of the issues it raises. I believe that a deeper investigation of the question is our best hope of getting whatever there is to be gained from a study of philosophical scepticism. At least one thing we can perhaps expect to gain is a more accurate understanding of how our familiar everyday knowledge actually works. Philosophical scepticism is a 'benefactor of human reason' in forcing us to pursue that question at levels we would have no reason to reach, or even to consider, without it. Whether there could ever be such a thing as a general account we would be willing to call 'a theory of knowledge' is a further and, it seems to me, still open question.

It is too much to expect a thorough unravelling of the sceptical reasoning here. The most I can do by way of conclusion is to indicate briefly what seem to me to be some of the most interesting lines of investigation and some of the difficulties to be faced. Even if no final or fully satisfactory diagnosis is yet in sight, there is much to be learned from pursuing the most sympathetic available accounts of the sceptical reasoning and the most promising attempts to get to the bottom of it.

What we need, in Stanley Cavell's words, is:

> a detailed working out of the skeptic's apparent progress from the discovery that we sometimes do not know what we claim to know, to the conclusion that we never do; or an investigation of his apparent assumption that our knowledge of the world as such is at stake in the examination of particular claims to know.[1]

That working-out will have to do justice to our sense of the force and depth of the sceptical reasoning, even if it exposes the 'progress' to its conclusion as ultimately only 'apparent'. It will also have to explain how the sceptical conclusion can seem so obviously to conflict with what we all ordinarily take ourselves to know. And it should account for what I have called the conditional correctness of scepticism: that the sceptical conclusion would be correct if the philosophical question to which it is an answer were legitimately posed. That will tend to focus attention on the first step of the traditional epistemological investigation—on how or whether a philosophical question about knowledge in general can get raised in an assessment of a particular piece of knowledge of the world around us.

[1] Stanley Cavell, *The Claim of Reason: Wittgenstein, Skepticism, Morality, and Tragedy* (Oxford, 1979), pp. 45–6. (Hereafter cited as CR.)

Cavell concentrates on that question by asking '*Is* the example the philosopher produces imaginable as an example of a particular claim to knowledge? What are his examples examples of?' (CR, 205). I think we are naturally inclined to reply that they are simply examples of knowledge (or at least putative knowledge). Descartes begins by investigating what he regards as an instance of knowing that he is sitting by the fire with a piece of paper in his hand. He finds a 'basis' for that knowledge in sense-experience, and then introduces a ground for doubt in the possibility that he might be dreaming. In Chapter One I tried to fill in some of the details, stressing the parallels between what Descartes does and our familiar everyday assessments. To be sure that we get the most from an exposure of scepticism we should examine it in its intuitively most persuasive form, in which it corresponds most closely to procedures we accept.

Despite the apparent correspondence between Descartes's investigation and ordinary investigations of particular claims to knowledge, Cavell thinks that if we look carefully we will find that the 'basis' offered for the claim to know in the philosophical case is 'not entered fully naturally' and that therefore 'the ground for doubt could in turn not be fully natural' either (CR, 191). It is also not fully unnatural and, given the philosopher's context, it is not absurd or something that can be ignored. But its lack of full naturalness is for Cavell a clue to a diagnosis.

To extend that 'unnaturalness' into a formidable criticism of the traditional philosopher's procedures and results Cavell thinks it has to be shown that the philosopher 'does not mean what he thinks he means', that the context in which he tries to conduct his investigation 'has itself prevented his meaning what he wishes to mean, what he *must* mean if his conclusion is to mean what he says' (CR, 193). That would not be simply to repeat the familiar charge that the philosopher changes or distorts the meanings of the terms he uses in his investigation. On the contrary; he conducts his scrutiny of knowledge in words whose meanings he shares with all masters of his language. Rather, what Cavell emphasizes in trying to understand 'unnatural' remarks made by philosophers is the way in which 'the *saying* of something is essential to what is meant' (CR, 208)—'the fact that what an expression means is a function of what it is used to mean or to say on specific occasions by human beings' (CR, 206). This idea, emphasized in the work of Wittgenstein and Austin, is the basis of a distinct form of criticism of traditional epistemology.

It is not that the philosopher cannot mean what he thinks he means because his conclusion is contradictory or unverifiable, as many have supposed. It is the conditions of saying something or even thinking something that he ignores, despite the fact that the words he utters mean just what they have always meant.

> 'Not saying anything' is one way philosophers do not know what they mean. In this case it is not that they mean something *other* than they say, but that they do not see that they mean *nothing* (that *they* mean nothing, not that their statements mean nothing, are nonsense). The extent to which this is, or seems to be, true, is astonishing. (CR, 210.)

Cavell holds that it is true of the traditional epistemological investigation.

In philosophizing it is apparently easy to forget that asserting something, for example, is something people do, and not just anything they do will be an assertion, even if it amounts to uttering a well-formed indicative sentence in a language the speaker understands. The same is true of telling someone something, or asking a question, or even simply making a remark. Each of those distinct types of action has its conditions. If those conditions are not fulfilled, no assertion, question, or remark will have been made. Offering a basis for a claim, or introducing a ground for doubt as a challenge to a certain basis, are also things we do, and they too have their conditions. A basis 'is a statement which supports a particular claim; the rejection of the claim through the countering of the basis . . . depends upon that' (CR, 205). What is the claim that the philosopher's 'basis' is supposed to support? We naturally assume that it is his claim to know that, for example, he is sitting by the fire with a piece of paper in his hand. Hence the point of Cavell's leading question: '*Is* the example the philosopher produces imaginable as an example of a particular claim to knowledge?'.

Cavell finds that it is not.

> *no concrete claim is ever entered as part of the traditional investigation.* The examples meant as illustrating what happens when we know something are not examples of *claims* to know something; to ask us to imagine a situation in which we are seated before the fire is not to ask us to imagine that we have claimed (to know or believe) that we are seated before the fire. I will say: the example the philosopher is forced to focus upon is considered in a *non-claim context.* (CR, 217–18.)

The philosopher invites us to imagine (or in Descartes's case actually finds himself in) a certain situation, and he then goes on to imagine a claim's having been made in that situation. A basis is then sought for that imagined claim, and a ground for doubting that basis is then introduced. But since the context originally imagined is one in which no concrete claim is made, when we try to follow the philosopher's instructions we are not really projecting ourselves imaginatively into a situation in which it has been claimed that something is known. There is only an imagined claim, floating free as it were, and not an engaged, concrete claim within the original context. The 'basis' supplied for the imagined claim 'suffers the same misfortune as the original claim it supports' (CR, 218). It is not entered as a specific basis of a specific claim. The 'ground for doubt' and hence the 'question' 'How do you know?' are therefore less than fully natural in the same way. Having been imagined, they seem to demand a reply, but since it is 'a non-claim situation, the conditions under which a request for a basis can be answered have been removed' (CR, 239). We cannot possibly answer what we nevertheless feel we must answer. 'But the reason that no basis is satisfactory, is not that there isn't one where there ought to be, but that there is no claim which can provide the relevance of a basis' (CR, 239).

The philosopher's failure to say what he means—what he must mean if his conclusion is to mean what it says—is not a mere slip or oversight on his part. He is forced into the plight Cavell describes. He must imagine a claim to have been made, since without a claim there would be nothing for his 'basis' to be the basis of, and so nothing for his assessment to assess. His investigation would then not even look as if it corresponded to our familiar procedures of assessing knowledge in everyday life. But to fully imagine that a concrete claim to knowledge has been made, he must imagine a context in which that claim is made. And that would require that he imagine in addition the specific conditions in that context that make a claim possible and make it the specific claim he considers in his investigation. His verdict in that particular case, made possible by those specific conditions, could not then be representative of our position in general. It would be context- or condition-bound, and would not have the kind of generality the philosophical conclusion needs. Cavell sums up the 'dilemma' he finds confronting the traditional epistemological investigation this way:

> It must be the investigation of a concrete claim if its procedure is to be coherent; it cannot be the investigation of a concrete claim if its conclusion is to be general. Without that coherence it would not have the obviousness it has seemed to have; without that generality its conclusion would not be skeptical. (CR, 220.)

This is not meant to be a full account. Cavell sees it as 'no more than a schema for a potential overthrowing or undercutting of skepticism' (CR, 220), and I have merely sketched the schema. But it promises a resolution of the right general form. It would show that the sceptical conclusion with the significance it is meant to have cannot be reached. The traditional philosopher must treat his particular case in a certain way in order for his reflections to be as obvious and as convincing as similar reflections would be in everyday life, but when the case is understood in that way it could never yield a general philosophical conclusion of the kind he seeks. He must misconstrue the significance of his particular verdict if his general conclusion is even to seem to follow from it. The necessity of that plight is what for Cavell would eventually explain how and why the traditional epistemologist could have come to imagine himself to be saying something when he is not—to be merely 'hallucinating' what he means, or to be under 'the illusion of meaning something' (CR, 221).

How far does Cavell's promising suggestion take us? We will need some way of showing that the traditional epistemologist must inevitably fall into the quandary Cavell describes. How is that to be shown? Cavell in his own account concentrates on the idea that 'no concrete claim is ever entered as part of the traditional investigation', but even if that were so it would not bring out the inevitability of the traditional philosopher's failure to say what he means to say. What seems most important for developing and defending Cavell's suggestion is the idea that any assessment the traditional epistemologist does manage to make in the examples he considers could not stand as representative of our epistemic relation to the world in general in the way he intends. His verdict in the particular case could not be appropriately generalized into his philosophical conclusion about human knowledge. Showing that that is so would not require showing that the traditional philosopher does not really manage to assess anything because there is nothing in his example for his 'basis' to be the basis of. It would be enough to show that the philosopher must inevitably misconstrue the significance of whatever particular assessment he makes. That would seem to provide a more plausible and more sympathetic explanation of how he could come to imagine himself to be saying something when he is not than the suggestion that he simply fails to see that he is not assessing anything.

But is it true that 'no concrete claim is ever entered' in, say, Descartes's assessment of his knowledge? The thing to do would be to look carefully at Descartes's reflections and see whether there is a claim to know something there or not. The quite general fact that asserting, remarking, claiming, offering a basis for a claim, and so on, all have their own special conditions is not enough to establish the point. We would have to know what the conditions of claiming something are, and why they must be fulfilled in order for a claim to be made, before going on to show that not all those conditions could be present in the kind of examples the philosopher considers. And an account of *claiming* alone, as opposed to judging or believing or asserting or assuming, and so on, would not be enough. It would have to be shown that the conditions of *none* of the ways of saying something or thinking something that could serve the philosopher's purposes could be fulfilled in the kind of example he must rely on. But what are *all* the ways of saying something or thinking something that could serve the philosopher's purposes? That is what a diagnosis along these lines would have to concentrate on—what the philosopher aspires to, and why he cannot reach it.

If he is to assess his knowledge, even in a particular case, must the philosopher imagine that a claim to knowledge has been made in the particular case he considers? It would seem that all he needs for his assessment is a particular instance of knowledge, or at least of what we would all regard as knowledge. He imagines (or finds) himself in the normal course of events sitting by the fire with a piece of paper in his hand. He then asks himself whether and how he knows in that situation that he is sitting there. Even if he makes no claim to know at the time that he is sitting by the fire, it looks as if he could still ask whether he did know at the time that he was sitting there, and discover a potential basis for any such knowledge, and then go on to assess the reliability of that basis. He might come to the conclusion that he did not know, perhaps that he could not know, that he was sitting there, even though he had made no claim to know it at the time. If so, the absence of a specific, concrete claim to know in the situation he is interested in does not seem to make it impossible for him to assess his position in that situation.

I described Descartes's project as an attempt to review his knowledge. He wanted to assess the reliability of everything he had accepted since his youth. It does not seem to me essential to that project, or even to his conception of it, that he has actually claimed at some time to know each of the things he wants to review. When I asked myself what I really know about the common cold I did not suppose that I had ever actually claimed to know each of those things I realized I had accepted for a long time. But still I could ask how I knew them if I did know them, what my acceptance of them is based on, and how reliable those bases are. I did not actually carry out the investigation, but if I did I might come to find that I know much less about the common cold than I have been unquestioningly taking for granted all these years.

In the same way, it would seem that an assessment of the kind the epistemologist engages in does not require an actual claim to knowledge. He might find that when he is sitting by the fire in the normal course of events he does not claim to know that he is sitting there; he finds in retrospect that he was simply assuming without question that he was sitting there, or taking it for granted that he was. In reading a murder mystery or deliberating in a jury-room, for example, I might come to realize that I have been assuming without question that a certain thing was impossible, and that I really have no reliable basis for thinking it is, although I never explicitly said to myself or to anyone else that it could not happen. I can retrospectively assess the position I was in and find it wanting. Any 'attitude' I could take to a certain state of affairs—any claim or belief or assumption or thought or anything else I could realize might be wrong or could be found on examination to go beyond what is justified—would seem to be enough to give me something to assess.

I do not mean to suggest that all is therefore well with the traditional investigation of knowledge. I want only to locate more precisely the reason why the sceptical philosophical conclusion cannot be reached. Cavell says it is because any claim to knowledge that the philosopher could assess carries with it specific conditions that would prevent his verdict's being appropriately generalized. That seems to me the right thing to try to establish. My present point is only that in order to establish it it would not have to be shown that no claim at all is made in the situation the philosopher investigates. If it looks as if he could assess his position even without a specific claim to knowledge having been made, the diagnosis will have to concentrate on showing that any assessment the philosopher does make could not have the kind of significance he thinks it has. I am suggesting that that is the crucial issue.

To show that no particular instance of knowledge that the philosopher might investigate could be taken as representative of human knowledge in general, or that no verdict he arrives at in any particular assessment could support a general conclusion of the kind he seeks about our knowledge as a whole, it would have to be explained what sort of general conclusion the philosopher seeks, and why he cannot reach it. It would not be enough to say simply that he seeks a *general* conclusion, because it is not true that the investigation of a particular concrete claim to knowledge cannot support a general conclusion about human knowledge. I might investigate a historian's claim to know that there were apples in Sicily in the fourth century B.C. and find that it is well supported. That shows that somebody knows something about Sicily in the fourth century B.C., and that is a general truth about human knowledge. Another is that no one knows the causes of cancer; it might be arrived at by scrutinizing the credentials of all past and current theories, hypotheses, and conjectures on the subject. G. E. Moore presents us with conclusions apparently closer to the traditional philosopher's concern. From his concrete claim to know that there are hands before him it follows that he knows there are external things. So it is a general truth about human knowledge that it is known that there are external things. If we feel that Moore does not thereby establish a general conclusion about human knowledge of the kind the traditional epistemologist seeks, it cannot be because his conclusion is not general. It is expressed in the very same general terms that the epistemologist would use to express the conclusion he is interested in.

What must be invoked at this point is the distinction between two different ways of speaking, or two different ways of taking the same words, that I have tried to draw attention to in several different forms in preceding chapters. Precisely how some such distinction is to be understood, and how a shifting from one side to the other might bc at work in the traditional epistemologist's reflections now become central questions in the diagnosis of scepticism.

Those questions are at the centre of Thompson Clarke's investigation into the 'representativeness' of the philosopher's particular assessment. By looking at how the raising of doubts or the introduction of certain possibilities can count against our knowledge in everyday life, and at how they are meant to work in the philosophical assessment, he finds that sceptical doubts are 'equivocal'; they can be understood in a 'plain' or a 'philosophical' way.[2] The distinction between two ways of taking what might be the very same form of words is crucial to an understanding of the traditional epistemologist's procedures.

I have tried to illustrate that general point, using some of Clarke's own examples. Another case, more relevant to the present issue, is this:

> Suppose a scientist is experimenting with soporifics, himself the guinea-pig. He is in a small room. He keeps careful records. Experiment #1. '1:00 P.M. Taking X dose of drug Z orally . . . 1:15 P.M. Beginning to feel drowsy. I am not focusing clearly on . . . 6:15 P.M. I've been asleep but am wide awake now, rested and feeling normal. *I know*, of course, *that I'm not dreaming now*, but I remember, while asleep, actually thinking I was really awake, not dreaming . . . . (LS, 758.)

The experimenter says he knows he is not dreaming now. It would be just as ludicrous to say that he thereby settles in the affirmative the philosophical question whether we can ever know that we are not dreaming as it was to say that the lecturing physiologist in Chapter Three settled the philosophical question whether we can ever know there is an external world. Those remarks are none the worse for not answering philosophical questions. They are to be understood as 'plain', and not 'philosophical' remarks. Clarke puts it by saying that the knowledge expressed by this experimenter who says he knows he is not dreaming is 'plain' knowing. We no more expect him to go on to explain how he knows he is not dreaming now than we expect a similar explanation to be added to a careful report of an experiment in chemistry. The question is not deemed relevant to whether the person knows.

How does the possibility that I might be dreaming actually work against my knowledge in everyday life? Obviously it will do so only if it really is a possibility—something that could be so—and it is incompatible with my knowing what I think I know. Those are at least necessary conditions of a successful challenge to knowledge by the raising of a certain possibility. We can begin to probe what makes the dream-possibility a possibility by reflecting first on a thought

[2] Thompson Clarke, 'The Legacy of Skepticism', p. 763. (Hereafter cited as LS.)

I might sometimes have while sitting by the fire: the realization that I might wake up in a few minutes and find that all this has been a dream. That certainly is a thought I can have. It does seem to represent something that could happen; I can scarcely deny that it is possible. And it could undermine my knowledge—if I did wake up in a few minutes and find that I had been dreaming, it would follow that I do not know what I think I now know about what is happening around me.

Clarke points out that in order for it to be a possibility that I might wake up and find that all this has been a dream, the possibility or the ground for doubt must be understood in a 'plain' way. When I envisage the possibility of discovering later that I was dreaming a few minutes ago, I envisage my coming to know something. To say that the possibility is understood as 'plain' is to say that the knowledge involved in it is understood as 'plain' knowing. If I think of myself as saying at that later time, 'I now know that a few minutes ago I was dreaming that I was sitting by the fire', I think of that as a 'plain', and not as a 'philosophical', remark. It would be just like the remark of the experimenter on soporifics, or the lecturing physiologist's remarks, or Moore's everyday assertions. What I imagine myself saying later is not to be understood as subject to the 'philosophical' requirement that I know then that I am not dreaming. It is not to be understood as an affirmative answer to, or even as relevant to, the 'philosophical' question whether we can ever know we are not dreaming. That later knowledge is not to be seen as vulnerable in the way that the possibility of my discovering that I was dreaming would show my original 'knowledge' to be.

Suppose the later knowledge-claim were understood in a 'philosophical', and not just a 'plain', way. Then that knowledge I imagine myself getting later—knowledge that I was dreaming a few minutes ago—would have to be invulnerable to the 'philosophical' challenge 'But how do you know you are not dreaming now?'. The 'philosophical' problem about dreaming arises because there is apparently no way of telling at any particular time that we are not dreaming at that time, so what could I say in answer to that question? I would be no better off for answering that question a few minutes from now than I am now. My later claim to knowledge would then be as vulnerable to criticism as my present claim is. So if I do not know now that I am not dreaming, I would not know then that I had been dreaming earlier either. But if I could not even come to know later that I had been dreaming earlier, the possibility I originally thought I was envisaging will have vanished; it will turn out to be no possibility at all. The possibility I originally envisaged involves my coming to know later that I had been dreaming. But if that later knowledge is understood as 'philosophical', I could never come to know that. In trying to imagine the possibility of coming to know that I had been dreaming earlier I would therefore be trying to imagine something that is actually impossible. There would be no possibility of the sort I was trying to imagine. Understood 'philosophically', as Clarke puts it, that possibility 'calls in question (negates) the very knowing it presupposes' (LS, 765). Only if the knowledge involved in the possibility is not called in question or negated in that way will there be a genuine possibility. So the possibility that I might discover in a few minutes that all this has been a dream can work against a present knowledge-claim only if it is understood in a 'plain', and not a 'philosophical', way.

It follows that the possibility that I might wake up and discover that all this has been a dream could not be used to bring *all* of my knowledge of the world into question in the way the philosophical sceptic intends. Even if that possibility succeeded in undermining a particular piece of putative knowledge, the result in that case could not be appropriately generalized into a sceptical conclusion about all of human knowledge. That is because it will be a genuine possibility that can work against a particular claim to knowledge only if it is possible to have the knowledge that is involved in that possibility. So it can undermine a particular claim to know only on the condition that there be some knowledge of the world that is not undermined or in question. That version of the dream-possibility is therefore unavailable as a ground for a general sceptical conclusion that says we can know nothing about the world around us.

There is no suggestion that the traditional epistemologist

is confused on this point and would make use of a possibility that clearly fails to serve his purpose. But reflecting on a familiar ground for doubt that clearly presupposes some undoubted knowledge can be helpful for the light it might shed on what looks like a quite different sort of possibility. The traditional epistemologist is concerned with human knowledge in general, and introducing only the possibility that I might *discover* that all this has been a dream will not give his conclusion the kind of generality he seeks. But there is another possibility at hand that seems to require no knowledge or discovery at all. I mean simply the possibility that I am dreaming now, whether I can ever come to discover that I am or not. The philosopher asks only whether it is possible that he is dreaming now, and how he can know he is not. The simple possibility that he is dreaming seems to involve no knowledge at all; even if he could never find out which state he is in, it does seem to be something that could happen. If that is so, then what prevented the earlier possibility of *discovering* that one was dreaming from supporting a general sceptical conclusion would not prevent this new possibility from supporting such a conclusion. It would seem that this version of the dream-possibility cannot be shown to call in question or to negate the very knowing it presupposes, since it does not presuppose any knowledge or discovery at all.

Clarke's investigation is directed towards showing that that is not so. He thinks the possibility that I might be dreaming—which appears to involve no knowledge—is a genuine possibility that would work against our knowledge only if certain things were at least knowable, if not actually known, in a 'plain' way. When I envisage the possibility that I am dreaming now—and not the possibility of discovering later that I am dreaming now—I do not have to suppose that I will ever know which state I am actually in. I might concede that it is possible that I will never know. It does seem possible for someone to go to sleep and dream and simply never wake up again, and when I imagine the possibility of my dreaming right now I might also imagine that perhaps that will happen to me. So there seems to be no obstacle to my acknowledging that I might be dreaming now and that I might never come to know that I am or that I was. The possibility I imagine does not seem to include any knowledge on my part about what state I am actually in. But still, Clarke argues, it does involve knowledge, or at least possible knowledge, on the part of someone. When I imagine that I am dreaming now I imagine that I am actually in a certain place and a certain position, and that the truth about where I am and what is happening in the world is something that others, if not I myself, could know. Descartes's evil demon, for example, whose aim is always to deceive me, is thought of as himself knowing what state I am in and what is happening in the world around me. And, as before, that knowledge, or possible knowledge, is understood as 'plain'. I do not suppose that it meets the 'philosophical' requirement for knowledge of the world.

Suppose it could be shown that such knowledge or possible knowledge is indeed involved in the possibility that I am now dreaming. Then, as before, that possibility could not be used to support a general sceptical conclusion. It would undermine a claim to know only on the condition that there be some knowledge or possible knowledge that is not in question. No appeal to that possibility could bring the knowability of everything about the world around us into question in the way the sceptical philosopher intends. I can suppose that I am dreaming, and that therefore I know nothing about what is going on in the world around me. I can suppose that many others are dreaming and that they therefore do not know either. I can even suppose that no one now left on earth is awake and knows anything about the world. But that would not mean that philosophical scepticism was true. Those 'empirical' or 'internal' or 'plain' truths about human knowledge do not state 'philosophical' conclusions about the human condition. They would be rendered false if one of us simply woke up, or if someone arrived on earth from elsewhere and saw what an unfortunate state we were in. No general sceptical obstacle to human knowledge could be derived from the dream-possibility if its even being a possibility involved the 'plain' knowability of facts about the world around us.

Does the possibility that I might be dreaming involve

or presuppose the knowability of facts about the world? If it does, we might be in a position to explain how the traditional philosopher who ignores that presupposition could think he has reached a general sceptical conclusion when he has not. We might see that the sorts of possibilities he relies on could succeed as they do in his particular assessment only if they are not understood to have the sceptical consequences it seems very natural to draw from them.

How is such a satisfying result to be secured? I hope I have given some idea of how complex the issues involved promise to be, and how deeply a successful diagnosis would have to go. For Clarke it would bring into question even something as rich and apparently powerful as that standard conception of objectivity, or of how it is possible for us to think about the objective world, that I attributed to the traditional philosopher in Chapter Two. If that conception were fully intelligible it would be possible for us to entertain the thought that we might be dreaming without having to suppose that anything at all is knowable about the world around us. That is perhaps another way of saying that for Clarke if that conception were intelligible scepticism would be correct. His idea to the contrary is that:

> it is inconceivable that I could now be asleep, dreaming, *if* no other outsider could know my real environs because in the same boat, for the same reason, because he, too, could not know he was not asleep, dreaming. Does Descartes's possibility even *seem* to make sense, if we ask ourselves how the Evil Demon, or God, could know that he, too, wasn't dreaming—and allow that neither could? (LS, 766.)

Does that possibility make sense under those conditions or not? Here we come up against the difficult question how we can tell whether a certain thing is conceivable or not. One thing to do is to try to conceive of it and see what happens. Of course, that is not conclusive, since what makes it possible for me to have the thoughts I am having might be hidden from me. I might be surreptitiously presupposing the very opposite of what I take myself to be conceiving. But if that is so in the present case it is at least not obviously so.

Could it be that I am now dreaming? Not only does the right answer seem to me to be 'Yes' but, more importantly, it seems to me that the possibility continues to make sense even if I go on to imagine that no one on the face of the earth or anywhere else could ever know that I *am* dreaming because they too could never know whether they were awake or dreaming. Adding the further thought that the truth about my state is unknown or even unknowable to everyone does not seem to me to affect the possibility I originally tried to imagine at all. Of course, I might be wrong about this, but how is one to tell?

Clarke is impressed by the fact that when we acknowledge and follow out the implications of the kinds of possibilities usually raised in the traditional epistemological reflections we do not explicitly specify that it is also unknowable to everyone else whether the possibility is realized or not. When we ask ourselves whether we might be dreaming right now we do not go on to insist that whether we are or not is something that no one else could ever know either. When we are asked to imagine an evil demon out to deceive us, or an evil physiologist who has cleverly wired up our brain to ensure that we know nothing about the world around us, we do not immediately ask how the evil demon himself knows that someone isn't fooling him, or how the physiologist knows that his own brain is not as cleverly wired-up as we are supposing ours might be. I simply entertain the possibility as originally described and go on to worry about its implications for me, for what I can or cannot know.

I think that is true. We do not usually ask ourselves the further question about what the others can or cannot know. And perhaps that is why the possibilities work on us in the ways they do. But it is difficult to see that it is essential to our acknowledging such possibilities as genuine that we refrain from asking that question or silently presuppose that others could know things about the world around us. When the question does arise about how or whether other people or the evil demon or the physiologist could know what is really going on, it seems to me that I can concede that they too could never know without thereby threatening the intelligibility of the possibility I am trying to conceive of. It seems to me that if I acknowledge the possibility that I could be in such a state and therefore not know what is going on in the world around me, and I realize that others could also be in such a state (as it seems to me they could), then those others would not know what is going on in the world either. We would all be in the same boat. That seems to me to be just as much a possibility as the original possibility seemed to be.

Descartes's *Meditations* are written in the first person, but when I read them I do not say simply, 'What a peculiar man René Descartes is. He cannot tell whether he is awake or dreaming.' If I find what he says at all persuasive, I recognize that his first-person utterances can also be uttered by me, so I see immediately that what he finds to be true about his own knowledge is also true about mine. And of course I do not think that René Descartes and I alone share an unfortunate epistemic handicap. The same thoughts that he and I have had can be thought by anyone, and everyone. If I see that my granting that it is possible that I am dreaming now has the consequence that I can never know whether I am awake or dreaming, and I see that everyone else is just like me in that respect, then I see that no one can ever know whether he is awake or dreaming. Even if I imagine that an evil demon or a clever physiologist has arranged things so that I cannot know what is going on in the world around me, it seems to me that those same thoughts would be just as applicable by him to himself as I find them to be to myself. If they are, then all beings to whom such thoughts apply would be in the same position. Reflecting in this way on the human condition would lead me to conclude that no one can ever know anything about the world around us—that scepticism is the right account of our position. If it is a condition of the dream-possibility's even being a possibility that philosophical scepticism not be derivable from it, I should come to realize in drawing the sceptical conclusion that it is not really possible after all that I might be dreaming right now. But in fact that seems to me to remain just as much a possibility as it ever did.

I stress the tentativeness of these thoughts. It *seems* to be possible that I am now dreaming even though no one could ever know anything about the world around us, I *seem* to understand what a dream is without having to suppose that someone must be able to know things about the dreamer's environment, but what *seems* possible and intelligible might turn out not to be. We need some way to demonstrate or illustrate the covert knowledge or possible knowledge that on Clarke's view must be involved in the dream-possibility.

In seeming to find the dream-possibility intelligible even though no one could ever know things about the world I am no doubt revealing my continued attachment to what in Chapter Two I called the traditional conception of objectivity or of how it is possible for us to think about the objective world. I think it is very difficult to free oneself from that conception or to see how or why it cannot be correct. On that view, whether I am dreaming or not is simply a question of which state I am in. What matters is only whether the conditions under which it would be true that I am dreaming are fulfilled. The truth of 'I am dreaming' does not imply anything one way or the other about whether anyone else does or could know what is going on in the world around us. So on that view it will be at least *possible* to dream even if no one could ever know what is really happening. Philosophical scepticism therefore could not be blocked in the way I have just been sketching. It could not be shown that when the philosopher generalizes from his particular assessment to a conclusion about human knowledge in general he inevitably denies or withdraws one of the presuppositions that make it possible for his challenge to work as it does in the particular case.

If it is true that the possibility of knowledge of the world must be presupposed by the dream-possibility in order for it to undermine our knowledge in the way it does, that traditional conception cannot be fully coherent. It cannot be the correct account of how it is possible for us to think about an objective world. To examine how the dream-possibility actually works would therefore be to examine the intelligibility of that conception. How can it be shown that some unproblematic knowledge of facts of the world is presupposed or involved in any genuine dream-possibility, or more generally, that the only possibilities that can threaten our knowledge must be understood in a 'plain' or 'internal' or 'empirical' way? That would be to show that the fully 'external' or 'philosophical' conception of our relation to the world, when pressed, is really an illusion, and not a way we can coherently think of ourselves at all.

I have tried to show how the Kantian view would block scepticism and supplant that traditional conception, but only by giving us a 'transcendental' theory which, if we can understand it at all, seems no more satisfactory than the idealism it is meant to replace. I have tried to show how verificationism would directly oppose the traditional conception by implying that everything meaningful could be known to be true, or to be false; that the 'empirical' way of understanding things is the only way there is. But I argued that that could be used to establish the incoherence of the traditional conception only if there were some independent support for the verifiability principle. And it remains to be seen whether any such support could itself be understood only 'empirically', while having the philosophical consequences it is meant to have. The challenge is to reveal the incoherence of the traditional conception, and perhaps even to supply an alternative we can understand, without falling once again into a form of idealism that conflicts with what we already know about the independence of the world or denies the intelligibility of the kind of objectivity we already make very good sense of.

Can that be done? Could any account satisfy us? We will not have got to the bottom of philosophical scepticism until we have answers to those questions.

Index

2007